THE ORIGINS OF
LOVE AND
HATE

By

IAN D. SUTTIE, M.D.

INTRODUCTION BY
ASHLEY MONTAGU

THE JULIAN PRESS, INC. • NEW YORK

PUBLISHED BY THE JULIAN PRESS, INC.
8 WEST 40TH STREET, NEW YORK 18
PRINTED IN THE UNITED STATES OF AMERICA

INTRODUCTION

By ASHLEY MONTAGU

The Origins of Love and Hate is one of the most original and important books in the field of modern psychology. Originally published in England in 1935 this extraordinarily original book has had a steady and continuing influence in that country. In the United States the book is known to very few of the persons who would most profit by it. To those who have had the privilege of reading it the book has come as something of a revelation.

Intended for an audience much wider than that of the professional psychologist, no time seems more appropriate for the publication in the United States of this great book than the present. Many of the leading workers in the various fields broadly covered by the term *psychology*, have independently been moving in the direction so interestingly plotted by the author in the present work, so that the book is likely to find a most sympathetic audience among them. The book should prove equally interesting to the general reader interested in the study of human nature.

As an old student of psychology and critical reader of the literature, no other work since I had first read Freud, many years ago, has made so profound an impression upon me as Ian Suttie's *The Origins of Love and Hate.*

Having been brought up in the teachings of Freud, I had become a devoted but not uncritical admirer of Freud. (In 1922 I presented six papers critically examining Freud's *Introductory Lectures* to The Critical Society at University College, London). Following much study and reflection I had come to the conclusion that several of the most interesting and fundamental of the Freudian concepts were both unsound and unsoundly based. For example, it became increasingly clear to me that not only was there not the slightest evidence whatever for the existence of a "Death Instinct," but that all the relevant evidence indicated the contrary, namely, that all natural drives were directed towards the maintenance of life and the avoidance of death. I had concluded that no one could properly understand the psychoanalytic system of Freud unless they understood Freud himself and the milieu in which he had himself been conditioned. I felt that the psychological system that Freud had created—without question the most significant in the history of mankind—was a masculine system, with woman, the mother, most strangely slighted, not understood, and underrated. Freud's psychoanalysis is a patriarchal psychology—the nature of women seems utterly to have escaped Freud, and he virtually confessed as much, and for this reason or rather the reasons responsible for this failure, he never quite grasped the true meaning of the relationship between mother and child or the meaning of love.[1] Freud's view of the origin and organization of the "self," the existence

---

[1] See *The Meaning of Love,* edited by Ashley Montagu, Julian Press, New York, 1952.

of a drive towards "destructiveness," the "cyclopean family," penis
envy, the biological determinance of the oedipus complex,[2] narcissism
as a normal phase of psychobiological development, and a number of
other Freudian concepts seemed to me open to serious question.

Students of human nature such as Karen Horney, Harry Stack
Sullivan, and Erich Fromm—all great admirers and intellectual heirs
of Freud—had paid Freud the tribute of correcting and carrying
further some of his ideas, it was therefore no new experience to find
Freud corrected in *The Origins of Love and Hate*. What *was* new
was the extent and the originality of the correction.

Nietzsche has somewhere observed that we accept a philosopher's
views not so much because we agree with him as because he agrees
with us. This is no claim to priority. I am quite sure that Suttie had
arrived at his views long before I had at mine.[3] What so greatly impressed me in Suttie's book was that he had independently arrived at
conclusions precisely similar to those which several others, including
myself, had in part arrived. Suttie, however, had made most of his
observations and discoveries himself and had stated them very much
more systematically than other writers.

One of the reasons why *The Origins of Love and Hate* is a book
which deserves the attention of all serious students of human nature,
is that it not merely corrects Freud, but corrects him *constructively*.
Suttie was no mere desk critic. He was a busy psychiatrist who was
much influenced by Freud, and who put the Freudian theories to the
test of experience; as he tells us in his Preface, he gradually came
to find some of them questionable. A fortunate opportunity gave him
a prolonged period of time during which he was able to think things
critically through and write this book. Suttie's discovery and replacement of the Freudian concepts by others which seemed to state the
facts more accurately, had gradually led him to a view of human
nature and its social development very substantially different from
that of Freud.

Where the cornerstone of the Freudian system is "sex," in Suttie's
it is "love." Where Freud speaks of "libido," Suttie speaks of "the
need for companionship." As Suttie points out, the application of the
latter conception re-orients the whole psychoanalytic dynamic. "It attributes to the mother the significance in rearing that Freud formerly
attributed to the father." Here, as in much else, Suttie anticipated
what was shortly to be discovered, what was in fact in process of being
discovered at this very time, by such workers as Lawson Lowrey, David
Levy, John Bowlby, Margaret Ribble, Ruth and Harry Bakwin, René

2 See Ashley Montagu, "Nescience, Science and Psycho-Analysis," *British
Journal of Medical Psychology*, vol. 18, 1941, pp. 383-404; also *Psychiatry*, vol.
4, 1941, pp. 45-60.

3 See Ashley Montagu, "The Origin and Nature of Social Life and the Biological Basis of Cooperation," *Journal of Social Psychology*, vol. 29, 1949, pp.
267-283; also Ashley Montagu, *On Being Human*, Henry Schuman, New
York, 1950.

Spitz, and others, namely, the critical importance of the mother in the psychic development of the child.[4]

The reader will soon become aware that Suttie writes as a scientist. He has no special axes to grind. His criticisms of Freudian theories are either true or false; Suttie modestly offers his own original contributions as "tentative formulations," "hypotheses." Whether his criticisms are true or false is objectively verifiable by anyone willing to take the trouble to check the facts. And therein lies the value and the beauty of both Suttie's criticism and his own original contributions, they are objectively verifiable. Many of Suttie's "tentative formulations" have already received the best kind of confirmation, namely, by independent workers who were in most cases not directly testing Suttie's theories, but someone else's or who established the sufficient relations in the course of some other work. I refer particularly to Suttie's conceptions of love, aggression, tenderness, the relation between personality and early conditioning and the relation between these and culture, and so much else that it would far exceed the space at my disposal to mention it. There are so many original ideas in this book that their exploration should afford American students of human nature a virtually inexhaustible source of research leads.

It is unnecessary to dwell here upon Suttie's criticisms of Freudian theories. The reader will judge their value for himself. In the light of my own studies I find Suttie's criticisms to be thoroughly sound ones, demonstrating an origin in a systematic theoretic bias of Freud —a bias which rather more seriously affected his theory than his practice. I believe that almost every critical reader will agree that there have been few, if any, more trenchant and more constructive criticisms of Freud than this.

Throughout his book Suttie takes the viewpoint of the social biologist with the emphasis on the social, the cultural, development of man, rather than on the individual development "of a self-contained entity independent of his fellows." I cannot imagine a book of more interest to the student of culture and personality. I envy the reader who comes to this book for the first time.

In its American edition it should be stated that the book is published exactly as Suttie wrote it, and that its publication in this country is due to the enthusiasm for the book of Mr. Arthur Ceppos, President of the Julian Press. The reader, I am sure, will add his thanks to mine, to Mr. Ceppos for making this significant book available to American readers.

Princeton, N.J.

July 1952

[4] For a full and admirable survey of the evidence see John Bowlby, *Maternal Care and Mental Health*, Columbia University Press, New York, 1951. This important volume should be read by every adult capable of reading.

CONTENTS

CONTENTS

CHAPTER III

Severity and extent of the social inhibition of tenderness—Evidence of
"the Theatre" and "Novel" of inhibition and of the need for "safety
valves"—Causes of taboo-on-tenderness—Abrupt psychic weaning; solecisms—Why these are so distressing—Conditions under which escape
is possible—The rejection of love and love-shyness—Tenderness taboo
is cumulative from generation to generation—Its ethical effects—Racial
character moulded by it—Puritanism and Tenderness Taboo—Stoicism and Cynicism are expressions of Tenderness Taboo—The impulses and feelings which undergo this repression—Distinction between tenderness and feeling *inhibition* and idiocy and dementia—
Cultural variations in the taboo on tenderness—Are paralleled by differences in rearing customs—The minimal taboo on tenderness—
Where defensive paralysis is unnecessary—The consequences of tenderness taboo for parenthood—Sex differences caused by the variable
incidence of tenderness taboo in the rearing of boys and girls respectively—"Sex war" and incompatibility as an indirect result of tenderness taboo—The tenderness taboo on regression acts as a positive obstacle to development and integration—Conclusions.

CHAPTER VII

REPRESSION AND THE JEALOUSIES

Is society artificial or natural,—Repression—History of the concept—
Its sexual reference—Sexual Jealousy and "Penis envy" regarded by
Freud as fundamental—Inadequacy of this view—Prohibition by *interference* and by *rejection* compared—Inhibition of fantasy—The Mother's "Imago" and ideal (super-ego)—Paternal suppression is ineffective—Endogenous and exogenous repression—Maternal rejection is
conclusive—Relative status, in child's eyes, of Father and Mother—
Social influences and cultural differentiations—Freudian selection of
evidence—Maternal character and its social determinants—Effect on
"Oedipus Complex"—Definition of endogenous and exogenous repression—Trend of Freudian opinion—Freud's limited conception of
the jealousies that disturb socialization of the child and the race—
"Cain" Jealousy—"Zeus" Jealousy, "Couvade"—Effect of these upon
character and social relationships of the sexes—Patriarchal culture is
the expression of envy of womanhood and of childhood—The Aranda
—Interpretation of certain customs—Zeus Myth—Laios Jealousy—Sum-
mary of jealousies.

CHAPTER VIII

ORIGIN AND NATURE OF SOCIETY

Validity of this Speculation—Freud's conflicting views of the origin of
society—Rational motives in socialization—Fear, "identification", "reversal of affect" as socializing motives—Freud's view of Group Psychology—Its contradictions—His doubts—Psycho-analysis cannot understand social life or love—or hate—Genesis of society—The "band
of brothers" and "the litter"—Work, Play and Culture—Secondary
differentiation of masculine and feminine minds—Relative unimport-
ance of sex jealousy as a social factor—As we know it sex jealousy is
itself largely derivative and morbid, not primal and universal—Freud's
patricentric theory over-emphasizes sex jealousy—"Social", and "do-

CONTENTS

CONTENTS

series" invalidate current classification—but demonstrate that the suggested groups (wish and frustration) are "natural" not artificial—Wish-frustration series are not so notable as changes in the same patient during the course of the disease—Mnemonic Diagram—Explanation—Health, frustration and morbid aim—Explanation—Affinities and contrasts—Value of Myers' interpretation of mental disease—Adler's interpretation of mental disease—Successive Freudian views of psychoses—Recent Freudian views of psychoses—their inadequacy—1st, over-elaboration of theory involved—2nd, social inadequacy of libido conception—Trend of Psychoanalysis towards social explanation—Views compared in this respect—Suggested mechanism of the initial psychopathic deflection of development.

CONTENTS

attempt to explain this without postulating love—He takes little notice of social behaviour in animals and interprets this anthropomor-
phically—His patriarchal bias—The affective meaning of the Theory
of Death Instinct—Speculative origin and delusional development of
the idea—Its absurd implications never noticed by Freud—His evasion of issues and disingenuous defences—use of obscure analogies
to avoid retractation—Uselessness of the theory—A gratuitous fantasy
—Bad Method—Freud's insistence upon the sexual origin of tenderness—He regards love as sexuality, goal-inhibited through fear and
repression—Tendentiousness of Freud—Conception of Narcissism a
denial-of-love—His pessimism—Conception of Sublimation likewise a
denial of love—Complementarity of Sex and Culture—*Three* interpretations are possible—Freud's selective interest in "latent" content
—His materialism—His belief in compulsion as the prime socializing
agency and civilizing force—and in the tyrant and superman—Sum-
mary of Freud's systematic error—His admitted misinterpretation of
anxiety, and insistence upon the material aspect of the separation
anxiety—His utilitarianism—He considers morality is based upon castration-fear—Automatic or spontaneous Repression—His negative conception of Human Motive. (Note D) (1) Posture in Coitus and
Freudian attitude to sex; (2) Over-valuation of masculinity; (3)
Röheim's doubts.

CHAPTER XIV

FREUDIAN PRACTICE IS A "CURE" BY LOVE 242

Freudian Metapsychology and Practice unrelated and even opposed—
and have to be supplemented by a very unsystematic *clinical theory*
—Original non-logical structure of Freud's Psychology—Its casual development—The Conception of Death Instinct split off clinical theory
from Metapsychology, and was followed by a more social tendency
in the development of the former—The concepts of Ego-ideal and
Super-ego embody the social instance—Their introduction expresses
love evoked by contact with patients—while the free speculations of
the metapsychology express Hate harmlessly—The Flight from Love
—Instead of theory *influencing* therapy; it cannot even explain it—
Factors in Therapy — Interpretation — "Overcoming Resistances" —
"Transference Neuroses"—The Narcissistic Diseases gain nothing by
the loosening of Repression—Freud's false conception of Expression—
The "overcoming of anxiety" and at-one-ment—"Mitigating the severity of the Super-Ego" is reconciliation with parents and their sub-
stitutes—"The Physician's Love heals the Patient"—The Physician as
mediator and as sacrificial victim—Unconscious motivations of "pas-
sive therapy"—The Physician himself is healed by love—Progress of
Clinical Theory towards the recognition of love—Play therapy—
"Active therapy" and the treatment of Psychotics are frankly "loving"
—Love is the common factor in all psychotherapy, however carefully
disguised—Sympathy and Compassion—Security with the mother—
"Overcoming hate with love"—Freud the Theorist and Freud the
Healer—He can tolerate children but not Mothers—His Thanato-pho-
bia—Note E Motivation of behaviourism.

THE
ORIGINS OF LOVE AND HATE

PREFACE

In our anxiety to avoid the intrusion of sentiment into our scientific formulations, have we not gone to the length of excluding it altogether from our field of observation ? Is love a fiction, an illusion of a weak mind shrinking from reality, and if so how and why should our minds (regarded as really incapable of loving) ever have created the " idea " of love? Science is concerned with the whole range of experience, but its aim is to formulate this *without* the bias of hope or fear. It must therefore exclude *wish and purpose* (so far as is humanly possible) from the scientific " interest " but not necessarily from the scientific " field·". We even draw a distinction in this respect between " pure " and " applied " science, and regard the outlook of the latter as being restricted by reason of its " practical " objectives. Even pure science, however, cannot function without a driving " interest " of which indeed it is an expression, but it is characterized by its aim to abstract this interest from any *particular* wish or purpose, so as to extend and organize knowledge in a way that shall be valid for all. While holding that our formulations can never be final, philosophic science holds also that they should be objective, i.e. uninfluenced by the limitations of the senses and the distortions due to feeling and tradition. If science had any philosophy of life it would be expressed thus : " We should wish what we see, not see what we wish." This attitude to reality probably constitutes the funda-mental antithesis of science and religion, but we must consider whether the scientific attitude is not itself a denial of a section of reality—a denial, that is, of a body of fact as well as of a " bias of interest " —a range of data, too, which vitally concerns us as psychopathologists.

It will not be denied that even the scientific mind is the product of evolution and culture, and that, while it has got rid of certain imperfections in itself, it may have done so at the expense of limiting its purview. Even within the field of scientific method this operation of abstraction is admitted to occur, as when primitive physics excluded from its study the " secondary qualities " of matter. It may be agreed, then, that certain data are peculiarly refractory to scientific method, and that certain states of mind are incompatible with the scientific attitude. If then one of these " objectionable " states is a psychological fact, e.g. sentimentality, it would tend to get less than justice from scientific study, and psychology would suffer for too rigid an adherence to the idealisms appropriate to physical science. (It is even rather absurd that some psychologists should idealize the formulations of physical science at a time when physicists themselves are not agreed as to the *Kind* of formula which is desirable.)

Surely the bankruptcy of science upon the problem of social integration leaves the field open for fresh hypotheses, and even suggests that materialistic, mechanistic science is at a peculiar disadvantage in dealing with the topic of human " attachments ". I would go further still and assert that science itself represents a flight from tenderness into a peculiarly sublimated form of intellectual " play ", and that in this psychological

INTRODUCTION 3

respect it is an antithesis to the Christian religion
which seeks to reconstitute the tender relationships
with the human environment which is lost in early
childhood.

When I began my studies of social behaviour
twenty years ago, however, I never imagined that
I would come to attempt to put the conception of
altruistic (non-appetitive) love on a scientific footing.
Rejecting the "ad hoc" and therefore sterile
hypothesis of a "herd instinct" both on biological
and methodological grounds, (A) I was nevertheless
early compelled to recognize that the psychoses
are essentially disorders of the social disposition ;
(B) and that all our theories of the construction
of the social group are seriously inadequate.
(G) Five years ago, however, I realized that the
infant differs more from our primitive ancestors
than we adults do, in spite of Recapitulation
Theories (C, D, E) and that this adaptation to
infancy (as I called it) implies an innate disposition
towards the social habit though not towards a
"Herd Instinct". (F) Nurture of the young and
"the social habit" appeared to me associated with
each other, and with the replacement of blind
instinct by intelligence, in their actual distribution
throughout the Animal Kingdom (G).

I had been compelled to reject the Freudian
Metapsychology on logical and biological grounds
from the time of its appearance (H, C, D), but it
was not until 1932 that I seriously questioned
Freud's sexual theory and the clinical conception
of the Oedipus Complex and sex-jealousy, paternal
repression and castration-anxiety, as the main
determinants of culture and character. In February
of the latter year, however, in studying the change
that had occurred in Teutonic culture and character
during the middle ages and particularly the history
of the witch phobia, I reached the conclusion that

repression was a function of love, not of fear, and
that the repressor of the "oedipus complex", etc.,
was the mother, not the father (F, J). My
theoretical standpoint was still dominated by the
fate of the Oedipus Complex, but I seemed to be
able to get a new and synthetic point of view towards
the data of animal behaviour, the evolution of
culture and the Psychoses, which Freud had been
unable to achieve. 1933 was mainly devoted to
psychopathology (M) and 1934 to a study of the
forces underlying social life generally, and particularly to the nature of the jealousies, etc., which
differentiate one culture and character from another.
I reached the conception of a Dimorphism of human
" nature " and Culture (of course never clear-cut
or absolute) and of the mode of interaction between
cultural conditions and the upbringing of the child,
which I had outlined two years previously, but then
merely on a " oedipus " basis (J).

To my mind the source of love now appeared to
be the need for food, etc., and not sexual desires
and sensations (G) ; and of course the original
object of love (as also of reverence) now appeared
to be the mother and not the father. Almost
immediately, however, I saw the possibility that the
biological need for nurture *might be psychologically
presented in the infant mind*, not as a bundle of practical
organic necessities and potential privations, but as
a pleasure in *responsive* companionship and as a
correlative discomfort in loneliness and isolation.
The Freudian conception of self-expression as a
" detensioning " process or emotional evacuation
now seemed to me false and in its place I imagined
expression as an offering or stimulus directed to
the other person, designed to elicit a response while
love itself was essentially a state of active harmonious
interplay. I now seemed to perceive a bias even
in the analytic standpoint and a definite limitation

in their method of investigation and of therapy (K, L). I had arrived at the idea that tenderness itself was tabooed in *our* culture and science—tabooed more intensely even than sex—and that even psycho-analytic investigation and treatment was sharply limited by this bias.

I had now brought conclusions based on animal behaviour and ethnology into relation with the data of psychopathology and the experimental evidence of psychotherapy. For the first time I felt it was in order to try out my working hypotheses systematically against the established theory of Psycho-analysis. This was all the more difficult because Psycho-analytic Theory is supported by the co-operative work of many specialists in widely different fields and presents a relatively integrated body of "explained" observations, extremely difficult for *one* individual, single-handed, to challenge successfully. The Freudians have all the advantage of a disciplined team working on the same hypotheses with definite conceptions and terminology. Against these advantages for interpretation and investigation, however, " team work " seems to hinder any critical philosophical investigation of basic assumptions.

English psychologists, who remain unattached to any " school ", suffer a great disadvantage in lack of co-operation or even of common understanding. Further (largely in consequence of this), they suffer in prestige and publicity and are stigmatized by psycho-analysts as half-hearted, eclectic and individualistic plagiarists of the Freudian discoveries. Neither their criticisms of psycho-analysis nor their own positive views had sufficient unity to lend each other support or to serve as a basis for further co-operative development. Nevertheless something tending towards a consensus of opinion, some common attitude, seems to be developing—a convergence not based merely on a negative attitude to Freud (due to similar repressions), but proceeding from positive observations from a slightly different standpoint and with different cultural antecedents. With an increasing sense of contact with these workers, and having, through the good offices of an individual, enjoyed (for a year or so) the leisure for a wide theoretical survey that psychotherapeutic practice does not permit, I felt emboldened to present an account of the tentative conclusions arrived at, even though this as yet must be extremely unsystematic.

Formally, the tentative theory I have formed belongs to the group of psychologies that originates from the work of Freud. It differs fundamentally from psycho-analysis in introducing the conception of an innate need-for-companionship which is the infant's only way of self-preservation. This need, giving rise to parental and fellowship " love ", I put in the place of the Freudian Libido, and regard it as genetically independent of genital appetite.

The application of this conception seems to re-orient the whole psycho-analytic dynamics. It attributes to the mother the significance in rearing that Freud formerly attributed to the father ; it lessens the importance attached to *individual sense-gratification* as motive and increases the significance of *social* desires and interests (i.e. it represents " expression " as an offering or stimulus applied to others not merely as a pleasant exercise of function). It denies the sexual basis of culture-sublimation and it relegates the Oedipus Wish and Sexual Jealousy to third place in primacy and importance as disturbers of social development and harmony. It seems that Freudian opinion is trending in this direction ; but no one seems to recognize that the logical conclusion is *that the Oedipus Complex, being largely contingent on particular modes of rearing and forms of family structure, culture and racial character must vary within wide limits—must be, as I said, Dimorphous.* In other respects also the theory here sketched produces widely divergent interpretations from those of Freud. A vast mass of difficult (even transcendent) hypothetical constructions are swept away, and a very considerable body of hitherto admittedly intractable problems are seen to have a possible solution.

In many other respects these theories seem to be of much wider applicability than Psycho-analytic Psychology proper. Economic, National and Racial sentiments now offer a promising field of research ; new possibilities are opened up in the Psychology of Religion and its evolution ; definite problems can be formulated in regard to the development of social feeling and " cultural " interest and new light is thrown on the bewildering variety of mental disease. As illustrations of this I have included two papers delivered and published elsewhere.

At the same time it must be understood that these are only tentative formulations, roughly applied over the whole field of human *and animal* behaviour. Their validity remains to be judged by their logical coherence, the scope of their application and the heuristic and practical value of the correlations and interpretations they suggest. This cannot well be done by one man, wholly apart from the possibility that attractive results (so far secured) may have been due to the use of an elastic *measuring-rod.* This is my excuse for bringing together results so far attained and for inviting the critical attention of a public wider than my own profession.

The present volume is largely based (Chaps. I to XII) on a series of lectures delivered to the Institute of Child Psychology this spring. It is therefore non-technical so far as the ability of the author and the nature of the subject will allow. The more recondite arguments and detailed evidence must be reserved for a later work which is in hand. Inevitably also there occurs a good deal of repetition, as the same subject must be looked at from different angles. Psychology does not lend itself to systematic presentation.

It may also be objected that the book is not a balanced presentation of data inasmuch as but little attention is given to morbid psychology, delinquency, etc., whereas stress is laid throughout on the social aspects and relations of mental process. There are, however, good reasons for this. Biological and Ethnological data formed the ground for my own departure from Psycho-analytic beliefs, and, further, they have certain special value for the psychologist.

First the facts are objective and can be checked by several observers, *unlike evidence derived from the analysis of patients*. The behaviour in question also appears under natural conditions and not under the artificial and uncertain influence of " transference ". But it has a third special value for us. It presents us with pictures of mental and social life departing widely from everything we are accustomed to take for granted. Thus it affords us *the only means* of criticizing our idea of what is " normal " and what is " natural " for mankind. It is impossible even to pretend to an understanding of human nature without knowing what varieties it *can* produce and under what diverse conditions it can develop *and survive*. Freud and Adler themselves naively regard as "human nature" or "instinct", traits and dispositions which may turn out to be the product in subtle ways of certain factors in *our particular culture*. Added to this, psychopathological data have the further disadvantages of being highly technical and extremely voluminous. Further a lifetime of observations can furnish a thorough study of very few cases, say two to three *completed* per annum. All sorts of practical circumstances too dictate the selection of cases for investigation, so there is no sort of guarantee that any observer has worked upon a " fair sample ". I preferred, therefore, to offer a tentative " try-out " of the group of related working hypotheses over other fields (which are indeed wide enough) and to reserve more detailed technical evidence and argument for a subsequent publication, in the hope that criticism and co-operation might test and perhaps develop these ideas.

My thanks are due to Miss J. M. S.. for help with the index, etc.

INTRODUCTORY REFERENCES

A. " Critique of the Theory of Herd Instinct." *Jl. of Mental Science*, 1922.

B. " Some Sociological Aspects of Psychiatry." (*Ibid.*), 1923.

C. " Critique of the Theory of Recapitulation." *Jl. of Neurol. and Psychopath*, 1924.

D. " An Irrelevant Accretion to the Freudian Theory." *Brit. Jl. of Med. Psych.*, 1925.

E. " Adaptation to Infancy." *Bulletin of Psychopathology* (private publication).

F. " The Mother : Agent or Object " (with Dr J. I. Suttie), Pts. I and II. *Brit. Jl. of Med. Psych.*, 1932-3.

G. Lecture (unpublished), B. Psych. Soc. (Med. Sect.), " Non-Sexual Factors in the Evolution of Culture and Character," Feb. 1934.

H. " Metapsychology and Biology." *Jl. of Neurol. and Psychopath*, 1924.

J. "Religion, Racial Character and Mental
    Health." *Brit. Jl. of Med. Psych.*, 1933.

K. "Theory *versus* Therapy : a Study of the
    Unconscious Motivations of Psycho-
    analysis." Paper (privately circulated)
    delivered to R. M. Psy. Assoc. (Research
    Group), Dec. 1934, and April 1935.

L. "Origins of Love and Hate." Paper (privately
    circulated) delivered Nov. 1934, to the
    Institute of Medical Psychology.

M. "A New Conception of the Psychoses."
    Paper (privately circulated) delivered to
    the Institute of Medical Psych., Jan. and
    Feb. 1934.

N. "Psychological Factors in War." *Year Book
    of the Commonwealth Institute*, 1935.

Papers not published are largely embodied in the
present work or will be in that ensuing.

CHAPTER I

THE BIOLOGY OF LOVE AND INTEREST, ETC.

MODERN Psychology is concerned with the motives of human conduct and the sources of enjoyment, happiness and misery. This contrasts rather sharply with what is called Academic Psychology which affords us rather a *description* of the adult self-conscious mind, and gives us little assistance in predicting or influencing behaviour and still less in the understanding of mental development and its aberrations. For all *practical* purposes we are dependent upon this modern " dynamic " and genetic psychology, which, broadly speaking, we owe to the pioneer work of Freud. Indeed twenty years ago we could have said with substantial truth that the only useful psychology was Freud's. Since then, however, there have been important developments and divergences of opinion. Other schools of thought have developed their own systems with independence more or less artificial. Even within the Freudian movement itself important dissensions have recently arisen, largely through the work of the child psychologists. Many vital tenets and conceptions, confidently held ten or fifteen years ago, are now formally abandoned. Freud himself has said, " We shall have to abandon the universality of the dictum that the Oedipus Complex is the nucleus of the Neurosis."

Everyday life and mental illness alike are now regarded as an attempt to " master anxiety ", and this anxiety itself is no longer considered to be merely frustrated sexual desire but is regarded as largely due to hatred and aggressive wishes. The task of healthy development is even described by Dr Brierly as " overcoming hatred with love ", and in many devious ways Psycho-analytic Theory is recognizing more clearly the social nature of man, and is no longer presenting his psychology as that of a self-contained entity independent of his fellows except in so far as his bodily appetites and gratifications demand their services. Psycho-analysis in fact is losing much that made it obnoxious to European philosophy, good sense and good feeling, but it still fails to take a wide enough view of its subject matter. This statement may seem outrageous to many who are acquainted with Psycho-analytic studies of Art, Biography, Primitive Custom, etc., but it must be remembered that psycho-analytic ideas are merely *applied* in these fields ; they are *developed* and *tested* almost exclusively in the consulting room.

From the widest scientific and philosophic standpoint we must consider the human mind as the product of evolution—that is to say as having had its definite function to serve in the survival of our species and in the attainment of our present dominant position. Later we shall find it necessary to consider mind from two other points of view also —namely as the result of the child's contact with members of its own family, and as the result of its parents' social and cultural relationships. The evolution of cultures and civilizations cannot be explained in terms of the individual minds which are its members. Nor should mind be considered in isolation from its social contacts. Psychologists are prone to describe a Mind as if it were an independent self-contained but standardized entity, a number of which, grouped together in some mysterious way, constitutes a Society. Anthropologists frequently make the opposite mistake and describe social organizations and behaviour with little reference to the minds which produce and are moulded by these institutions. The separation of the science of Mind from that of Society is arbitrary and was originally dictated by practical convenience and the tastes and fancy of the student. The two sciences must be pursued in relation to each other, for mind is social and society is mental. Finally the whole study of human behaviour must be correlated with that of the social animals both on the grounds of the evolutionary relationship of species and of the common purposes in life and the different means of attaining these.

We must first, then, direct our study to the relationship between the Human Mind and those of animals which *might be* similar to those of our remote ancestors. Formerly, Comparative Psychology was the playground of the Victorian Arm-chair Theorists who cheerfully attributed much of their own ill-understood mentality to the higher animals and even the social insects. Mind in those days was regarded as mainly concerned with the intelligent pursuit of rational purposes and/or with the instinctive performance of some biological task satisfying some need or *condition of survival*. Worse still, these old psychologists reconstructed the mind of the *infant* in terms of this false conception of *animal* mind. The child and primitive adults, they supposed, were alike and but a stage removed from our pre-human ancestors who in turn were regarded as very similar to the higher animals, although, as we shall see, the very opposite is the case. Accordingly the infant's " disposition " was regarded as a bundle of instincts some of which, like sex, remained latent till adult life (!), while others had to be disciplined and held in control by education and civilization.

If ever a doubt arose as to the forces which brought about this supposed *subjection of animal impulses,* one or other of three different explanations was offered.

(1) Religion and the Will of God was cited, though it did not well explain *animal* society or the fact that primitive peoples conform far more closely and rigorously to tribal custom and moral codes than civilized Christians do

(2) " Reason and Utility " were popular as an alternative explanation ; though here again it was difficult to understand how a species of animals like our pre-social ancestors could foresee the advantage of social co-operation without culture or experience, could negotiate such a social contract without language, and could adhere to the bargain without moral impulses.

A third type of explanation of man's social character suggested that a change had occurred in his inherited constitution ; in other words a chemical change in the germ plasm. According to this " herd instinct " theory, man is different from birth from non-social animals. The theory however really explains nothing and has been utterly useless, adding nothing to our knowledge and presenting an illusory solution to the problem. Further it presents the difficulty of forcing us to suppose that the same variation has occurred in at least twenty-five different species of insect and in a very great number of species of birds and mammals ; whereas man, the most social of all, has the greatest difficulty in maintaining his adjustment to social life.

It will be no matter for surprise that, with such conceptions of the infant mind and of the forces moulding upbringing, no progress was made in the understanding either of the child or of society. Such conclusions as these early speculators arrived at were wrong in every material respect and wholly useless as working hypotheses for further investigation. When we actually study the facts of social life comparatively, in order to see if social differ from " solitary " animals in any respect *other than this habit*, the important fact emerges that social animals as a rule nurture their young and conversely that nurtured animals tend to be more or less social. The social disposition seems to be a modified continuance of the infant's need for the nurtural parent's presence (even when the material need is outgrown). Into it enters also nurtural or parental impulses, but there is no need to postulate a special social instinct.

We need in fact only suppose· the child is born with a mind and instincts *adapted to infancy* ; or, in other words, so disposed as to profit by parental nurture. This is not an unreasonable supposition, but it implies the conclusion that the child mind is *less* like that of primitive animals than is the adult mind. It is less like animal mind since it is adapted to a milieu and mode of behaving vastly different from that of free-living, self-supporting animals. Instead of an armament of instincts—latent or otherwise—which would lead it to attempt on its own account things impossible to its powers or even undesirable—it is born with a simple attachment-to-mother who is the sole source of food and protection. Instincts of self-preservation such as would be appropriate in an animal which has to fend for itself would be positively destructive to the dependent infant, whose impulses *must* be adapted to its mode of livelihood, namely a pseudo-parasitism.

We can reject therefore once and for all the notion of the infant mind being a bundle of co-operating or competing instincts, and suppose instead that it is dominated from the beginning by the need to retain the mother—a need which, if thwarted, must produce the utmost extreme of terror and rage, since the loss of mother is, under natural conditions, but the precursor of death itself. We have now to consider whether this attachment-to-mother is merely the sum of the infantile bodily needs and satisfactions which refer to her, or whether the *need for a mother is primarily presented to the child mind as a need for company and as a discomfort in isolation.* I can see no way of settling this question conclusively, but the fact is indisputable that a need for company, moral encouragement, attention, protectiveness, leadership, etc., remains after all the sensory gratifications connected with the mother's body have become superfluous and have been surrendered. In my view this is a direct development of the primal attachment-to-mother, and, further, I think that play, co-operation, competition and culture-interests generally are substitutes for the mutually caressing relationship of child and mother. *By these substitutes we put the whole social environment in the place once occupied by mother—* maintaining with it a mental or cultural rapport in lieu of the bodily relationship of caresses, etc., formerly enjoyed with the mother. A joint interest in *things* has replaced the reciprocal interest in *persons* ; friendship has developed out of love. True, the personal love and sympathy is preserved in *friendship* ; but this differs from love in so far as it comes about by the *direction of attention upon the same things* (rather than upon each other), or by the pursuit of *the same activities even if these are not intrinsically useful* and gratifying, as is the case with much ritual and dance, etc. The interest is intensified even if it is not entirely created (artificial) by being *shared* ; while the fact of sharing interest deepens the appreciation of the other person's presence even while it deprives it of sensual (or better of sensorial) qualities.

This is my view of the process of sublimation ; but it differs very greatly from that of Freud and his enormous " team " of expert specialists. As far as anyone can tell, Freud considers that all the infant's desires for the mother, and the gratification it receives from her, are of a sexual nature. Indeed it is probable that a strict Freudian would define all pleasure or satisfaction as " sexual ". These longings and urges are called " skin ", " eye ", " mouth ", and other " erotisms " to indicate their essentially *sexual* nature. At a certain age, Freud tells us, they become organized under the supremacy of " the genital zone ". That is to say they become " sexual " in the " proper " and popular meaning of the word. Having become sexual—according to Freud—they have also become incestuous (directed towards other members of the same family) and hence lead to jealousy. The Oedipus Complex is thereby established. Undergoing repression next from fear of the rival's displeasure and revenge, these sexual wishes (for the parent of opposite sex) become goal-inhibited ; that is to say become a de-sexualized love. Or they may be deflected to the parent of the same sex, thereby constituting homo-sexuality, and then sublimated as friendship. The wishes themselves may be altered, distorted or symbolized *beyond recognition* and this " displacement " from the original biological objective is imagined as the basis of culture-interest in the race and (presumably) of sublimation in the individual. (Freud, *Introductory Lectures*, p. 290.)

Freud's view seems to me inadequate to explain the mechanism of the development of interest or its very early appearance in childhood, that is to say, its appearance before the maturation, repression and sublimation of sexuality can be imagined to have taken place. Further it is certain that the Freudian ideas in these matters cannot explain the constitution of society. Society in fact never was instituted by an aggregation of independent adult individuals, nor even by the growth of a single family by polygamy, group marriage, exogamy or otherwise. Society exists already in the group of the children of the same mother and develops by the addition of others to this original love-group. Neither does culture arise by the thwarting of sex-impulse and its deflection to symbolic ends. (Freudian Sublimation.) Still less does it arise through rational co-operation in the pursuit of the material necessities of life. Necessity is not " the mother of invention " ; Play is.

Play is a necessity, not merely to develop the bodily and mental faculties, but to give to the individual that reassuring contact with his fellows which he has lost when the mother's nurtural services are no longer required or offered. Conversation is mental play, but it is long before the child completely outgrows the need for bodily contact. Even many adults retain the need for caresses apart from sexual intentions and gratifications. Nevertheless cultural interests do ultimately form a powerful antidote to loneliness even where there is no participator present in person ; that is to say, cultural pursuits have a social value even where " the other person " is imagined or left unspecified.

We can now clearly understand why man has become virtually the only cultural animal and hence by far the most sociable. We can also understand from the same considerations why Man has developed an aggressiveness, a competitiveness and a complex morality in which also he is unique. The neo-Freudians, approaching this point of view, no longer refer to human life as a struggle for pleasure, sense-gratification or self-expression (detensioning) as formerly. They see the master-motive of humanity as the "struggle to master anxiety" and further recognize this dread to be one of "separation". Still, they endeavour to retain a materialistic, individualistic interpretation of separation-anxiety ; but, more and more, psychologists are convinced that it is really a dread of loneliness which is the *conscious expression of the human form of the instinct of self-preservation* which originally attached the infant to its mother.

It is as if the process of evolution had taken back with one hand a portion of the benefits conferred by the other. Man has to be thankful for,

(1) his prolonged and sheltered immaturity which provides leisure and a respite from the struggle for existence, in which to *experiment* with development and with behaviour ;

(2) he has to thank the extreme plasticity of his instinct of self-preservation, not only for his adaptation to infancy, but for his capacity to deflect interest from the satisfaction of appetite and from the procuring of defence and the means of existence, to activities we call cultural, which in turn have *incidentally* procured for him a tremendous mastery over all nature except his own. Against these benefits (of the opportunity to develop and to learn and the interest-disposition to do so) we must set the very equivocal power to love and the need for love. While this provides the incentive and conditions for *learning* by experience and for accumulating knowledge from generation to generation and so of building up an immortal tradition, at the same time it drives man so hard as to make him anxious, aggressive and inhibited. Man is the only *anxious* animal. When nature produced him she found herself with an "explosive" on her hands which she did not know how to handle. For all our language, cultural achievements and our family life, our love-need is still seeking new

techniques of social relationship. In this search for the security and satisfaction of social integration (fellowship) we are constantly driven into false channels which we will have to study presently.

To sum up the evolutionary antecedents of man, we may say the principal features that distinguish him from other (even social) animals are :

(a) The extreme degree to which the definite, stereotyped, specific, instincts of " self-preservation " of his pre-human ancestors are " melted down " or unfocussed into a dependent love-for-mother, which in turn becomes need for others and finally parental " love " and interest, social feeling, etc.

(b) The prolongation of the period of immaturity between organically nurtured infancy and matehood and parenthood. This, as I said, along with the social need, affords both the opportunity and the incentive to co-operative activities not concerned with the material necessities of existence, and which may therefore develop indefinitely on free *playful* and *experimental* lines. The organic bodily relationships of infancy, matehood and parenthood can be imagined as affording security and satiety to this social need, and in them, moreover, the interest of each party is absorbed in the other *person* rather than directed upon " things " and *joint pursuits*. Further, adulthood has its practical, material cares that demand close attention to business and the rigorous adherence to well-tried customary methods of getting things done. The practical man is notoriously stereotyped—a creature of habit and opposed to all innovation. Practical shipbuilders told us a century ago that iron ships could not float. We can therefore conclude that the period of *youth* is not only that of mental development in the individual, but is the reason for the development of that distinctively human product, Culture.

(c) The fact (mentioned in (a)) that in man a collection of instincts is replaced by a relatively aimless and plastic curiosity, attachments and interest, is of course the reason why this play period can be turned to such account. Non-appetitive " interest " combined with need-for-company (they may even have the same origin) to apply the drive to the cultural pursuits of knowledge for its own sake, and to the development of a tradition which can be accumulated indefinitely.

These three characteristics then represent the advantages that the course of evolution has conferred upon man. Respectively they make him *social*, *educable* and *progressive*. At the same time evolution has left man with so little definite biological guidance in the form of instinct and with so much drive towards association and experiment that he has become *unstable and pervertible*. Other distinctively human characteristics are thus accounted for, namely man's anxiety, his arbitrary social customs and his liability to psychogenic mental disorder. Now we can see why man has been set a peculiar task which to some seems to offset his advantages— namely the task of understanding and mastering himself. This is what gives to modern psychology its peculiar importance and makes it a matter of urgency that it should be widely and critically studied by every citizen and not relegated to the specialist.

Having presented a synoptical picture of the fundamentals of human nature as I see it, it is, therefore, only fair to show how this compares with the broad outlines of the Freudian view. The difference will be found to turn largely, but by no means wholly, on the meaning attached to the word sexual.

I see in the infant's longing for the mother an expression of what in free-living animals we call the self-preservative instinct. Consistently with this, I see in anxiety and hate an expression of apprehension or discomfort at the frustration, or threatened frustration, of this all-important motive. Freud sees the infantile attachment as sexual and indeed sensual, while he regards anxiety and hate as proceeding from a separate independent instinct for destruction *which even aims to destroy its possessor.* The latter theory of Death-Instinct has produced the greatest dissensions in the ranks of Psychoanalysts themselves, and has been shown to be completely untenable and self-contradictory in many ways. (Refs. F, H.)

Again the period between infancy and adulthood appears to me to be dominated by an almost insatiable social need, which uses the plastic energy of human interest for its satisfaction in play. Freud sees this period as one of repression of the (by now definitely *genital*) sex impulses on account of their incestuous aims. Interest for Freud is just a substitute for *or sublimation* of sexual yearnings, and friendship is sexuality which has become "*goal-inhibited*" by the definitely genital wish becoming repressed. He accounts for the supposed stronger cultural " drive " in the male sex on the supposition that the Oedipus Wish (sexual desire for mother) is stronger and better repressed than is the girl's corresponding desire for her father. It seems to me that man's cultural need is greater than woman's, inasmuch as he can never look forward to the bodily functions of maternity and lactation by whic h evolution has conferred upon women the virtual monopoly of the child. In a later chapter I will deal with the evidence of this and other jealousies which are much neglected by Freudians.

Further comparison of views must be deferred until after a consideration of the subjective aspect of the infant's mind.

NOTE A.

THE BIOLOGY OF HATE AND ANXIETY

In organisms which are not born in a state of nurtural dependency the emotion of anger is little more than an intensification of effort to overcome frustration. Anger and fear are thus closely akin in their function as in their physiological mechanism, the former aiming to attain an end, the latter to avoid a danger.

I am suggesting that in animals born or hatched in a state of nurtural dependency the whole instinct of self-preservation, including the potential dispositions to react with anger and fear, is at first directed towards the mother. Anger is then aimed, not at the direct removal of frustration or attainment of the goal of the moment, still less at her destruction, but *at inducing the mother to accomplish these wishes for the child.* Instead of being the most desperate effort at *self-help* it has become the most insistent demand upon the *help of others*—the most emphatic plea which cannot be overlooked. It is now the maximal effort to *attract* attention, and as such must be regarded as a protest against unloving conduct rather than as aiming at destruction of the mother, which would have fatal repercussions upon the self.

Hatred, I consider, is just a standing reproach to the hated person, and owes all its meaning to a demand for love. If it were a desire (or appetite for destruction for its own sake), I cannot see how it could be focussed so definitely upon one individual and as a rule upon a person who is significant in the subject's life. I would say " Earth hath no hate *but* love to hatred turned, and hell no fury but a baby scorned," for hatred, except for a preferred rival or a rejecting lover, does not seem to exist. At bottom therefore hatred is always ambivalent, always self-frustrated.   It has no free outlet, can look for no favourable response, and this is why it is so important in Psychopathology.[1]

In the same way the " instinct " of fear must be modified to suit the conditions of nurtured infancy. The helpless infant cannot flee or perform any avoiding reactions efficiently so that the emotion of fear can find useful expression *only as an appeal to the mother*.   As in the case of anger, the response expected and desired is not an identical emotion on the part of the mother.   Either anger or apprehension on her part increases the corresponding disturbance in the child's mind.   Where the child is afraid it is reassured by her confidence and serenity, but not by her indifference and neglect, which is perhaps the worst of all for the child. Neglect of the fear-appeal is extremely traumatic.

---

[1] In a measure it must undergo *automatic inhibition* or repression, and this process is already being dimly perceived by clinical analysis.

CHAPTER II

A SCIENTIFIC CONCEPTION OF LOVE, HATE AND INTEREST

WE must now endeavour to paint a picture of life as it probably appears from the infant's point of view. This must of course be largely a matter of guess-work, since memories—even if recalled under deep analysis or hypnosis—must be influenced by the adult medium through which they are expressed. However we do know something of the conditions which limit the infant's appreciation of its surroundings. For example it is unable to use its eyes together—to fixate—in such a way as to get stereoscopic vision with a sense of depth and distance. Further, lacking the experience of reaching for things and of locomotion, it cannot to begin with have any idea of space, and this will for a time retard the building up of an orderly mental picture of the rooms, passages, etc., in which it has been. For the infant, therefore, people will not "come and go", they will "appear and disappear" as for us they still do in dreams and in supernatural fantasies.

People themselves have not in the infant's eyes the distinctive features which for us constitute them personalities ; though certainly it is probable that the infant is instinctively attracted to the mother by smell. Language, too, is meaningless for the infant except for tone-modulation and rhythm, which probably evoke emotional responses just as smell evokes appetites from the beginning. In the light of such knowledge of the conditions limiting the infant's experience and its stock of memories, we can, with some probability, interpret infant behaviour.

Such a picture of the infant consciousness differs from the " blank page " of the philosopher Plato as much as it does from the " blooming, buzzing confusion " which William James imagined. According to the view put before you in the first chapter the mind has a general directing purpose from the beginning, and consequent anxieties and resentments when this is frustrated. The purpose is not clear in the infant's as in our own minds ; it carries as yet no idea of the desired satisfactions and dreaded dangers. The child's wishes are rather *states* of pleasure or of need and discomfort passing over into equally aimless *states* of anxiety and rage. By calling them *states of rage* I mean to emphasize that they are not anger *at anyone* any more than they are caused by need of *anything* that the child knows of. They are, in other words, not merely inarticulate but *undirected*, and *objectless* wishes.

From the known conditions of infant life then, we can infer with great probability that the infant, to begin with, cannot appreciate the distinction between itself and its mother. It *discovers* its body by degrees, realizing that in some way an impulse to move is accompanied by felt or seen movement ; in other words the wish and the act are experienced as one. By *contrast with the self it must gradually distinguish the " not-self "* which restricts its movements and acts in a way not expected or wished by itself. The self makes its first appearance as it were, as docile but rather helpless ; the not-self emerges as powerful for pleasure or for displeasure, and by this last possibility it stands out as an inharmonious part of experience. Sometimes it conforms to wish and gratifies need ; sometimes the agency, now perceived as external, acts in disagreeable or unanticipated ways. The very birth of self-consciousness then, for the helpless infant, must be attended by experience of wish and frustration, by gratifications, longings and by *anxiety*, rising at times to angry instinctive cries and struggles directed at the newly discovered " others ".   This process to my mind is " psychic parturition ", the distresses of actual birth forming but a small part of it.   It is responsible in my opinion for that apparently baseless anger that Freud attributes to an " instinct of destruction " ; and further, we must suppose that relatively trivial differences in handling, in the responsiveness of nurses and mothers, may produce great differences in the child's first impressions and reactions, and hence upon the whole future development of temperament.   The important thing to remember, however, is that consciousness of *self* as isolated from and independent of the rest of the world is probably associated with some measure, however trivial, of anxiety and resentment *from the* very beginning, but on the other hand (in my view, as against Freud's) it is also associated with loving feelings towards others as well as with angry claims upon them.

There is another all-important differentiation of experience which must be made by the infant mind about this time and probably in connection with the distinction of self from not-self.   It is the distinction between what is actually being experienced and what is only remembered or " fantasied ".[1]   The

---

[1] It is perhaps the essential character of consciousness that it is not just a picture of what is happening at one instant of time, or, in " learned " language, an *infinitely thin cross-section of process*.   Consciousness introduces the time-dimension as a reality, linking the no-longer-existing past with the actual present in what is called perception or recognition, and forecasting a merely " possible " future on lines influenced by wish or purpose. " Process " and " purpose " are thus inseparable in our own minds from the very beginning, and it is little wonder that man has in his theorizing about nature endeavoured to interpret *external happenings also* in terms of such purposes as are known to him and has consequently formed a theistic or animistic conception of the universe.   It is significant in this connection that the repressed " unconscious " mind is said to be *timeless*, suggesting that the loss of " span " is one of the factors in repression.

actual process of events, however, can rarely coincide with our own purposes. The actual present situation, besides having sensory reality, always differs from anything the infant remembers, because its experience is constantly expanding. Further, the future which actually does eventuate must often differ from that of its hopes and expectations.

Disappointment must actively stimulate the distinction of the self from the not-self which frustrates wish and purpose, or, in other words, prevents or delays the remembered and desired pleasure repeating itself *as a sensory experience*. The instinctive way of dealing with this frustration has already been dealt with—namely the cries expressing discomfort and need, anxiety and finally rage. We have now to notice an alternative technique called fantasy gratification. In this the infant *enjoys directly* the pleasurable *memories* of past gratifications, cutting out or paralysing the disturbing wish or need for the *actual sensory experience*—and in this way becoming (so far as its mind goes) to some extent independent of the apparently un-co-operative. " not-self ", or external environment.

This method of dealing with frustrated need by fantasy or " pleasure thinking "was early recognized by Freud, and distinguished from the instinctive method of coercing the real world by " magic cries and gestures " (affecting the mother) which formed the beginning of " *reality thinking* ". Reality thinking finally leads to the coercion of present impulse in favour of future gratification or to avoid the anger of others (morality). The " pleasure principle " and the " reality principle ", however, seem nowadays to be used rather as descriptive terms than as denoting two different forces or compartments of mental process. The distinction, however, is very important and should be clearly understood, since fantasy thinking is a very important factor in realistic mental development, in the formation of ideals and ambitions and in planning the future. *Only where effort exhausts itself in fantasy or finds adequate satisfaction therein does this mode of activity lead to trouble ;* e.g. morbid self-sufficiency and finally the isolation of dementia precox ; otherwise the temporary " cutting out " of the urgent desire for sensory satisfaction serves the good purpose of liberating *thought* for play, experiment and reflection.

I have presented you with a conception of the primal state of infant mind as being unorganized and undifferentiated in the highest degree. At this phase the distinction has not yet been made between self and mother, the whole of experience is " immediate " ; self and not-self present no antitheses. Impulses function in isolation and hence there is no " control " by " opposing " impulses. Each function brings its own gratification and hence Freud calls this phase of development Auto-erotic. Thereby he implies the self-sufficient, self-regarding nature of the infant's striving and enjoying, and also that all its pleasures are to be regarded as of a sexual nature.

The main significance of this phase seems to me however to lie in the infant's naive acceptance of all experience as unitary and in its inability to discriminate other selves. I therefore place the emphasis upon this aspect by calling it the phase of Infantile Solipsism, thereby relating it to the Metaphysical Theory which regards the existence of other minds (than that of the thinker) as an *inference* (and hence challengeable) rather than as an absolute *self-evident* truth. To my mind the most important aspect of mental development to be elucidated is the *idea of others and of one's own relationship to them.* Freud's interest, however, centres on the nature and inter-relationships of the *impulses seeking expression*, or rather, as *he* conceives it, evacuating or " detensioning " (his own word). Hence the terminological difference.

Freud finds that this first stage (auto-erotic, as he calls it) gives place to one in which, the self having been more or less defined, both love and hate are directed towards this. The self is the object of love as in the myth of Narcissus and is defended from the hypothetical Death-Instinct (desire for death) by the " projection " of this latter wish *against others*, in an altered form, namely that of an Instinct of Destruction. After this the " Narcissistic stage " is supposed to give way, gradually and variably, to one of object love or Allo-erotism. Sexual wishes (now in strict sense of genital thoughts, feelings and impulses) next undergo repression, and (*a*) persist as goal-inhibited love or tenderness, and (*b*) are sublimated (before or after repression), emerging as symbolic substitutes, displacements, etc., etc., and forming the root and energy of Interest, and Culture.

As against this conception of the development of Human Mind, I hold that the primary state (Solipsist), where there is no discrimination of " other " from " self ", gives place *directly* to one in which love and anger are both directed towards *others* (mother). The love of others comes into being simultaneously *with the recognition of their existence*, or, in Freudian language, the perceptions which are integrated as the first recognition of mother are " cathected " with love *from the very beginning*. The narcissistic phase has no real existence ; it is partly an inadequate conception of the solipsist state and partly the product of fantasies, of longings and *of resentment* [see Chapters XIII and XIV]. This I shall show later when I reject the *inter-related* conceptions—namely that of Death and Destruction Instincts, that of Expression as a mere discharge or " detensioning " of impulse, and that of Pansexualism.   All these, as I shall show from many lines of approach, make up one systematic error on Freud's part traceable to definite bias.

I consider then that love of mother is primal in so far as it is the *first formed and directed* emotional relationship. Hate, I regard not as a primal independent instinct (see later), but as a development or intensification of separation-anxiety which in turn is *roused* by a threat against love.   It is the maximal ultimate appeal in the child's power— the most difficult for the adult to ignore. Its purpose is not death-seeking or death-dealing, but the preservation of the self from the isolation which is death, and the restoration of a love relationship.

I find reason to believe that this primal love (and its obverse, anger), while it subserves self-preservation by maintaining the nurtural relationship to the mother, is something more than the sum total of organic needs and gratifications. Further the insistence that the latter are sexual (even in Freud's extended use of the term) obscures from our minds certain vital distinctions and has been a potent factor in the needless elaboration of Freudian Theory. I believe the love-bond to the infant mind has the quality of tenderness from the beginning. It is not sexual desire degenitalized (" goal-inhibited ") by repression as Freud would have it.   True, many of the nurtural gratifications and caresses which originally *mediated* love are dropped in the course of development. Love becomes much more a mental sympathy than a bodily relationship. But if this were (as Freud holds) merely a matter of the unconscious self-denial of the aims and gratifications of love, surely hate (privation—resentment) and not tenderness, would result.   True again, too sudden and violent a denial of the physical manifestations of the mother's love does produce this very phenomenon (see later on " Tenderness Taboo ") ; but tenderness itself could not be *produced* by rejection. The infantile tenderness, with some difficulty, and to a variable extent in different cultures, can unite itself with sex, but it does not originate from this by a process of mutilation.

Again I disagree with Freud by denying that Sexual Love for the Mother, *rejected and repressed*, becomes Interest-in-Things by a process of deflection and symbolic substitution. This branch of Sublimation (tenderness being the product of the other) I consider arises in the following way. Originally the Baby-Mother bond is vaguely and intuitively appreciated by the former as mutual absorption. By degrees the baby's expanding activities and sense-impression change the character of this bond. A service rendered to the baby's body and a caress are originally indistinguishable by it, but the baby's perceptions of and interest in its own body and its immediate surroundings grow rapidly under the influence of the mother's ministrations. In this way it develops Interest-in-Itself, the process Freud misconceives as Narcissism. It is of course arbitrary to say at what point the *companionship of love* becomes the *companionship of interest*, but there is no doubt that the feeling-relationship of the companions does change *as attention ceases to be absorbed wholly and reciprocally each in the other and becomes directed convergently to the same things.* Co-operative activities, identical or complementary attitudes to outside happenings, build up a world of *common meanings* which marks a differentiation from simple love wherein " the world " of each is the other person. The simple direct bond has become a triangular relationship wherein external objects form the *medium of play.*

Of course the primal love relationship need not cease with the development of the Interest Rapport ; but the latter can become highly differentiated from the " love " from which it took origin.   Thus new interest-relationships can be formed with play-fellows without the preliminary establishment of love. Further, they can be formed with persons unknown, and finally, they differ from the love rapport in that they may embrace any *number of participators*, becoming, if anything, *more intense thereby* [i.e. they are less jealous and possessive]. Although, therefore, there are all grades of feeling from love to interest (e.g. interest *in* the other person or persons), to discover the exact process of differentiation is vitally important to our understanding of social life.   Freud's conception of the origin of interest in sublimation of sexual impulses which have been denied their organic satisfaction is admittedly obscure and incomplete.   I think that, like his theory of the cognate subject of tenderness-development, it is totally inadequate to explain the facts and can only be upheld by supplementary theories and explanations which pile conjecture upon hypothesis.   The function of the interest rapport has this in common with love that it affords a sense of companionship and dispels that of loneliness.   It is thus social not sexual in function or in origin.

I might now summarize the differences between Freud's conception of mental development and my own.   Our starting points (hypothetical conceptions of infancy) are not, as I have said, very dissimilar.   On the left the diagram represents " Freudian " development, on the right my own view of the equivalent phases.

The differences are not isolated points of disagreement in observations, formulation or inference such as might result from differences of personal ability

DIAGRAM ILLUSTRATING THE THEORETICAL DEVELOPMENT OF
THE AFFECTIVE DISPOSITION, ACCORDING RESPECTIVELY TO
FREUD AND TO THE HYPOTHESIS HERE PRESENTED.

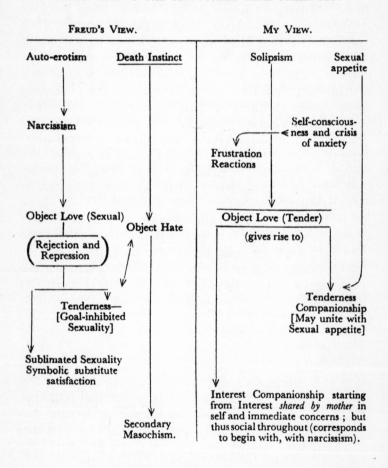

or experience.   They are not the random result of
pure *errors* on Freud's part or on mine.   They form
together a systematic, logically coherent, divergence
of opinion, indicating a difference either in standpoint or in bias or in both.   In later Chapters
[XIII and XIV] I shall endeavour to convict Freud
of a definite bias and to indicate its general nature
and source.   Here I shall merely explain how from a
fallacious metaphysical starting-point Freud has
(in my opinion) been led into a series of related
errors.

Freud conceives all motive (*a*) as a " letting off
of steam ", an evacuation or detensioning, and
(*b*) as a quest for sensory gratification.   Anxiety,
he consequently thought, arose when an *outlet* was
denied and tension consequently rose.   (Significantly this latter conception has recently been
admitted to be erroneous.)   Man's conative nature
Freud depicts as very little more purposeful than
an explosive ; indeed he explicitly stated that life
is no more than the attempt to attain death and
dissolution by a particular way.   Human social life is
regulated in so far as the " explosions " of impulse
produce painful and terrifying consequences to the
originator.   Man is a bundle of energies seeking
to dissipate themselves but restrained by Fear.
Against this I regard expression not as an out-
pouring for its own sake, but as *an overture demanding
response from others.*   It is the absence of this response, I think, that is the source of all anxiety and
rage whose expression is thus *wholly purposive.*[1]
Even the sexual act aims to elicit response ; and
surely the aims and satisfactions of maternity
transcend the evacuation of the mammary glands !

Concurrently with this view of the nature of
impulse and expression Freud denies the existence
of love as a primal and independent need for

[1] See Note A, Chap. I.

expression and response. Having done so, he is
unable to account for the manifestations of an
anxiety and anger which *to him* appear unprovoked
by any *material* frustration or privation. He is
forced then (" insensibly " as he says himself) to
regard this aggressiveness as proceeding from " a
primal, independent instinct of destruction ". On
this point again we find a significant disagreement
among the Freudians. We are thus introduced to
mankind as a collection of independent individuals
seeking, within the limits of individual safety, to
release their impulses (reduced tension to zero), and
over and above this to destroy themselves and their
fellows *for destruction's sake*.

Still regarding the individual as an absolutely
separate entity, Freud considers that, so far as it
develops the power to love, it first loves itself—
Narcissism. As I would have it, the elements or
isolated percepts from which the " mother idea " is
finally integrated are loved (cathected) from the
beginning (in the solipsist phase) so that object-love
is coeval with object perceptive. I thus regard love
as social rather than sexual in its biological function,
as derived from the self-preservative instincts not
the genital appetite, and as seeking *any state of
responsiveness* with others as its goal. Sociability I
consider as a need for love rather than as an
aim-inhibited sexuality, while culture-interest is
derived from love as a supplementary mode of
companionship (to love) and not as a cryptic form
of sexual gratification.

The conception of love and hate here outlined
appears to me therefore simpler, more coherent and
more consistent with the facts than that of Freud.
It was not arrived at deductively but by the
convergence of a number of lines of inductive study.
Further divergences from Freud will appear and
will be summarized in a final systematic criticism

of the Freudian Theory, and an attempt made to explain its inferiority to the *clinical work* of psychoanalysis. We must first, however, consider more fully the evidence bearing on my conception of love and interest and consider what picture of human mental development this working hypothesis affords us and what contribution it offers to the solution of certain outstanding human problems.

So far as the term narcissism *describes* a form of behaviour or state of feeling it is very well chosen ; but I do not consider that it represents an actual phase in the development of love. It seems to me that Freud has confused two things. Partly he has not thought out the implication of the auto-erotic or solipsist phase, wherein states of satisfaction, " beatitude ", etc., have the appearance of self-love (though, even here, I hold that the rudiment of " other "-love is present). Partly he has mistaken the *interest* the baby develops in its own body and immediate concerns under the attentions of the loved mother for an actual love-of-self. The bodily self acquires a value over and above its capacity for yielding sensory satisfactions *in so far as it is the object of the mother's interest*, and the first plaything *shared* with her. To begin with this state of affairs can hardly be distinguished from love itself (reciprocal absorption), but it acts as the nucleus and starting point of future *interest*-development or sublimation.

I thus regard the states of feeling and modes of behaviour which Freud conceives as Narcissism, not as an intermediary phase in the development of love as he thinks, but as an off-shoot from it.

CHAPTER III

BENEVOLENCE, ALTRUISM AND HEDONISM

IF we postulate the existence from infancy of a social need, then the " pilgrimage to maturity " assumes for us an aspect different from that which we obtain by looking backwards from an anxious, competitive adulthood. The greed and hate, " the ape and the tiger within us ", " original sin ", proclaimed by Freudians and the theologians alike as characteristically human, appear as fictions of their own social mal-adjustments and of their " forced " or " false " maturation. In the beginning of life none of the transactions between mother and infant could be distinguished *by the latter* (even were it endowed with adult mind and power of expression) as " giving " or as " getting " in the sense of " losing " or " gaining ". The mother gives the breast, certainly, but the infant *gives the mouth*, which is equally necessary to the *transaction* of suckling. The fact that there is a transfer of substances from the mother's to the child's body is immaterial to the child's mind, *if the milk comes " willingly "*. It never thinks of this as " the mother's sacrifice " or feels under a burdensome obligation. (From now on I will use the word " gift " in a wide sense to cover not merely material offerings but also such " gifts " as approbation, attention, interest, etc.) There should be no conflict and even no separation of the " interests " of mother and child. Still less is it possible for the child to *offend* the mother ; all its acts are absolutely acceptable ; it is both " free " and " good " in a sense that has given rise to the myth of the golden age (though there may be some historical truth behind this) and has contributed much to the idea of Paradise, and the aspirations after Utopias. In this ideal state anxiety is at a minimum and resentments are only transient. There is no abiding sense of insecurity or of grievance. But the exigencies of life itself—(for example the advent of a second baby), or of culture (e.g. cleanliness-training), or of civilization (e.g. the working mother who must leave her babies), interrupt this happy symbiotic relationship. The baby finds its acts *occasionally* unacceptable, and the mother's " gifts " to it conditional or even unpleasant. Until these conditions are understood and a satisfactory habit adjustment has been made, the infant must feel insecure and irritable.

The infant now appears to feel for the mother a mixture of love-longing, apprehension and anger that is called *ambivalence*. It is extremely uncomfortable because obviously none of these emotions can get free expression ; even the enjoyment of suckling may be seriously interfered with. The " separation-anxiety " is in full force, and henceforth all effort (not directly concerned with survival and appetite-gratification) is devoted to " the Mastery of Anxiety ". Freudians still talk as if this process were one of " resolution of endopsychic conflict ", or even of an immunization to the feeling of anxiety, i.e. an acquired tolerance. They employ also the phrase " overcoming hate with love ", which, since they believe hate to be a separate instinct, independent of love, must mean *repression*. This again seems inconsistent with their other view that life is a struggle to attain peace by the release of impulse (the so-called " detensioning function of the psyche " as expounded in " Beyond the Pleasure Principle "). These inconsistencies—as they appear to me—seem to arise because of the Freudians' obstinate determination to leave out of account social situations and hypothetical social motives. They wish to account for the whole process of mental development in terms of what goes on within the individual mind itself, with a minimum of reference to any stresses of adjustment between one mind and another and involving the interplay of both. I, on the contrary, would say that " mastering anxiety " and " overcoming hate with love " refer to the *situation* between the child and the mother and later to its substitute relationships with its whole social environment. The child's attempt is *primarily not* to secure an endopsychic adjustment of conflicting feelings, but to remove the *cause* of the anxiety and hate by restoring harmonious social relationships. When the social disagreement is removed the feeling rapport can *change back from anxiety and hate into love and security*, not " overcoming " the former by the latter, but *re-transforming them into the latter*. The " release of impulse " *in some measure* is necessary to this ; but the aim of the anxious psyche is not merely the peace and sensory, selfish gratification of self-expression by detumescence but the *direction of these pleasurable activities upon lines that will be acceptable to others* (i.e. responded to favourably) and the control of the resentments that are aroused by frustration. Thus purposes that might be called moral, or at least " guilt sensible ", are present from the very beginning of directed behaviour. It is true that infantile guilt cannot contain the elements of shame, remorse and pity, which characterize the adult consciousness of guilt. Primitively it is much more personal, more closely allied to anxiety, though tinged with grief and longing and tending more directly than anxiety to reconciliation. Thus I put a social interpretation upon these three processes, " mastery of anxiety ", " overcoming hate with love " and " release of impulse ", which Freudians regard as the characteristic master-motives of human mind. By so doing I not only overcome the inconsistency between these formulae themselves, showing how they are but different aspects of the same purpose (the love quest), but I avoid two fallacies which have seriously disturbed the development of Psycho-analytic Theory. The first of these is already *admitted by them to have been an error*—namely, the idea that anxiety is nothing but frustrated sexual desire. The second—the theory of Death-aggressive Instinct —is admittedly a very unsatisfactory explanation of sadism and masochism (which is its only empirical justification), while it has caused serious dissensions among psycho-analysts themselves (see later).

The social interpretation I put upon early child strivings, brings my view very much more closely in line with Adler's than with Freud's. I disagree with the former, however, in his view that the quest for power is a primary and universal characteristic of human nature. I regard the struggle to excel as an *anxiety-reaction to a particular mode of upbringing* and hence *contingent* upon certain cultural influences. I further consider that Adler's conceptions, like Freud's, are influenced by the materialistic and aggressive character of our own tradition. They concentrate attention upon the material *services* of which the child is deprived (or threatened to be deprived) without regard to the probability that some of these material services, e.g. washing, are accepted by the child *more in the light of a caress than as a practical utility*. In their emphasis upon " mastery " and " excelling " too, Adlerians seem to accept the Freudian idea of aggressiveness and egoism as fundamental, whereas I regard this as merely one mode, and secondary at that, of recovering the sense of social security which is lost on the emergence from the unconditional love of (indulged) infancy into disciplined childhood. I feel, in fact, that both Freud and Adler accept the traditional view that the child is a " bad " animal that is forced in its own interests, by external threats and compulsions, to become " social " or " good ". (The Adlerians of course do recognize a " community feeling " ; but I have seen no definition of this or suggestion of its origin and genetic and other relationships to other instincts.)   I on my part have come to regard the desire to love, to give, and " to be good " or " co-operative " as influencing the appetites from their very first thwartings.   Doubtless the tendency of this social feeling is, to begin with, towards a continuance of infantile parasitism ; but there is neither greed nor malice, " the ape or the tiger ", in this, for the infant is helpless to give *in our material sense*.   It has only its pleasure and goodwill, and these it gives freely.

Be that as it may, it is not to be doubted that very early in life the infant in our culture discovers that the benevolence of others is whimsical or conditional and that its own gifts in turn are apt to be criticized and rejected.   This I call the Crisis of Anxiety and I agree with Adler that the child's " choice " of adaptation, its character, its " neurosis " (or, if any, its " psychosis ") depends upon the rôle in life which *at this time* seems to it preferable to itself and more acceptable to others.

Automatically, as a matter of its inborn constitution, the child's frustrated social love turns to anxiety (at a later age it may turn directly to guilt as the child feels it ought not to have asked for what the mother has refused or offered what she rejected), and then to hate if the frustration is sufficiently severe.   But hate of a loved object (ambivalence) as I have said, is intolerable ; the love relationship must be preserved as a matter of life or death. and there are various means of doing

this.   First, it may be done by the preservation of
the lovability of the first loved object—the mother
(see later).   An alternative is to abandon the
mother, *as she now appears in reality*, for the mother as
she once appeared and as she is remembered.   This
involves the technique of *taking refuge from reality
in fantasy*, to which reference has already been made.
It is true that the child may seek a " good "
substitute for the " bad " mother in the nurse or in
the father ; but towards this substitute the same
demands will be put forward and the same struggle
renewed.   Yet it is true that to the progressive
transference of dependency to others than the
mother, the normal person owes much of his
success.   A fourth alternative is found in the
Adlerian technique of power (or in possession),
which involves aggression, coercion, anger and
love-protests on the part of the child.   These
alternatives might be restated as imaginary explicit
declarations of the child's own intentions by itself.

I.   The *Preservation* of the lovableness of the
mother.   " Mother *is* good and kind ; if she does
not love me that is because *I* am bad."   From this
starting point is developed what is called by some
people   " inferiority   complex ".   The   ultimate
extreme is " melancholia ", where the patient has a
sense of utter unworthiness.   We find the same
developmental motive in the Augustinian Theory
that unbaptized infants go straight to Hell forever
and that God is *right* to ordain this.   On the other
hand this feeling is the stimulus to idealisms and
to the wish to become " what mother loves ".

II.   The *regression* to the pre-moral infancy might
be expressed thus : " I *will* be a baby again, because
mother is only kind to babies," or, as a variant,
suggested by experience of illness in childhood,
" Kiss it and make it well," or " Mother nurses
sick people *like* babies."

The former *regression* (to babyhood) under fantasy leads to a great deal of infantility of character in adult life, and, where it involves the *complete turning away from reality*, we find the condition of Dementia Precox which is responsible for the filling of perhaps one-third of all asylum accommodation. The lesser degree of regressiveness, namely the utilization of illness, its exaggeration or manufacture —produces hysterical invalidism. Here fantasy flourishes *but does not obscure reality*. The patient still craves and intrigues to obtain the attentions of *real* people, and does not withdraw into a dream world of her own.

III. The third technique of renouncing mother might be stated thus : " *You* are bad ; I will get a better mother than you." (The Paranoiac says in effect to his *social environment*, " You have denied me the rights I was born with, you hate and conspire against me, *I am good* and you are bad.")

It leads to the adoption (by the child) of the father as *the* parent, whereas he had previously had little significance. If it does not interfere with sexual attitude in the boy or produce excessive " father fixation " in the woman, it can be looked on as normal, as it ultimately leads on to the adoption of the whole social environment in lieu of mother.

IV. The fourth mode of dealing with the separation anxiety is that of seeking security by substituting the *power to exact* services for the spontaneous, " free ", love of infancy. The child who adopts it might be imagined as saying, " You *must* love me or *fear* me ; I will bite you and not love you until you do." " Delinquency " is largely a product of this technique, which, carried to its highest point, plays an important part in producing " Paranoia ". See Note A, Chapter I.

This disease is characterized by the retention of an excessive egoism and self-importance along with a suspicious and overbearing attitude towards other people. The paranoid combines the naive ego-centricity of the child with the arbitrary power and irresponsible privilege of the " bad " parent *as known to the child mind*. Apart from producing abnormality, however, it is true that the reliance upon power in lieu of love characterizes and perhaps vitiates our whole culture and tradition.

One other mechanism that operates at this early and critical phase of life is what is called " phobic substitution ". Another is the impulse to earn love by *becoming what is wanted*. A particular form of phobic substitution has already been mentioned, namely the desire to exonerate the mother by condemning the self. Hate and fear, however, can be displaced in other ways from the loved object, for example, the whole blame may be put upon " the rival ", perhaps the father or the younger baby. The more constructive way of earning love by becoming what is wanted is the strongest incentive to character development, though it is capable— *if directed by childish misunderstanding*—of producing lamentable results, e.g. of turning a girl into a would-be boy, or vice versa. The failure of other techniques for obtaining love leads to the defensive technique I have described as " tenderness taboo " (Chapter VI).

This account of the directing forces which start human development along so many different lines is much nearer an Adlerian than a Freudian inter-pretation. Freud considers that the whole vital force motivating appetite and social behaviour alike is of a sexual nature—libido. At least he frequently writes in this sense, though occasionally and inconsistently he makes casual references to "ego instincts", love, etc.—conceptions to which, however, he gives no real functional place in his theory of mind—using them only as descriptive conveniences. Freud considers that the character of a person develops from his psycho-sexual attitude and that the form of his mental illness (if any) can be explained by the manner in which this diffuse and primitive sexual urge organizes and directs itself. At first, as I have already explained, it is imagined as directed upon the self in narcissism, later it is directed upon others as object love, but still with a view to the attainment of sensory or fantasy gratification or the avoidance of material danger. Libido is also supposed to undergo transformations *in its mode of expression*. To begin with, it is supposed to be dominated by *sucking* interests, or rather by sucking and then by biting. These are therefore called the Oral Phases. Next the libidinal development is dominated by excretory impulses, "expulsive" and "retentive", and this period is termed accordingly the Anal Phase—First and Second. By degrees genital feelings and impulses get control of the developing libido so that sexuality proper (as we know it and use the term) appears—the Phallic Phase.

On this theory of human development a certain amount of libido was supposed to remain arrested at each level of development, so that the resultant character was a composite of all these fixations. A heavy fixation at the first oral level is supposed to produce Dementia Precox ; if it occurs at the second oral, Melancholia results. Paranoia was due to this happening at the First Anal Phase and Obsessional Neurosis to fixation at the Second Anal. Hysterics were supposed to have reached the genital level, but not to have emerged into the normal object-choice of adult sexuality and so on. So little reason, however, could be given for incidence of these hypothetical "fixations" that they were supposed to be largely determined *by heredity*. Consequently the theory could neither *explain the mechanism of treatment* nor suggest any effective means of preventing these fixations. In fact it seems that analysts are just quietly allowing these conceptions to fall into disuse or at least into the background of theory, while laying more and more stress upon the *overcoming of separation-anxiety* as being the directing motive of human development (i.e. social purpose is tacitly displacing mechanistic cause as fundamental motive). Now I have suggested that this conception is only a clumsy psychological way of describing the child's efforts to retain or regain pleasant relations with the mother ; that is to say separation-anxiety is merely the felt discomfort at an inadequate social adaptation. These supposed phases of libidinal development would then appear to be merely means of adjusting to the mother's demands in regard respectively to sucking and weaning, to excretory pleasures and prohibitions and finally to the growing prominence of genital feelings. The supposed " phases of libido development " on this view would *no longer* appear as stages determined by inborn forces in the same way as bodily development is determined. They would rather appear as *responses* on the child's part to a changing relationship between itself and the mother ; and this relationship in turn is largely determined by the rearing customs imposed by culture and civilization. Character and mental disease would then appear not as the automatic expression of internal developmental forces operating with little regard to the environment, but as responses on the part of the mind to the social situation in which it finds itself.

This difference in theory is really highly characteristic of the different attitudes to life of Freud and Adler respectively. The former endeavours always to treat the individual as a self-contained and self-determining entity—the latter regards him always as dependent upon his society. That is to say, Adler, in contrast to Freud, always frames his explanations to account for a changing or strained rapport between the subject and some other person or persons. There can be no question but that in this matter Adler's conception of his problem is truer—less artificial—than that of Freud as the recent trend of Freudian theory is showing. My criticism of Adler is that, having stated his problem correctly, he does not push his inquiry more closely into the true nature and beginning of mind, but accepts the " competitive ego " and " community feeling " as universal and elemental —the starting point of all development and incapable of analysis—and henceforth confines himself to practical interests. He is in fact *wiser* than Freud but less scientific—less given to scrutinize supposedly fundamental conceptions.

It appears indisputable that an understanding of the nature, origin and relations of love and hate is the key not only to the interpretation of psychopathy and of individual character but to the understanding of culture. You will observe that in both the Freudian and *the Adlerian theories, the root-motive of human life is taken to be the " advantage of the individual "*. While Adler explicitly allows the importance of " the other person ", he sees the latter only as the " subject " or minister to the egoistic individual. For him socialization is a *keeping in check* of egoism, a restriction of self-assertion enforced from the outside (i.e. by the remonstrances of other people), not by any natural goodwill or altruism inherent in the individual. The conception of community-feeling is only employed " ad hoc ". Freud's outlook upon life is even more ego-centric, since his idea of ultimate enjoyment (and hence purpose) is merely that of sense-gratification and the *exhaustion* of impulse. He also makes much of the power-quest ; for him this is the attempt to recover the infantile omnipotence, the reduction of all other individuals to the service of the self.   In the last resort, then, the philosophy of life of these two thinkers is agreed that the goal of life is self-assertion and self-seeking, limited only by fear of unpleasant consequences or retaliation.   Both think gain is the essential appeal of the " reality-sense ", that is to say the reason why it becomes an actual motive directing or inhibiting natural impulse.

It seems to me that an alternative view is possible—in fact, that we can turn this whole philosophy outside in and still use all its formulae with increased effect.   Instead of seeking other peoples' love for the sake of the power it confers upon us of getting them to do things for us (i.e. making them our servants) it often comes to be the other way about.   We get them to do things, perhaps needless things, for us in order to be assured of their love.   That is to say, it is possible that we seek to influence, impress or please other people for the sake of demonstrating to ourselves that we are loved.   In other words we seek power as a means to love (through neurotic anxiety), not love as a means to power.   The primal state is not one of omnipotence, for omnipotence implies the consciousness of self as distinct from mother, which differentiation (as is known) cannot exist in early infancy.   Prior to this differentiation of the self from the not-self, as I have shown, there can be no question of power, nor of a conflict of interest or wish nor any awareness of the distinction between gain or loss.   The interactions between mother and infant are entirely pleasurable or unpleasurable and convey no sense of advantage or defeat to either side.   Displeasure and anger therefore are not at this stage transformed into hates or grudges.   Even after the differentiation has been made and the

c

infant begins to know its mother as a separate, independent, being or agency, there are still *moments of reunion or at-one-ment in which interaction is in no way competitive*. In these moments there is no question of a "balance of trade" of benefits conferred or *obligations incurred*. It is not even " *more* blessed to give than to receive ", for every *gift is* in fact a gain ; every transaction liquidates itself immediately ; the baby is *solvent* and there is literally *no occasion* for anxiety. Power at this moment is as meaningless as *credits and debits*. There is no *criticism*, so that " goodness " and " badness " are non-existent. This is the age (or the " moment ") of innocence.

It is important to realize that the emergence from this paradise is not felt merely as the refusal of the mother to *give* the breast, caresses, attention, etc. Just as the original intercourse with the mother was at once both a giving and a getting without distinction between the two, so the anxious sense of separation seems to the infant as much a *rejection of its own gifts* as a refusal of the mother to give. The rejection of the child's " gifts ", like any failure to make adequate response, leads to a sense of badness, unlovableness in the self, with melancholia as its culminating expression.

The refusal of the mother to give to the child leads to anxiety, hate, aggression (which Freud mistakes for a primary instinct), and the quest for power which Adler mistakes for an equally fundamental and inevitable characteristic of human nature. The abstraction of the *responsive state* of love into giving and getting, with a possible balance of gain and loss, is an artificiality of our anxiety-ridden minds which cannot get away from the analogy with *material transactions*. Both Freud and Adler appear to regard aggressive and even antipathetic feeling as welling up spontaneously within the individual irrespective of its environment. I regard it as a product of a particular relationship to environment, namely one of refusal *and rejection* by the mother or, more generally, non-responsiveness. In practice the emergence from primitive infancy and the consequent anxiety and anger reactions may not be entirely avoidable, but there is no doubt from a comparison of upbringing and its results under different culture conditions that it is variable within wide limits.

Now many people would argue that it makes no difference whether we regard aggressiveness and antagonism as inherent in human nature (as supposed by Freud and Adler), or whether we regard it as merely a *potentiality, evoked by almost inevitable circumstances*. In any case (they would argue) it *will* appear, and in any case it does so because man is born with the capacity for reacting in this way. This is quite true, but it is always necessary to have our *theory* correct, irrespective of whether *we can* see at present that it makes any *practical* difference or not. I think further that it does make both practical and theoretical differences (even in the present state of our knowledge), whether we regard aggressiveness as an *appetite* like hunger, which must assert itself in all circumstances in response to *internal* processes, or as a merely *reflex response* like fear which (theoretically) need never have been evoked at all as it is contingent upon environmental stimuli.

As an example of the difference it makes to assume a primary appetite of aggression I would say that this assumption has led Freud to accept hatred and violence as inevitable, and to suppose that the wisest possible human policy can do no better than find socially harmless targets for this unavoidable hatred. The same philosophy of life has led Adler to feel that the baby must be forced into " co-operation from the earliest possible moment ", so that I suggested to him (without evoking any protest on his part) that his ideal of upbringing was that the child should receive the minimum of unconditional love which was compatible with its survival ! In other words he would introduce the child to the anxiety of *conditional* love at the earliest possible moment. Both Freud and Adler therefore regard the infant as " bad " by nature and as having to be made " good " or " social " by external compulsion, or else allowed outlet for its badness. I consider that the germ of goodness or of love is in the individual (of every species which has evolved a nurtured infancy) from the very beginning, and that our traditional method of upbringing frustrates this spontaneous benevolence and substitutes a " guilt-anxiety " morality for natural goodness. I consider further that the traditional attitude is so deeply ingrained in Freud and Adler's outlook on life that they cannot admit the existence of love as other than a prudent avoidance of the anger of others. Theoretical results of these views will be further considered in the chapters on Psychotherapy, etc.

I hope, therefore, you will be willing to try out the supposition that the infant brings the power and will to love with it ; and that, even in the separation-anxiety and angry protests, it pursues one or other of two courses,—either it aims to recover that love rapport in which there was no competition, no grudging, no suspicion, no balancing of advantage and disadvantage ; or on the other hand it renounces the pursuit of this kind of spontaneous love relationship for the substitute one of power. These are the two strands of development, the latter of which has almost exclusively absorbed the attention of Freud and Adler. I call them " strands ", for both aims are present in the thread of life from the first moment of self-consciousness. They do not lead towards different goals as do those to which reference has already been made. On the one hand we have the " strand " or factor of egoistic dominance, which mainly occupies psycho-analytic attention, on the other hand we have the attempt to overcome anxiety, not by gaining power over the love object, but by restoring reciprocal relations with its object ; not by enforcing claims but by making oneself lovable. It is true that Freud now and then refers to the morality-enforcing fear as " fear of losing love " ; but it is only very slowly that this social point of view is affecting the originally individualistic standpoint of Analytic. Psychology.

The baby then not only starts life with a benevolent attitude, but the Need-to-Give continues as a dominant motive throughout life, and, like every other need, brings anxiety when it is frustrated. Our adult, grudging, materialistic minds have decided that the baby gets the best of the partnership with the mother, and we talk of the mother's sacrifice ! The mother-child relationship however (to the child's mind) is a true, " balanced ", Symbiosis ; and the *need to give* is as vital, therefore, as the *need to get*. The feeling that our gifts (love) are not acceptable is as intolerable as the feeling that others' gifts are no longer obtainable. Yet one or other of these two feelings may dominate an individual life. The former feeling (of unwantedness) plays a dominant part in anxiety and frustration symptoms, the latter likewise contributes to aggression. To some extent the two anxiety ridden impulses might be respectively equated with the " repressor " and the " repressed ", so that the process of psychotherapy appears from the point of view as nothing but the *overcoming of the barriers to loving and feeling oneself loved*, and not as the removal of fear-imposed inhibitions to the expression of innate, anti-social, egoistic and sensual desires.

NOTE B.

CLEANLINESS AND ETHICS

In our culture one of the most important (because earliest enforced) adaptations is that to cleanliness, etc. Interference with evacuatory impulses has most important repercussions both upon interest development and upon social-moral attitudes. Of course this field has been systematically explored by psycho-analysts (notably E. Jones in this country), but, I consider, with a prepossession attributing greater importance to sensual values than to associative needs, and with an insufficient appreciation of the significance of the priority in development of this adaptation over that concerned with genital taboos.

The baby feeds because it must—it has no option of long delay. It feeds to please and satisfy itself ; and normally its feeding is uniformly encouraged by those in contact with it. With the evacuatory function it is different in two respects. The baby has a certain choice and control ; and the exercise of this volition early affects the reactions of those who are " training " it. Here then is its *first* experience of power—and that power the all-important one of pleasing or displeasing. With that sense of power and significance comes also the rudiment of responsibility, anxiety and hostility. This experience first elevated the infant into a moral being open to reward or blame. The earlier experiences of power—the " magic cries " and gestures of Freud, are subjectively I believe more automatic techniques than this ; they are not based upon a clear perception of the difference between " the self " and " the others " ; they belong to the " solipsist " phase, and are therefore not concerned with the love (or hate) of others.

I do not think that at this stage the infant has a sense of pride or of " property " in his evacuations, nor do I attribute the same significance as most Freudians to the sensory gratification or " creative significance " of the act as affecting the child's *primary* interest in excreta. If we take the view— to which I have no objection—that these are the first " property " and incentive to possession then we must also admit (as I have argued elsewhere) that in our culture the Institution of Property is social (i.e. other-regarding) *ab initio*—in other words that individual possessions were not only to use and enjoy but *to give away to* or withhold from others.

It is difficult for anyone but a nurse or a practising psychotherapist to realize the importance to the infant of these functions, which for us have become so much a matter of course and so little a matter of pleasure, reflection or *serious* discussion. Yet we ought to remember the smallness of the baby's world in which quite a little matter may loom large. We ought to remember that these are *first* impressions of life and the *foundation* therefore of organized experience. The only infantile experience of comparable sensory and affective value is that of feeding *which is followed by sleep*. Evacuation is much more a waking function and is followed by *washing*, etc., an experience which must convey the most vivid possible realization of the separate existence and independent activities of *other people*.

We are naturally averse to allowing such significance in mental development to a function which plays so little part in *our* social, cultural and economic system. Yet, without postulating repression, we can account for the difference between adult and (alleged) infantile interests very clearly. There is no " hush hush " convention in the early rearing. The " good " nurse or mother is not merely tolerant ; she is genuinely interested in these functions and freely shows anxiety and approval to the child, *never* disgust for the legitimate function. There is nothing to suggest to the child that the mother's interest in these matters at this period is not equal to (and on some occasions greater than) its own, or that it has any radically disapproving quality. How could the child imagine any aesthetic-conventional ideals superior to its mother's ?

But a change takes place in the mother's attitude, a change which—if too sudden and unexplained— is shattering to the infant's confidence in what it has learned and to its feelings of importance to other people. The mother professes disgust for the very functions upon which the infant had relied to hold and cultivate her liking. This change in the very basis of the child's love-worthiness as felt by itself, must be shattering to its confidence (*a*) in other people, and (*b*) in its own acceptability to them. This is the " crisis of anxiety ".

Summing up, we may say that cleanliness training and washing are therefore more important factors in the development of social disposition and interest than even feeding for the following reasons :

(1) Evacuation is critical, orgastic in fact, whereas feeding brings a *gradual* detension of hunger.

(2) Evacuation is followed by the interesting and sensual experience of handling, washing, attention, and, to begin with, by approval. Feeding, by contrast, is not accompanied by attention to the outside world (which indeed is all but invisible during feeding) and further it leads quietly and insensibly to sleep and not to the vivid waking experience of washing.

(3) As a rule, until weaning, the breast is always given willingly, whereas in our culture the maternal attitude to excreta is more equivocal, and the baby must feel her original appreciation change into intolerance—which must be anxiety-provoking in the highest degree.

(4) In the matter of suckling the baby has little power to choose ; hunger drives effectively, or death eliminates the recalcitrant. The experience of maternal pleasure-displeasure however can teach it sphincter-control quite early, and this control affords the *very first experience of social* power. With this (limited and, to begin with, uncertain) power of affecting other people's *favour* expressions, there must go a sense of responsibility. Love is no longer unconditional, but it is " up to " the baby itself to " earn " it. Food as stated in (3) is never conditional in this sense until the period of sweet-giving or withholding.

For all these reasons I judge the functions of excretion to have an enormous influence on the very foundation of (social) character. This in no way denies the sensual significance of the functions, called " anal " and " urethral " erotisms by the Freudians ; but it does shift the main emphasis from its organic and sensual meaning to its *social* significance.

CHAPTER IV

PSYCHOLOGY OF LOVE AND ITS VARIANTS

I CONSIDER that the child wakes up to life with the germ of parenthood, the impulse to " give " and to " respond " already in it. This impulse, with the need " to get " attention, recognition, etc., motivates the free " give and take " of fellowship. Any inhibition upon giving (*which we usually misconceive as a primary selfishness*) is probably the outcome of frustration and anxiety, so that the child tends *naturally* to adopt " parental " and " fellowship " attitudes to others. These virtues do not require to be extorted *from* or *forced upon it* ; but if the mother suffers from love-anxiety herself she may seek, gratuitously, to *exact* love from the child and thus unwittingly may set the child the example of anxious self-seeking even though there be no trace of *material* selfishness in her conduct. She may in fact slave herself to death for the child and *deny herself* everything in the unconscious need to evoke *recognition of her goodness*. But a true gift should never establish a claim or obligation. The neurotic (the sufferer from separation-anxiety), however, cannot take love for granted, but must constantly solicit the little signals which betoken its existence. It may even be the case that major services and sacrifices are quite unsatisfying to the neurotic, because he is intuitively aware that circumstances such as desperate need, etc., extort these kindnesses even *from the indifferent* as a matter of duty. *The tiny acts of attention however are gratuitous*, spontaneous, and thus are satisfying evidence of an active state of love. *Courtship* is wanted in fact and not merely potential or conscientious benevolence. It seems to me that a mother whose love-need is of this constant, urgent character, is able to achieve a paradoxical reaction in her child by over-indulging it so that it comes to take services and attention for granted, while in spite of her love she leaves the primary separation-anxiety unappeased or even aggravated by the rejection of its uncultural " gifts " (e.g. cleanliness training), and by her demands upon a demonstrative love and consideration which are beyond the child's feelings and power. The importance of this lies in the fact that *it can explain love-anxiety in the best-loved child*, and also account for the perpetuation of neurosis from generation to generation.

Before describing the further process of maturation of mind and the obstacles which have to be overcome and the blind alleys to be avoided in " growing up ", it is necessary to have a clear conception of the nature of the emotions and of their inter-relationships. According to academic psychology, a sentiment (by Shand's definition) does not consist of one kind of emotion only, but employs a number of different emotions all in relation to the same thing, person or purpose. Thus : " I *love* her and therefore *hate* my rival. I feel *sorry* for her, and *guilty* that I could not prevent her misfortune." There we have four different emotions functionally constellated round one and the same object and brought into play *according to the aspect presented by it or to our relationship to it*.

This view of Shand's is accepted as a great advance on the old view which imagined a number of different emotions, brought into play by appropriate stimuli as one might play separate notes on a piano. You will also note that though

Shand's definition of sentiment does not state that emotion is nearly always *socially* related (by exception, *disappointment* about food might lead to *anger* under circumstances not involving other people), still the vast majority of sentiments will be found to be connected with social attitudes— originally at least.

Freud, as I have shown, adheres to the older *kind* of view in regarding 'love and hate as wholly independent of each other in their origin, as conflicting in " ambivalence ", and as *uniting* in sadism and masochism. I do not take this view, but regard hate as the *frustration aspect of love*, as " tails " is the obverse of " heads " in the same penny. I consider that the most true and *useful* way of regarding the infinitely varied forms of human emotion is as *interconvertible forms of one and the same social feeling*. I do not mean that anything like the physical " law of the conservation of energy " will necessarily be found to hold good for the transformations of emotion ; but there is something like a quantitative equivalence expressed in the saying " Earth holds no hate like love to hatred turned."

The greater the love the greater the hate or jealousy caused by its frustration and the greater the ambivalence or guilt that may arise in relation to it. This is a truism ; but why should we hesitate to draw the inference that in the social emotions we are dealing, *not with a number* of hypothetically abstracted primary emotions blended together in an endless variety of ways, but with one and the same love-urge, expressed under the stimulus of *different relationships to the loved object*.

Thus " *love threatened* " becomes anxious, that is to say partly transformed into *anxiety*. So far as it is *denied* it is transformed into *hate*, while external interference (supplanting) switches it into *jealousy*.

In the same way its rejection—the conclusive refusal by the loved object either to accept or return it—converts it into *despair* ; the feeling of *unworthiness* of a lesser degree makes it *guilt* or *shame* ; the loss of the object, under circumstances not inspiring resentment, induces *grief*, while sympathy with that object's suffering transforms love into *pity*. In all these constellations of emotion we can, as I say, observe a rough quantitative equivalence wherever one form of feeling comes to replace another ; and on that account, and because no agreement is possible as to the number of primary feelings which exist, it seems to me better to suppose that we are dealing with a single " fund " of love-energy capable of endless transformations of quality or aim, even into the apparent opposite of love—hate.[1]

The psychology of the love disposition is even further complicated by the changing personal relationships to other people involved in the process of maturation, from dependency through the fellowship of play and of interest to parenthood. Its thwartings, and the cultural channels into which our mode of upbringing forces it, produce still further modifications of love, among which the principle (of course) is the power-quest in all its numerous forms. The quest for " admiration ", for example, is one of the earliest adopted of all the false starts or blind alleys of social development. " Possession ", in our social system, offers another unsatisfying, but more substantial mode of social integration. Like admiration it is an unbalanced or unilateral relationship. That is to say it is not mutual, not reciprocal ; *one* party *only* is the benefactor or the " superior ", the other is the

---

[1] We might say, in the most abstract terms of all, that *anxiety* is concerned with the inadequacies of other people's responses or overtures to us, while *guilt* is produced by a felt inadequacy of our own responses to others.

conditional beneficiary who, as it were, must pay tribute or remain under " obligation ". Such a relationship, since it is not equally satisfying to both parties—not wholly responsive—must be unstable. The bond is dependent upon extraneous circumstances, e.g. wealth or social position, good looks, wit or " moral " qualities. Such a bond is of course contingent upon many circumstances, and, even if it were secure, the rapport seems to lack the satisfying, reassuring, qualities of intrinsic personal liking (love) or of genuine common interests (fellowship). Anyone can satisfy himself of the substantial truth of this from his own experience. Consider the value of an unexpected gift or token of remembrance or appreciation from a relative stranger. It has the disproportionate value that we have already noted as appertaining to the small but spontaneous acts of attention or consideration which signify personal regard or tenderness. Even in regard to some exciting or moving event, the *participation* as a spectator *with* some perfect stranger who is appreciative adds greatly to our own appreciation of the experience. The psychology of crowds depends upon the fact that *shared experience intensifies interest and produces that pleasant reassuring sense of social integration which we call love*, and which both Freud and Adler leave out of account in favour of sex and of power-emotions respectively.

Exception will doubtless be taken to my inclusion of unamiable and antagonistic emotions as variants or frustration-reactions of love itself; but the close relationship of love with jealousy and anger on one hand and with unhappy feelings culminating in despair on the other is a matter of everyday observation.

It seems to me doubtful whether a state of *absolute personal* hatred can exist. A rival may excite continuous rage by virtue of his rivalry ; but this would cease on his defeat, as is shown in sex rivalry in animals. If he is preferred by the loved object, he must be *esteemed* to some extent, and in any case the hate is not strictly personal dislike ; it is contingent upon a relationship of persons rather than on intrinsic personal qualities.

Originally anger is a technique of self-preservation (being little more than mobilization of extreme effort directed to obtaining one's ends by one's own exertions)—and, like the rest of this instinct, it is adapted to infancy and becomes there the extreme, desperate, appeal for attention (i.e. for getting others to meet our needs for us). (See Note A, Chapter I.) " Goodness " may be neglected and ignored by complacent parents, but naughtiness and anger compels attention (i.e. response) of *some* kind, which is better than none at all. From this root develops the technique of " teasing " and the need for the reassurance of punishment ; it being intuitively felt that " anger " is not " indifference " and that parental discipline demonstrates anxiety, not dislike. That is to say parental displeasure is a proof that the child is able to thwart parental love and therefore that the parent does love it.

Aggressivity is therefore a technique or mode of love-seeking, it is *not merely pressed into its service* as the Freudian Theory of sadism suggests. A love-quarrel puts a *tension* upon the feelings of each for the other and thus heightens the sense of the other's presence. Even although intrinsically unpleasant, the *rapport* is thereby rendered more vivid and *reassuring*.

Bodily love is expressed by the nurtural *mutual* services of baby and mother [trophyllaxis in insects, etc.] and later in life, by sexual union. The original *organic* relationship of baby and mother is extended indefinitely in fondling and caresses, but even this is not the specific basis of love ; what might be called "thoracico-laryngeal" love, expressed by laughter and many vocal emotional calls, serves to maintain the rapport between mother and child, and later, between members of a group. This relationship may be obstructed by differences of wish or even by physical separation, so that the love-need, by frustration, is *intensified* as anxiety, as anger (just described), as guilt (e.g. masochism) and as grief, all of which *intensive metamorphoses of love* are deliberately exploited for pleasure in art, play, fiction, etc., thus displaying their positive origin and value, i.e. that they are not *merely* responses to pain.

Besides these forms of love in the individual there are differences in the response relationship between the participators in the love bond. Pure *unison* of response by "organic sympathy" is found in associations of a most primitive type—e.g. fishes. In its highest form we find it in the emotionalism and unitary enthusiasm of crowds. But the child does not want an emotional response in the mother *which is identical with its own feeling*. Thus a response of "confidence" to its "fear" is comforting *provided* the child feels that its anxiety has been fully appreciated (though not strictly "sympathetically") by the mother, i.e. that it has "got across" and met with full response. Again the child's anger is primarily excited by wants (e.g. milk) and is satisfied, not by sympathetic or reciprocal anger, but by the opposite, namely the positive form of love—tenderness. We must then recognize that love-relationships present still further variety and complexity according to whether the responses are " in unison " or in (appropriate) " harmony ". All the states moreover are extremely vague, impossible to introspect and very difficult to identify as between two different " subjects ". (See further Chapter I, Note A, and Chapters IX and XII.)

We can compare, identify and name our colour-experiences by pointing to the same object and agreeing upon a word to denote our optical sensations. But this simple procedure will not detect colour-blindness—a qualitative difference in sensation. It is infinitely more difficult to compare love emotions and thus to be sure that we all attach the same meanings to the words supposed to denote them. This is manifestly so ; for, in the first place, an *experimentally devised* situation would excite interest not love, unless it took the subject by surprise. In the second place people's character and disposition react so differently to the same situation. The exact observation and experimental study of love therefore is impossible, and this is a bar to the conception of " *love* " *as distinct from the relatively definite appetites* being accepted and employed by science. Science has, therefore, an all but unavoidable tendency to equate love with the organic appetites subserving and express- ing it.

There is another and perhaps more potent reason however why love still remains the affair of poets, romancers and the religious—not of science. The disposition of love is the centre of all the bitterness of human nature and this leads directly to the denial of the existence of love. A clinical example may make this clearer. I have said that the need to give love and to have it accepted is as real in its way as the need to have our bodily wants satisfied, though certainly privation in the former case does not lead to bodily death. One of the most grievous of possible experiences is that of having to accept grudging service, since the unwilling servant shows no satisfaction in our pleasure—rejects our love responses and manifestly refuses to love us. A natural outcome of such an experience is a distrust of love-relationships and a tendency to demand a *wholly* unselfish love. That is to say the subject *looks for self-sacrifice in others as the only satisfactory evidence of their love for him* ; he values the gift by its cost to the giver. Now to give lovingly is *pleasant* to the giver, not painful ; it brings its own reward. When this is discovered by the kind of recipient we are considering it immediately deprives the gift of all value as a source of pleasure and of reassurance. Its material value alone remains to him. *Yet he can feel no confidence in the continuance of the spontaneous benevolence he demands, rejects and denies,* so his dissatisfaction swings round to the opposite extreme and paradoxically he now demands that people shall *enjoy* loving him.

Cynicism and Asceticism appear to be the twin offspring of this temperament which demands a love from others which shall afford the givers no pleasure and which therefore is undeniably unselfish and " genuine ". The cynic observes that amiable behaviour brings pleasure and concludes that it is done for this reason. For him this is merely an inverted form of selfishness and hence worthless. The sole motive he can see is the pursuit of pleasure in accordance with the demands of one's own nature. This view finds philosophical expression in Psychological Hedonism.

The ascetic, like the cynic, feels that love is not *real* if it is pleasurable. Self-sacrifice and self-denial for him also are the measures of goodness. Instead however of denying, like the cynic, the existence of what he craves, he endeavours in his own practices to achieve the absolutely selfless devotion of his ideals. But the pleasure of giving will creep into ascetic practices unless prevented by anger and anxiety, so there is a tendency always to intensify the " mortification of the flesh ". Naturally so false an attitude to life proceeds from and intensifies a warped love-disposition, and so the real ascetic is rarely a good " fellow " or a good citizen. Cynic and Ascetic alike prove the biological truism that it is not possible to love without pleasure. Their error lies in their original neurotic demand for this impossibility.

CHAPTER V

THE FUNCTION AND EXPRESSION OF LOVE

BESIDES our own anxiety and the egoism and materialism that develops out of it, there is another thing that hinders our perceiving the reality of love, namely, it appears to have no bodily organs or functions. This is however a mistake, as I mentioned in the last chapter. The larynx *is* such an organ and, along with the complex mechanism of emotional expression and the nerve centres by which these are organized, must be regarded as the organic basis of love, though less definite and conspicuous in the anatomical sense than the reproductive system. The emotions borrow, as it were, the *use* of organs whose primary function concerns individual survival, and turn them temporarily to purposes that are definitely social, though sociability in turn has its own survival value. The expression of emotion in fact has little or no biological value *except as a means of communication*—of keeping individuals of a group "en rapport" with each other. Even the expression of anger has the general tendency to *obviate* struggle rather than to aid in the destruction of an opponent. While such expressive mechanisms as phonation (voice) are of use in courtship, they are not *necessary* to this function. They are, however, of fundamental importance in maintaining nurtural, social and playful associations, and so justify the view that the latter have motives and purposes genetically distinct from reproduction.

Thus the tear glands which originally protected the eyes from dust come to be employed in "crying"; the respiratory apparatus in laughter. The facial muscles and those which control blood-vessels and hairs are also brought into the service of *expression*, and none would deny that this is true of the larynx, though it is quite possible that originally this was a mechanism for coughing and, so for protecting the lungs. We must emphasize that *expression* is essentially a social process, and, though it may serve the interests of the individual, it also establishes *rapports that are intrinsically pleasurable.* The baby undoubtedly gets pleasure from using its larynx and from purely *expressive* exchanges with its mother. Do we improve our understanding of this pleasure and of its biological origins and functions by saying that the pleasure consists of erotic sensations in eyes and ears (Eye erotisms)? I think not, and presently I will argue that all the *elements* of expression—meaningless in themselves like single *letters*—are *intuitively apprehended together* as one meaningful *word*. That word is love, and it signifies to the mind, not the anticipation of organic pleasures to come, but a sense of security and companionship which is pleasant *in itself*, and which certainly plays a part in life from very early days, even if it is not truly instinctual. And it might very well be a true instinct, for the maintenance of the child-mother rapport is vital to all nurturing species. The larynx, etc., could easily be dispensed with so far as the mating function is concerned, and in fact is often unused; but it is of vital importance for nurtural associations with which it is very generally associated. It is therefore not right to overlook the fact that there *is an organic basis to non-sexual love, with satisfaction feelings* (vague certainly) *involving respiration, circulation and digestive functions* and investing these with a secondary meaning and utility. These naturally are most prominent in such situations as being-in-love, etc., but are not wholly confined to this. There are bodily mechanisms concerned with feelings of anxiety and affection referring to other people, and not to the satisfaction of the appetites we share with non-social animals. These feelings and the nervous mechanisms which produce them are located more in the chest than in the abdomen (vagus and sympathetic nerves) and least of all in the sexual organs, though these also are readily affected in the expression of love. But this is no reason for supposing them to be the centre and origin of the love disposition as Freud implicitly does.

Freud indeed deals with the state of being-in-love and with " the oceanic feeling ", which, he admits, he himself is " *unable to experience* "(*Civilization and its Discontents*, p. 21). He feels he advances our knowledge of the former state by describing it as a " libidinal cathexis " of the " object " (i.e. mental image) at the expense of the " ego " ! He admits that the lover, from over-valuing the sexual object (i.e. the loved person), goes so far as to lose any clear distinction in his own mind between himself and the beloved. Freud writes " Against all the evidence of his senses the man in love declares that he and his beloved are one" (Ibid., p. 11). A little further on he clearly sees that the " oceanic feeling ", wherein the boundaries of the ego seem lost and the subject feels at one with the whole world, represents at least a partial return to the primal state before the discrimination of self from mother. (Freud refers to this as the " detachment of the ego ".) The curious limitation of his thinking is however immediately betrayed, for, dealing with this state as a motive for religion, he finds it quite inadequate as a " source of energy " as it does not seem to him to be the " expression " of " a strong need " (p. 21). " The derivation of a need for religion from the child's feeling of helplessness and the longing it evokes for a *father* seems to me incontrovertible " (my italics). " I could not point to any need in childhood so strong as that for a *father's protection*. Thus the part played by the 'oceanic' feeling, which I suppose *seeks to reinstate* limitless *narcissism*, cannot possibly take the first place. The derivation of the religious attitude can be followed back in clear outline as far as the child's feeling of helplessness. There may be *something else behind this, but for the present it is wrapped in obscurity.*" (My italics.)

There *is* something else " behind this ", namely the child's need for the *mother's* love ; and the " obscurity " to which Freud refers exists only in his own mind. Freud has, for reasons to be suggested later,[1] two blind spots—one for " the mother " and one for love ; and he has recently been compelled to admit the existence of the former scotoma. In his paper on " Female Sexuality ", 1932, he has to acknowledge to the child-analysts that even for the little girl " the father is nothing but a troublesome rival ", which · is a striking contradiction to the passages quoted in my preceding paragraph. The Freudian position at the moment is in a state of flux, full of contradictions and in active *though covert* retreat from the pan-sexual theory ; so we need not hesitate to proceed with our own hypothesis, that in all his social activities—Art, Science and Religion included—man is seeking a restoration of or substitute for that *love for mother* which was lost in infancy. We will have the additional advantage, in pursuing this working hypothesis, that it offers us at the same time a prospect of solving the problem

[1] Chapters XIII and XIV.

of *hate* which on the Freudian theory is made inexplicable and untreatable.

At the same time we will have to bring this conception of love into relation with sex, since we deny that the latter is its origin. It seems to me that the complete passion of love integrates genital appetite with that " love " or tenderness which is the descendant or derivative of infantile need. It utilizes it, as it were, as a means of restoring the lost sense of union with the mother ; for sexual intercourse and suckling are alike and unique in this respect, that in neither should there be any difference or conflict-of-interest between the partners. It is as absurd to consider who gives and who gets, or who gains and who loses, in the sex act as it would be to propound these questions in regard to suckling. The act or rather its culmination, is totally reciprocal, otherwise it becomes associated with anxiety. It restores the free give-and-take of infancy . where there is as yet no doubt of " welcome " or " acceptance ". Hence its extreme value in allaying morbid anxiety (a value which helped to mislead Freud himself as to the relationship of sex and anxiety) ; but hence also the ease with which anxiety in turn hinders its consummation. Here again we are able to explain an admitted Freudian error, namely, the mistaking of anxiety (morbid) for unsatisfied libido. It is of course unsatisfied *love*.[1]

I cannot of course present here much evidence for this view ; but I would call attention to a very significant reversal of our own sex-ethical sentiment

---

[1] It would be as absurd to regard the sex act as having a selfish " detensioning ", evacuatory motive as to say that a woman desires maternity for the drainage of her mammary glands. To Roheim's surprised discovery that " the penis is not a weapon ", I would add the observation that the child is not merely a " breast-reliever ". It is a failure in the love-response-factor in coitus which produces anxiety, not a failure of sensual satisfaction.

which Professor Malinowski reports from the Trobriand Islands. Intercourse between young unmarried people there meets with no disapprobation, provided reasonable decorum and prudence is observed. But the forging of bonds of *affection*, e.g. by mutual services, conversation, caresses, or eating together, is felt to be justified only by formal marriage. I interpret that (with Professor Malinowski, I think) as showing how separable the sentiment of love is from the genital appetite, since our culture represses the latter while Trobriand culture censors the former in an equally selective manner. Of course " the taboo on tenderness " (see Chapter VI) is not confined to the Trobriand Islanders. Indeed, it is the leading feature of our own culture and the main reason for the substitution of the power-technique for that of love. The substitution however is not complete ; a need for love remains, even although many of its manifestations have now acquired an aggressive egoistic character which disguises their true meaning.

We must, in fact, for peace of mind, either feel ourselves loved or in a position ᴐ be loved ; and we must ask ourselves " How ıs the comforting conviction of being loved arrived at ? " Words will not produce it, though pitch and timbre of voice are important. Quickness of response, readiness of understanding, sympathetic emotional responses, even laughter—(not of the malicious-pleasure sort), posture, the width and shape of the palpebral fissure (eye), dilatation of pupil, amount of fluid in the eye as well as facial colour and expression, all these and other signs which *individually are meaningless*, are intuitively apprehended as a harmonious whole, and so produce in us some reaction which is both pleasant and encouraging. (Notice how words meaning heart or stomach are used in all languages to denote love-feeling.)

Not that this reaction must always take the form of *reciprocal love* ; it may be merely an *enhanced interest in things* or a general feeling that life is worth living.

A deliberate attempt to reproduce the signs of love is always ineffective. The actor by " living his part " produces the *genuine article*, love-feeling, and any self-consciousness or deliberate simulation would be manifestly artificial. Equally a *conscious attention* to the individual signs of love or to verbal protestations " leaves us cold ", with no conviction of the sincerity of the feeling. Only, as I have said, by a *subconscious and collective apprehension* of the signs as a meaningful whole and *by the automatic response this awakens in us* (N.B.—cordiality is another significant word as indicating some vagal-autonomic disturbance) do we ever reach that rapport we indicate by the words " I love ". The whole mechanism of love-responsiveness is put out of action by attention or deliberation of any kind

This is a very important point of view for theory and for psychotherapy, for love is somewhat incongruous with the scientific interest and it is even incompatible with conscious attention. It cannot be introspected, while objectively it is vague, intangible, silent and with no *obvious* function as I have just shown.

From our own practical point of view the necessarily subconscious and involuntary nature of love has this significance, that if we do not like a patient we are hopelessly handicapped in treating him. No amount of technical skill, theoretical knowledge or conscientiousness will atone for the absence of a sympathetic understanding and the capacity to " put oneself in the patient's place ". Here is where the analysts both excel in practice and fall short in theory. By their severe training they remove many unnecessary intolerances and prejudices on their own part ; but by their idealization of passive technique and disavowal of all responsibility—still more perhaps by their pessimistic theory and philosophy of life, which idealizes the freest practicable expression of sex-drive and hate—they represent as unhuman, impersonal and purely technical, their relations to their patients, in striking contradiction to the saying attributed to Ferenczi : " It is the physician's love that heals the patient." One is tempted to ask " What kind of love is to be employed ? "

Before proceeding with the consideration of the craving for tender relationships and the inhibitions this arouses, a clinical note will illustrate more clearly the significance of tenderness or affection in everyday life or psychotherapeutic relationships and the importance of discovering whether this tenderness is a derivative of sex or not. About two years ago I took on a patient of nineteen years who had had systematized delusions of persecution (involving her parents) since the age of seven (Paranoia). Under these circumstances she had formed neither friendships nor interests. There was nothing in her life of interest to her except " people " and of them she saw only the worst side. Her whole existence was an offensive-defensive struggle for power and revenge against everybody—" to destroy the world." She loathed and despised " sentimentality " ; any-thing but ruthless egoism is, to her, hypocrisy or weakness. It makes *her " sick " and angry. But* for fear (which is an attribution to others of her own destructive rage), she would have been a moral imbecile.

When sufficient improvement had been obtained with this unpromising material to secure co-operation, she opened a counter-attack upon me which had some justification. That she had no love in herself, never could love and was entirely unlovable, she explicitly allowed (and sometimes with pride) ; but, she said, with truth, that I had not loved her "*well enough to make her well*"

I had taken her on, she said, partly out of pity that a young girl should spend the rest of her life in a madhouse. (Fifty years she estimated ; but she would have fought herself to death by exhaustion in five.) She said I had had a *scientific interest in her which* was equally useless as a means of satisfying her need of love (whose existence she denied). I had, perhaps, done it as a " *sporting effort* " and kept her on because " I did *not like to admit defeat* " ; I had done it out of " *humanity* " and a " sense of *duty* ", which she disliked most of all. " *I found her a great burden* " and " *wanted her to break away* " ; " I was *afraid of her* ", etc. Every imaginable imperfect motive she explored (and most of the above had, as I had to admit, an element of truth in them) to explain my persistent effort to help her ; but what she wanted, parental feeling, she could not or would not see in me.

Even when I came to realize what life had meant to her, and to admire the Luciferian struggle she had put up, my *genuine sympathy and liking* brought her no reassurance apparently, *since she had no emotional response of her own* (see pp. 73-74). Now and then, with a flash of terrible insight, she realized that this was so, and that it utterly cut her off from people, comfort, security and interest. She would watch my face to catch expressions of love, hate, contempt or boredom ; she would weigh my words. Naturally from this conscious, intellectual, scrutiny nothing emerged which satisfied her. Whatever the " radiation " of love on my part, her own " detector " was hopelessly out of order, and, as I have said, conscious attention is unable to read the complex signs of emotions, of liking and interest. They have to " resonate " by organic sympathy in

the subject in order to " get across " at all and her
emotions were absolutely blocked by hate.   As I
have said above, unless a love-response is aroused in
ourselves, the love of others cannot be *felt*.   Only
the objective fact of my being ill moved her at all
(whereupon she became definitely parental), and
she was careful to explain that it was not that she
cared in the slightest for me, but that my death
would leave her absolutely without anyone to
talk to.

Nevertheless it became apparent that this
unloving attitude was an artifact of her disease and
that although her love was as " egoistic " as a baby's,
the craving for love was there and in some way this
" greed " still seemed to carry the beginnings of
liking and consideration.   Now and again the
envelope of cynicism, contempt for love and for
cultural interests, and the glorification of a predatory
" Ishmaelite " attitude to the world was broken
through and revealed a horror of loneliness and a
passionate desire to be like and loved by other
people and belong to them.   The whole paranoid
mask in fact was a defence (only *slightly, a compensation*) against (*a*) an unloving world (as the child
saw it) and (*b*) against the pain of isolation and
against the longing for tenderness and security, and
the dread of the rebuff to which " snivelling " or an
equivalent appeal would expose her.

The kind of love she needed and her attitude to
human relationships is well indicated by her
appreciation of the character of Barrett of Wimpole
Street.   She sympathized with him " as one
paranoic to another " ; and she liked his strength
and possessiveness—approved of them, in fact.
To be loved like this, she felt, was to be secure not
only from loneliness, but, through his strength and
discipline, from her own dangerous impulses.   Of
course the " Girl's Oedipus Complex " played its

part, but the filial attitude was predominantly of an infantile, pregenital character.

It became clear to me at the same time that I myself had a positive intolerance to " mawkish " sentiment and " babyish " tenderness, and that in fact my correct, practical, " frozen " attitude had been maintaining her anxiety and paranoid rage. This intolerance of sentimentality (I use the derogatory term to indicate the bias which is embedded in our very language) was no revelation to me. It appeared the most natural, rational and practical attitude possible. The world, our world, could not be carried on upon any other footing than that of strength and independence. I was surprised, however, that any plea for sympathy should occasion me embarrassment and impatience, whereas sexual and excretory interests in the patient leave me undisturbed. Why, if tender feeling is a sublimation of sexuality, should it evoke a more active repulsion than its supposed origin ? It is not objectionable to the family or injurious to the group ; tenderness could not evoke sex jealousy. The answer is clear : because it is *childish* and the adult has been compelled to " put away childish things ". But surely if we are dealing with children (i.e. irrespective of their calendar age where psychopathy is concerned) we should have no intolerance of infantility ? We must come to terms with the patient, if not on his own grounds, at least on ground *that is attainable by him.*

I immediately began to study both the patient's and my own defences and came to the conclusion that there is a *taboo on tenderness* every bit as spontaneous and masterful as the taboo on sex itself. True, the repression of tender feeling and wishes from consciousness is more variable and less radical than the repression of sexuality (though Freudians exaggerate the completeness of the latter in *normal* people).   But the insulation from disturbing stimuli which would evoke sympathetic tenderness, and the 'inhibition upon response to such as *do* get across, appeared to me extremely strong and significant.

CHAPTER VI

THE " TABOO " ON TENDERNESS

In the Introduction I suggested that Modern Science had a positive aversion to anything savouring of sentimentality. While in the physical sciences this justifies itself on methodological grounds, in psychology it has been carried to such an absurd length (e.g. Behaviourism) as to betray an underlying bias of anti-emotionalism. Yet it may seem incredible that so harmless and amiable emotion as tenderness, the very *stuff* of sociability, should itself come under a taboo. Our religious professions exalt love above all the virtues and condemn the unloving life, though our outspoken *prejudices* centre round sexual morality mainly and our laws concern themselves greatly with property. Further Freud has laboured to show that tenderness is itself a derivative of sexuality (goal-inhibited), and so any embarrassment at sentimentality or intolerance of pathos might be interpreted as due to an incomplete " disinfection " of the sexual root motive of tenderness. This, too, squares with the fact (true to our culture) that men show less tenderness and more sexuality than women, or, as Freud would say, the latter are more goal-inhibited by a more repressive upbringing and by the special difficulties of the girl-child in sexualizing her love for mother. (Incidentally, however, this would imply that men have less sublimated culture-interest, since sex-outlets are freer to them.) Altogether the view that tenderness is more or less an artifact and that a-sexual love is a myth of the idealists is fairly well established in our tradition and everyday life. The idea that tenderness is a primal independent reality and that it undergoes repression will seem untrue and even absurd unless supported by much evidence. Where can we find it ?

The most typical example (indeed proto-typical) can be found in the " gang " of larger or smaller boys who idealize what is called euphemistically " manliness ", in contradistinction to "babyishness" and " girlishness ". The ideals of such a community are intensely antifeminist as indicated by the coining of such opprobrious epithets as " milk-sop ", " cry-baby ", " mummy's boy ", etc. On the positive side this ego-ideal holds up " toughness ", aggressiveness, hardness, etc., as prime virtues. Power, violence, cunning and crime have such a fascination for these children that (when, in due course, they arrive at Fleet Street) every burglary is " daring " and every swindle is " clever ". Obviously this state of mind is a *reaction* against the sentiments related to the mother and the nursery, from which (mentally) these children have just emerged, in all probability unwillingly. The suggestion arises that the whole of this character-formation is a revenge upon and a repudiation of the " weaning " mother, on the defensive principle of " sour grapes ".

Another feature of this phase of character-development is worth noting from the social point of view, namely the tendency to form "brotherhoods" or secret societies. We may conjecture that the social need of these juvenile outcasts from the nursery draws them together as a " band of brothers " united by a common bereavement (see Chapter VIII for a further consideration of this social phenomena and of Freud's view of the " out-casting "). There is a very general tendency to " rationalize " the process of socialization on the grounds of the material advantages (in the way of

D

efficiency) that may be derived from co-operation. But these secret "brotherhoods", juvenile or adult, have no practical *purposes* whatever. "Brotherhood" itself is declared to be *the purpose* of the greatest of all "secret" societies—the Freemasons. In point of fact, too, we find that juvenile gangs or societies are formed *first* and decide upon their objectives afterwards, as is amusingly urged by the practical Huckleberry Finn against the romantic Tom Sawyer. Social integration is, in fact, an end-in-itself and not merely a means to practical ends ; the brotherhood is constituted for its own sake.

These little boys when grown up and " civilized ", have no less inhibition in expressing and embarrassment in receiving cordial regard. Sentiment makes them " squirm ". " It is simply not done." It is " wet ". So that expressions of liking and esteem have actually to be disguised more carefully than a smutty joke. One very common " cover " for expressions of warm or tender feeling is mock abuse. Quite outrageous epithets are employed as terms of endearment. Chaff, practical jokes and horse-play further serve to express and disguise affection. How are we to interpret this ? As goal-inhibited homo-sexuality reinforced by instincts of destruction and inhibited as a sadistic play ? Is teasing of this kind merely *hatred*, repressed and released under the excuse " It is all in fun " ? Very often it is ; but it seems to me that this explanation will not cover all cases. Affection, which either is not sexual or of which the sexuality is efficiently repressed in this shamefaced way, is, if tendered too effusively, rejected with embarrassment and some such protest as " Don't be silly ". Why should a harmless and conventionally innocent emotion come under such a genuine taboo ? Is the phobic censure of homo-sexual off-shoots so remorseless that even the

most highly "*disinfected*" derivatives of this instinct
are repelled as tainted ?   If so, why does any human
activity escape taboo ; and, above all, why is the
taboo on tenderness so variable in its incidence as
between different individuals, between the two
sexes and between different cultures ?

Before attempting to answer these questions let
us collect further samples of aversion to and
concealment of sentiment, and of indirect and
surreptitious indulgence in this.   On the supposition
that there is a social reaction against tenderness and
feeling generally, we would expect to find that these
forces seek safety valves and express themselves
under various disguises and excuses, which evade the
prohibition.   We do in fact find much of such
evidence showing how strong is this taboo and
consequently how important are the impulses
subjected to it.

How can the pay of nurses be kept so low in view
of their hours and the nature of their work ?
Presumably there is an invisible remuneration—the
right to act sympathetically (although, of course, no
emotion must be *shown*).   The exhibition of
tenderness is permitted to the mothers of young
children, but " goo-goo " talk is rather reprehended.
It embarrasses us.   Why ?   Because there is a
taboo on tenderness or anything else that savours of
infantility.   A *man* may take a condescending
interest in children (under the guise of amusing
them) ; but how many men can exhibit a real
tenderness for *babies* ?   Yet some young boys will
play with dolls and, as I show elsewhere, the envy
of motherhood is one of the most potent factors in
culture evolution.   Yet again with " pets " we find
a permitted release of tenderness, but only on
conditions ; for here again we find the tenderness-
taboo stronger in men than in women *in our culture*.[1]

[1] Pets are adopted children, meant to remain so.

(This is correlated with the fact that the sex taboo is stronger in women, but not in the simple manner of extra goal-inhibition by women. Rather I would say that *men* had substituted sex for love. Even the psycho-analysts are now recognizing this.) The dog can match the man in the dignified " reserve " of its devotion. Indeed the sheepdog's relation to its master is sublimated (!) to a mere colleagueship of practical interests. Here, however, where it is not forbidden, the dog is often pathetically grateful for a little caressing. (In parenthesis, while human attachment to animals *may*, by Freudians, be attributed to repressed and deflected sexuality (" fur fetishism "), how does psycho-analysis account for the reciprocal attachment of animal to man ? It certainly cannot all be put down to sexuality, and it is certainly related to the treatment the animal has received when very young.) To return : the exuberant affection of a puppy can be tolerated, or, rather, ignored ; after all *we* are not responsible for its ridiculous antics, and our dignity is not affected. It is however rather " unmanly " to like cats, though this indulgence is, rather condescendingly and mockingly, permitted to lonely women.

I have already mentioned the tenderness craving that enters into love-making. Here again towards lovers we find a social attitude of contemptuous tolerance. Is this due to sexual envy or blame, or is it due to a recognition of the regressive nature of the sentimental as distinct from the passionate component of human love? We dissociate ourselves from the " weakness " or " madness " of lovers by applying to them such epithets as " spoony ". We regard lovers as " smitten by disease ", and in general show less respect, if less active reprobation to tenderness than we do to sex itself. In fact we excuse tenderness or sentimentality in this case *on the grounds of its sexual intention and tendencies.*

Examples of this inhibited social behaviour and embarrassment at harmless emotions could be multiplied indefinitely did space permit. The unsatisfied need for tenderness and for a sentimental play of feeling which results from this social inhibition constitutes the main drive to alcoholism. In a later chapter I will show the significance of love hunger as a motive to the " flight into illness " and the widespread incidence of " disease " of this origin. The uncontrollable feeling aroused in some great disaster seeks a religious or quasi-religious outlet since these are " licensed " by popular prejudice. Yet even Christianity is stigmatized as weak and childish since it avowedly cultivates tender sentiments. National idealisms show the same bent. Economic practice and the ideals of daily life express our admiration for " hard shell ", hard-boiled, hard-bitten men who have " steeled their souls ". A great if slangy vocabulary has sprung up to discriminate between the character and conduct which is emotionally responsive and that which is not so, and the balance of approbation trend always towards the latter. All this bespeaks a cultural antipathy to a range of feeling and emotion which is socially harmless.

If we take it that the theatre, music, etc., has the function of meeting the interest and emotional needs left ungratified in everyday life (just as the dream " fulfils " frustrated wishes), we must infer that the privations imposed upon tender feeling are almost as important as those imposed on sex. Indeed it seems possible that refuge from tender feeling and pathos generally is being sought in sex and that this flight is expressed in some people's intolerance of " good " music and delight in jazz excitement. At any rate this sphere of activity will afford evidence to test the hypothesis here put forward in the following lines : " Does the

' sickly ', ' sloppy ' sentimentality of the Victorian Theatre and Concert Halls and of the pantomimes of pre-war times express the sexuality that became goal-inhibited under the repression of these times, or is it an ebullition of tender feeling that is equally repressed in a puritan, patriarchal, community ?"

On the supposition that the latter question can be answered in the affirmative, we must consider what possible forces and mechanisms could conspire to inhibit an apparently harmless and even valuable impulse. I would answer this question tentatively as follows.

What we call tender feeling and affection is based not on sexual desire but upon the pre-oedipal emotional and fondling relationship with the mother and upon the instinctual need for companionship which is characteristic of all animals which pass through a phase of nurtured infancy. In our culture in particular the brusqueness of the cleanliness-training, the frequent and prolonged separation of mother and infant and the mother's own intolerance of tenderness (the result of her " puritan " upbringing) bring about a precipitate " psychic parturition ", attended by an anxiety, acquisitiveness, and aggressiveness which is reflected in our culture and economic customs and attitudes. This process of parturition or psychic weaning must be intensely painful even where not aggravated by jealousy of a supplanter. The measure of this pain can perhaps be found in conscious memories of solecisms and blunders, which are attended by an acute sense of shame years after they are committed. We really regret these stupidities more than we do " crimes ", because they meet with ridicule and exhibit us as children under the criticisms of adults. It seems to me that these painful memories may act as cover-memories for all the rejections and prohibitions which attend psychic weaning.

The distress of this process must after all be far greater than that attending sexual repression ; for, in the case of psychic weaning, the child is being deprived of *something it has enjoyed "from time immemorial"* ; while in sexual repression it is merely being forbidden something that is reserved for "grown-ups". To the anger attending the thwarting of tenderness-feelings must be added the grief for the loss of the mother and above all the anxiety caused by her *changing attitude*. This hits at the very foundation of the sense of security. The child discovers that what it has painfully and obediently learnt does not after all satisfy the parent who exacts these sacrifices, that its childish ways of pleasing are no longer acceptable and that there is really nothing on which it can depend. The very root of its sense of security and justice are struck at by the denial of baby caresses, and by the rejection of those offered by the child, for we must remember that touch is a more fundamental reassurance than sight or sound. This fact must be of some importance in deep analysis, wherever the physician deliberately avoids being felt, seen *or heard*. But it must be of supreme importance in the determination of culture and character, since upon it depends the first orientations of ego-idealism and ambitions.

It seems probable that this psychic parturition is relatively painless and harmless under one condition only, namely, *that the child's resources in companionship and play-interest increase "pari passu" with the separation from the mother and the loss of the direct love-caressing-interest in her. Where separation outruns substitution, anxiety and anger appear.* Unless the interest in the self, shared with the mother from the beginning (Narcissism ; see Chapter II) develops in secure and widening circle *before the direct tenderness and nurtural love-relationship is seriously threatened*, anxiety must appear ; and the child then turns back from the developing Interest-Companionship to insist upon, and hold on to, the companionship-of-Love, much as an army must turn round to defend its threatened Base of Supplies. That is to say the child will easily renounce more primitive enjoyments and security *if offered a more social but equally secure substitute.* But we find that circumstances and certain peculiarities of temperament cause the mother unduly to accelerate the psychic parturition. One by one the attentions formerly enjoyed by the infant are withdrawn and this is appreciated by the child mind as a withdrawal of love, and more important still, as meaning that its love and itself are not wanted or welcome to the mother. The child must then either (1) develop companionships and interests in lieu of the contracting love-absorption (normality), or (2) fight for its " rights " and/or (3) find surreptitious regressions or substitutes (Delinquency and Psychopathy), or (4) submit and avoid the pain of privation by repression (the Taboo on Tenderness). In the latter event the avoiding reactions tend to spread (as will phobia proper) in order to exclude all reminders of painful loss and all incentives to *"dangerous" appeals or indulgences.* Such a counter-rejection of love or *self-weaning from affection* serves an obvious defensive purpose. As I see it, this protective indifference is essentially a " sour grapes " kind of self-comfort—a self-insulation from love hunger by the " cultivation " of a "loveshyness "—but it *demands a psychic blindness to pathos of any kind*—a refusal to participate in emotion. It can be carried to such a point that the individual is not only " steeled against " the appeal and suffering of others, but he actually dreads appealing to their sympathy, and may, for example, conceal illness for fear of making a " fuss " or " scene " One can only suppose that the privation of love is here recognized as so inevitable, yet the longing remains so painful, that the whole conflict is forced out of mind. Anything that tends to re-arouse it (pathos and sentiment) is therefore resented exactly as the prude resents an erotic suggestion and for the same reason. The taboo upon regressive longings extends to all manifestations of affection until we can neither offer nor tolerate overt affection.

The repression of affection seems therefore to be a process likely to be cumulative from one generation to another. The mother who was herself love-starved and who, in consequence, is intolerant of tenderness, will be impatient of her own children's dependency, regressiveness and claims for love. Her suspicion and anxiety really amount to a feeling (rooted in self-distrust), that children are naturally bad (St Augustine !) and require to be " made " good by disapprobation and the checking of all indulgence of " babyishness ". This creates a corresponding anxiety in the children about retaining approbation and winning more. The child feels too early that love must be *deserved* or *earned*, and excessive anxiety may easily reach the point of despair.

This on the one hand constitutes a temptation to abandon the struggle in favour of regressive dreams (Dementia Precox) or to cultivate invalidism (Hysteria). Or, on the other hand, it may lead to a jealous competitiveness, the quest for power, position, " prestige ", possession. Love has now become aggressive, anxious, covetous. Unintentionally the mother has imparted her own inhibitions (on tender feeling) to her children, has substituted the ideal of duty for that of good-fellowship and established a morality of guilt and distrust in place of that of benevolence and confidence which I maintain would have developed naturally.

D*

The "hard", puritanical, character thus developed is intensely jealous and intolerant. For the indulgences we have been forced to renounce ourselves, we will certainly not permit to other people. We are in effect jealous of the child we affect to depreciate, we dread that it will be a " molly coddle ", and force, in turn, our own children to " grow up " *too quickly to allow them time to outgrow their childishness.* We make them " serious "—preferring " success " to enjoyment— efficient competitors in the struggle for existence, but we do this in ways apt to increase the intensity of the tenderness taboo to a point hardly compatible with the maintenance of social living.

This philosophy of life is idealized in Stoicism, which avowedly seeks a defence from suffering by eschewing desires that expose us to privation and rebuff. More typically however it produces a competitive materialism which cuts out " playful " and cultural interests as trivial or actually (if guilt plays much part as in Puritanism), " sinful ". Since there is no natural satisfaction obtainable in such modes of life we naturally find that they tend to intensify themselves. The Stoic becomes the cynic, the Puritan becomes morose, intolerant, anti-Christian in every essential respect, a ruthless " favourite " of a ruthless God.

We may get a clearer picture of the nature of this (hypothetical) taboo on tenderness by an analogy with ether-waves. These form a continuous series according to their wave length and produce at different points of the scale the effects we know as Radiant Heat, Light, Magnetism, " Wireless " waves and certain radiations from atomic disruption, etc. Only a few of these are perceptible to the senses ; the majority are discoverable only by indirect means. In a comparable way we could imagine human mental " energies " as ranging from the sense-experience of appetite and gratification and such organic relationships as suckling and sexual intercourse, through the definite, crude, emotions such as hate, fear, grief and joy of which we are vividly aware, up to the highly abstract and mental rapports of cultural interest, culminating perhaps in pure mathematics. Between the crude and definite emotions on the one hand and the abstract interests on the other, there is a great range of affective reactions of which we are habitually unaware and which are consequently very difficult to name or to recognize on account of their vagueness and of the fact that people who are mentally well take them for granted. They represent reactions to a range of situations occurring in everyday life and not distinctively characterized ; and consequently it is difficult to think or talk about them. They are not quite " emotional ", yet they are far more vital and less abstract than interest-in-objects which have no significance for bodily appetites. They form in fact a sort of vital background of *enthusiasm*[1] for all social and cultural activities rather than a bodily experience or object of mental interest, and are entirely dependent upon these being *shared*. Perhaps the best word to designate this level of response (companionship) is feeling or " meaning " or perhaps we might say it represents the unconscious liking between the co-operative and competitive participators in interest.

It is in this field of feeling or meaning-interplay as well as that of direct personal cordial appreciation that the taboo on tenderness manifests itself. It is not a definite lack of feeling (as in idiocy), nor a

---

[1] Enthusiasm and its opposite, " boredom ", must be regarded not merely as intensifications or subsidences of interest-in-things, but as largely dependent upon the social rapport which supports this interest. Leadership is dependent upon this fact.

withdrawal (as in Dementia Precox), so much as an *inhibition* which dulls the social responsiveness of the individual and may come to be *known* and deplored by him. He cannot tolerate " warm " or demonstrative relationship ; he gives all his friends the " frozen mitt " ; he takes refuge in formal relationships, abstract interests and sensuality, and usually he does not like " good " music or " good " literature—yet he knows, dimly or clearly, his lack. He is an uncomfortable friend or relative and an unhappy man.

Apart from these individual variations in responsiveness and spontaneity of feeling we find wide and general differences between the people of different cultures in this respect. We actually find, for example, that the taboo on friendly relations can become *explicit* even while sexual indulgence is regarded as harmless. Professor Malinowski reports of the Trobriand Islanders that while it is quite in order for a girl to sleep with her lover, it is regarded as improper for her to be too friendly (e.g. to prepare food) before marriage. They regard this very much as we are supposed to regard pre-marital intercourse. If their civilization were like ours presumably they would consider a restaurant bill good grounds for divorce ; the Sunday papers would print the menu and the Bishops would talk of the decay of morality and the dangers of neo-paganism. Still they do not carry the taboo on tenderness anything like so far as their neighbours and trading relatives the Dobuans, whose ideals of civic conduct would qualify them for Broadmcor even in this country. This latter people profess an ethical attitude that would justify the Freudian metapsychology. They consider the only worthwhile object in life is to get the better of your neighbours and the only means of doing so are force, fraud and sex-appeal.

A study of the conditions of upbringing in these peoples shows a pseudo-matriarchy—a state of affairs in which, in spite of nominal matrilineal inheritance of property, the actual mother can have no confidence, no stability and no dignity in the children's eyes.   The emergence from the kind and sheltered world of infancy into the ruthless competitiveness of the adult life of this people must be accompanied by stresses, resentments and regressive longings with which the mothers are quite unfit to deal.   There is not space to analyse the effects of the complex conditions of rearing, but the evidence is compatible with the view that the racial character of this people does not result from the release of natural badness so much as from the acquisition of hardness and the repression of a childish (natural) friendliness and generosity which cannot survive under ultra-competitive conditions.

At the opposite extreme of racial character we find certain African peoples whose children, Audrey Richards reports, hardly ever quarrel.   They can hardly be said to undergo any weaning compulsion, are protected from supplanting anxiety and jealousy with the most elaborate care and are not subjected to any cleanliness training, because, the mothers say, " It would be so cruel.   They will learn for themselves in good time."

In this culture also, the sex taboo and sex secrecy is extraordinarily light, so that the difference (from Dobuan character) cannot be due to this factor.   It seems to me that the child is able to reach maturity without developing anxieties, resentments, regressive longings for a lost happier state, etc., and without having to immunize or insulate himself from tender feeling.   Where the child has not been wounded by the refusal of love or by the rejection of his own, it does not need to develop a character " hard " and " cold ", contemptuous of enthusiasms and incapable of loyalties ; it does not develop a defensive inhibition of and unresponsiveness to feeling.

Another important consequence follows. The undefended, unreserved character makes a far better parent. Not having any anxious regrets for lost childhood to repress (or not repressing them) such an adult has no aversion to children or embarrassment under their attention and appeals. He makes effective contact with children because he has a childlike or feminine mind. He makes a better parent. There need be no lack of strength, resolution or penetrative capacity in mind, he has merely not cut out what our culture teaches us to despise. Have we not mistaken a mere desertion or suppression of the open mindedness of childhood for maturation, manhood, and regarded this negative quality—a defensive reaction—as good in itself, very much as aggressiveness is idealized by Fascism ? The fact that we do so gives us more than a hint as to the origin of sex differences in temperament.

These " secondary " sex characters have generally been assumed to result from the physiological characters of the organism, but a number of facts suggest that this factor in character development has a much more limited influence than we had tacitly supposed. We find highly " masculine " (as we think) mental characters in physiologically feminine women and vice versa. Further the differences in character between men of different cultures (alluded to above) are paralleled or exceeded by differences in the character and ideal of womanhood. Broadly speaking the greatest differences are found in patriarchal cultures where the woman becomes the protégé or toy of the man. Under matriarchal cultures, such as that of ancient Teutondom, no distinction was made between the virtues proper to a man and those of a woman.

Brynhild is depicted in the authentic sources as equal to Sigurth in every respect.

It is quite conceivable then that features of our mode of upbringing, which I have vaguely generalized as a tenderness taboo, create an artificial mental differentiation and consequent emotional barrier between adult males on the one hand and women and children on the other. Women, of course, can never, consistently with their rearing functions, lose touch with the child so completely as is possible for men. Besides the prospect of having children of their own, their own development differs from that of their brothers in that neither the Oedipus wish nor custom can ever bring about the same kind of cleavage between themselves and their mothers and they may even be associated with the latter in the care of younger children. There is no need to postulate an instinct of maternity when we find the disposition and the habit developing unchecked from infancy, and this is bound to have an influence upon the formation of the general character of women.

My point is that the taboo on infantile activities, gratifications and relationships to mother, the condemnation of regression, spreads to harmless and even necessary feelings and attitudes of mind. It artificially differentiates men from women, making them bad comrades and throwing the women back upon a dependency on their children, thus further widening the breach and aggravating jealousy. But its worst effects lie in separating parent from child. The former, unconsciously resisting and defending himself from regressive longings, is impatient with childishness and forces the child to grow up and to abandon its naive, unguarded, emotional relationship to social environment. Such a parent, while denying the " right to childhood ", presents to his children as the goal of life an adult nature and relationship which is unattractive to the child's mind or even productive of anxiety and depression. " If that is all maturity has to offer ", we might imagine the child feeling, " I had better stay as and where I am." Thus a puritan intolerance of tenderness increases the unconscious regressiveness it hates, and interposes unnecessary moral obstacles in the way of the maturation it designs to accelerate. It forces development to proceed by a violent change with repression instead of by gradual process. It does not produce really mature minds, but merely a hardness and cynicism with a core of anxious, angry, infantility. It loses the generosity of the child without acquiring the stability and integration which should belong to the adult.

At any rate it appears that the notion of a taboo on tenderness, related as it is to the general hypothesis of the nature of love which this book is sketching out, throws new light upon certain facts of character-differentiation between men, women and children and between different races, and places them in a new relationship. As such it seems worth working out.

CHAPTER VII

REPRESSION AND THE JEALOUSIES

THE fundamental question we must ask ourselves is "Is society a spontaneous expression of human nature, or an artifact of force?" Freud unhesitatingly and explicitly states that it is the latter. Society for him is maintained only by the dominance of the "leader" over guilty and frightened "followers", just as social behaviour in the individual is (in his eyes) the outcome of repression by fear. We must of course remember the distinction between suppression by coercion, operating at conscious levels, and repression, which is entirely an unconscious process. In the process of socialization of the group however the two mechanisms operate "in parallel" to produce somewhat the same result.

The starting point of Freudian (and indeed of modern) psychology is the conception of repression, not as a passive subsidence of memories, but as the forcible and purposeful splitting off of certain mental processes and contents from the stream of consciousness and also *more or less* from the determination of our waking behaviour. The investigation of the surreptitious influence of the resulting "unconscious mind" has been the main task of psycho-analysis. As has already been said, the development of social feeling, as also that of culture-interest, are regarded as dependent upon repression, so that the whole Freudian social theory rests upon the manner in which repression was supposed to be brought about.

The contents and processes of the unconscious mind *which first attracted attention* were of a sexual nature. Those which were next elucidated were also regarded as sexual by an extension of the meaning of that term. The more recent developments of psycho-analytic theory have not had time to affect its fundamental concepts, which still rest upon and represent these primitive observations and interpretations. Its conceptions of the origin and nature of society have also this basis, and have not been re-oriented to its developing psychology. It is therefore no wonder that they are one-sided.

Granted the premise that it is sexual wishes which undergo repression, it is quite logical to suppose that it is fear of a stronger rival which instigates this repression. Sexual jealousy must then be regarded as the mainspring of all control, be it social (as taboo)—or endopsychic (as inhibition and repression). Consistently with this, it is reasonable to imagine that this control is sanctioned by a threat directed to the sexual function, "castration" which would permanently remove the organ by which sexual desires can be gratified. Further, since these organs are not conspicuous in the female, it is intelligible that they should be envied by her, as, in fact, *under certain circumstances*, does happen to a very important extent.

Freud's psychology then leads him to emphasize two jealousies as being of prime importance in the development of the fabric of society, namely :

(1) Sex jealousy, enforced by castration fear.
(2) Penis envy on the part of the women for the superior " complete " males.

As I will show later these are only two, and *not the most important*, of a whole group of jealousies which play an important part in the development of society. Here I am concerned only to show that Freud's false emphasis proceeds naturally from his inadequate conception of the wishes undergoing repression and of the motive forces which achieve it. He says that—the boy early " perceives that the father is the principal obstacle " to the gratification of his incestuous wishes towards his mother. I maintain that this is not universal as Freud imagines, but is *contingent* upon certain circumstances affecting the mother's character and affective relationships to son and husband respectively.

The efficacy of a prohibition is the greater the more the prohibitor is loved as well as feared, for, besides the power to inflict material punishment, the loved object has then the power also of withdrawing love and of substituting anger, dislike, contempt, etc., *any evasion of which punishment is* impossible. Only the loved object can wield the separation-anxiety in its true sense. We can even find cases where the prohibition is perfectly effective although the prohibitor is weaker than, or even dependent upon, the person whose wishes are denied. Here there is no question of fear or punishment, the only fear is loss of love, and when we consider the effects of this fear in enforcing renunciation, we find them greater than the effects of any material apprehension. Thus, for fear of disgrace the soldier will sacrifice life, that is to say, for love of his good repute. Where, in a moment of impulse the forbidden wish has actually been indulged, remorse may lead the offender to seek the utmost punishment as a means of atonement with the loved object. Such conduct as this would be inconceivable if self-control were actually based mainly upon the fear of punishment and the rational desire of gain and comfort. We cannot understand such conduct on the supposition that it is ultimately motivated by selfish fear and not by love.

So much for conscious behaviour. We maintain, however, that for fantasy the same holds good, that love, not fear, is the dominant inhibitor. Indeed, since fantasy is quite secret (our own affair), there is no reason at all why we should fear to indulge it, were it not that in the indulgence of *condemned* fantasies we are conscious of a painful contradiction within our own thought processes. Thus, to take the eternal incest-question, a *fantasy* of incest with the mother, if it is agreeable in itself, could be indulged without risk of the father's vengeance. But, if the mother imago has acquired ideal beauties, and if her sentiments are known to be irreconcilably opposed to any such thoughts, then, even the fantasy, instead of being pleasant, is painful. While, therefore, the dread of the father might lead the child to *conceal* his incestuous fantasies (reticence), *his feelings for his mother would lead him to renounce them or repress them* (Repression). The typical Oedipus suppression to which Freud attaches such importance, namely the paternal inhibition, should lead to *reticence, not to repression* ; but the maternal prohibition, I suggest, extends its sway *at least as far as the unconscious*. The maternal objection cannot be evaded ; gratification without *her* knowledge is inconceivable. Father *might not know* " about baby and mother ", but mother must *always* know, since her own person is concerned. Concealment from the mother is unimaginable to the infant, and not even desirable to the child, since in *itself a guilty concealment constitutes a painful separation*. Even in the unconscious, I consider, it is only by a " splitting of the imago " that incestuous fantasies can be indulged.

From the beginning of infantile life, the mother is the first " object " to be defined clearly in the infant consciousness as a being independent of the child and all-important for its pleasure or pain. Thereafter her imago (the child's idea of her) undergoes many transformations in the course of the child's development.   Thus the mother may be imagined at one time as the complaisant slave of the child's magic cries and gestures, and at another she may appear as a terrible exacter of obedience ; her imago ranges from that of the feeding-cleansing nurse to that of the aloof, ideally pure and unapproachable goddess who cannot be imagined in connection with naughty or " vulgar " things. Hence she is supremely important, not only in the formation of the very first idealisms, but also in building up the child's first idea of *itself* and its first ambitions and purposes ;   that is to say that the mother has not only the predominant rôle in repression and denial, but she is of equal importance in the positive, constructive side of upbringing. The effects upon the child of her personality and relationship to other members of the family are therefore enormous and infinitely variable.

I suggest that the *patriarchal suppression*, the dread of the jealous father, only comes into operation in certain families and in certain cultures as a *complementary variable to the maternal repression.*   Only in so far as the latter is weak has the paternal authority to be mobilized to its assistance.   When it has to be evoked, patriarchal suppression never completely takes the place of the deficient maternal repression.   The Oedipus wish, if thwarted *by the father, not by the mother*, must find expression either in art, religion or in neurosis—the three fields in which Freud *has* demonstrated the sublimation or " return " of this complex.

It will not do, however, to speak simply of maternal and paternal repressions, for, from the genital phase onwards, the incidence of these repressions is different for boy and girl respectively. In the case of the boy, the jealous father may not be loved at all ; the father may be regarded as an interferer, an interloper or an outsider.   A complementary state of affairs can never arise between the girl and her mother, the mother can never be a real " outsider ". I think, therefore, it might be of value to distinguish, not as between paternal and maternal repression, but between those repressions which are due to the will of the loved and desired object itself—which I would call " endogenous "—and those arising from the fear of an intruding third party. The latter I call " exogenous ".

In regard to the Oedipus wish, my suggestion is that the maternal rejection is a vastly more effective repressant than the mere paternal " castration threat " of the earlier Freudian exposition. Not only has it priority *in time* over the latter, not only does it occur *at a more plastic phase of life*, but it is more logically conclusive and is backed by graver sanctions. It is more logically conclusive because the infant cannot imagine a gratification without mother's knowledge, though it might imagine a gratification in father's absence *if mother were willing*. Mother, for a variable time, has for the infant the prestige of all her previous victories over his uncultural wishes. She is " omnipotent " and " omniscient " ; she inspires all his ethical and aesthetical ideals and repugnances. If the infant thinks of the mother as repudiating incest, *he cannot proceed to the next phase of the Oedipus fantasy*, which implies that " if father were away " or " if I were stronger " mother " would be willing ". The idea, " mother would never consent ", is the conclusive barrier to the Oedipus wish, even at fantasy level. If, on the other hand, the mother is imagined as the (willing) property of the strongest, then indeed the child may form fantasies of rescuing her, or capturing her, from the father.

The relationship between mother and father is crucial for the other two sides of the affective family triangle. If the once omnipotent mother is discovered to fear father, *a fortiori*, the infant must fear him also. Indeed, the infant inevitably assesses or " cathects " his surroundings *from the mother's point of view* ; he approaches the world through her eyes. The father is then, for the infant, *what the mother's reactions make him out to be.* In sympathy with the mother the infant adopts her attitudes of fear, hate, love or admiration. The child also understands that the father has some power of commanding the mother's love and covets that power ; much then will depend upon what it conceives that power to be. If the father esteems the mother the infant's regard for her remains unshaken ; if he dominates her and she accepts his dominance, *might* will certainly seem to the infant not only *right* but virtue, the true way of winning love. If the mother loves the father, then the infant must also love him, and this, in concert with *her* rejection of the incest wish, will protect the father from the infant's Oedipus jealousy and hate. On the other hand, if the mother defers to the father as the sole source of authority, a very different affective attitude is inspired in the child. All these " ifs " indicate the possibility of difference between families and *even between cultures*, and we have to explore these differences in the next chapter. The principal " if " that concerns us at the moment is this : *if* our suggestions are valid, how have they not been forestalled by Freudian research ? How is it for example that in *The Ego and the Id* (p. 45) Freud writes : " The parents and especially the father, were perceived as the obstacle to realization of the Oedipus wishes, . . . ? " My suggestion amounts to this, that the mother, and (*in certain cultures and families*) *to a lesser extent* the father, are perceived as the main obstacle to the Oedipus wishes.

I have to make good this suggestion of the primary, paramount, importance of the mother's will against the enormous weight of evidence that supports the Freudian interpretation in psycho-pathology and ethnological psychology. Obviously I cannot make good the whole of my case within the limits of this book, but I can at least suggest two reasons why the Freudian principle, largely valid as it is, has prevented its exponents from appreciating the still greater importance, as I allege, of the underlying maternal repression. As I see it, maternal repression, if on right lines, is *so effective* in producing unconsciousness and renunciation, that *no recognizable Oedipus symptoms erupt*. In this case there is no " return of the repressed ". Freud's principle of patriarchal repression accounts for the neuroses ; maternal repression accounts for the quiescent cultures, " the people who have no history " ; it accounts also for a very large group of strictly matriarchal religions whose character is diametrically opposed to the group of aggressive, triumphant, religions that have a semitic, patriarchal, origin. True, as we shall see, the quiescent cultures and the matriarchal cults have largely gone down before the aggression of the guilt-ridden religions, which must needs atone for sin, and propitiate the " outraged father ", by compelling others to worship him. So we have come to live in a patriarchal culture, and I suggest that this forms one reason why the *first* analytic discoveries have been largely confined to what might be called the *Oedipus diseases* (neuroses) and the *Oedipus cultures*, since these are much the most conspicuous and, *on account of the essential weakness of patriarchal repression, most easily yield their secrets to analysis.*

Again, Freud's own antecedents lie in perhaps the most patriarchal of all cultures, a circumstance which, along with his pre-occupation with the neuroses, naturally led him to discover the paternal repression first. Armed with the Oedipus principle, he immediately found himself surrounded with problems it would solve. He interpreted the symbolic Oedipus pictures which confronted him without, it seems to me, concerning himself much with the, to him, relatively featureless " background " or the " canvas " upon which they were painted. Nevertheless, as I suggest, it is only where there were inadequacies in the maternal repression that the father-son antagonism received its real motivation and the Oedipus conflict was instituted.

I will show presently that in patriarchal cultures many circumstances concur to relax the maternal repressions and to bring the typical Oedipus Complex into prominence. As compared, for instance, with Nordic cultures, early child-bearing is commoner in patriarchal cultures and so also is age-disparity between wife and husband. The companionship and reality-interests denied to women she must compensate for in her relations with her children. Women in patriarchal cultures are prouder and more passionate mothers, over-tender to their sons, who largely constitute their own claim to social esteem. Lack of self-esteem as *women*, over-deference to the pater-familias, over-valuation of the male, all these circumstances tend to substitute paternal for maternal authority. In paternal cultures, too, the Oedipus wish must ripen more quickly, before the child has well learnt the lesson of renunciation of other wishes and before he has developed the companionship of reality-interest as a resource to fall back on. The repression of the infant's sensual feelings for the mother is almost impossible prior to weaning—if only because the distinction between the forbidden and the permitted is here too artificial and complex for the child ; perhaps it is even *unnatural*.   Thus a premature sexualization of these wishes, or a retarded repression in other respects, robs the *child of the chance of solving his problems one at a time*—an essential if the infant is to have *time* to get his substitute interests.   Finally, under patriarchal conditions, the mother *allows the child* to perceive the father as the chief obstacle to its exclusive possession of herself—sexually or otherwise.

Not only is it most difficult for the child in these circumstances to achieve renunciation and repression, but *his parents are not able to help him.* The mother has remitted some of her influence to the father, yet the latter lacks the prestige derived from weaning and excretory training ; he lacks also the primary nutritive and sensual bonds she has established during suckling, washing, etc., which, as has been pointed out, are invaluable for enforcing renunciation.   There is no *instinctive* love for the father ; he is loved, if at all, because mother loved him, feared because she fears him, hated because he interferes between mother and baby. The typical Oedipus " setting " is established on the weak foundation of paternal repression.

So I speak of endogenous repression, where the wishes of the loved person herself directly oppose those of the lover—the opposition in this kind of repression arises *within the love relationship and not from the interference of an outside party*, as in the exogenous, or Freudian repression proper (if indeed this ever effects true repression at all).

It appears as if the latest developments of Freudian theory trend towards recognizing implicitly the predominant importance of this, endogenous or maternal, instigation or repression. Psycho-analysis is attributing an ever greater pathogenic significance to the very earliest periods of life, before the discrimination of self from mother, and hence long prior to any recognition of paternal jealousy and anger as a possible source of danger to the child. Any repression in the pre-Oedipal phase must obviously be initiated by the mother herself, i.e. it must be endogenous, and not due to the psycho-analytically supposed dread of the jealous father's intervention.

Owing, then, to his starting point, personal antecedents and many other circumstances, Freud's original conception of repression was one-sided. Accordingly he was pre-occupied with sexual struggles and the only jealousies that he originally found worthy of serious attention were :

(a) The Oedipus (sex) jealousy of sons for fathers, and,

(b) The penis envy of women for the supposedly superior male.

But there is abundance of (ethnological) evidence to show that these are neither the earliest, the most important or the most universal of anti-social motives. I have already mentioned the Cain jealousy, (c), the control of which is the ethical "leit-motif" of the Mother-cults. I will also point out presently that the jealousy myths of matriarchal peoples are predominantly concerned with struggles among the children for the mother's favour, and not with the jealousy of sons and fathers. The Cain jealousy naturally tends to be the earliest and most powerful in individual development. Certain primitive peoples, e.g. Bantu, take elaborate measures to counteract Cain jealousy.

But the course of evolution itself has created one other great source of jealousy (d). By specializing the female for child-bearing and lactation it has given to her a virtual monopoly of (organic) parental functions and gratifications, at least so far as infancy is concerned. But apparently this evolution has not been accompanied by any reduction of the parental or associative impulses in the male, who among non-mammals shows himself quite as able and zealous in nurtural activities as the egg-layer herself—indeed often more so. This disparity between wish and the organic capacity to satisfy it expresses itself in certain abnormalities of individuals and particularly in certain primitive customs.

Couvade—still practised in Western Europe, etc., consists in a mock childbirth by the husband while the wife is " lying in ". This is usually regarded as a magical means of making delivery easier, but it might be interpreted as an expression of unconscious desire on the part of the husband to share in the production of the child, and so to become co-proprietor with the mother of the child.

Since the affective relationships of the parents to each other and particularly any difference in their attitude to the children affects the latter profoundly, any competitiveness in indulgence or severity is a matter of the very highest importance. I will press the point of this masculine jealousy of women, particularly as it is the very reverse of Freud's conception of penis-envy and suggests that the latter may be an artifact of special cultural conditions. The lack of maternal hopes, anticipations and satisfactions in man's own life has already been noted as perhaps accounting for his more intense creative and cultural interest, possibly also for his more aggressive and possessive temperament, for his greater delinquency, greater sexuality (if it is a fact) and conceivably even for the gradual political and economic predominance of the male sex.

Patriarchal culture and sentiment itself and the anti-feminism in which Freud shares might likewise be an expression of this hopeless envy. An example of the evidence of its existence might be offered :

(1) The Aranda (a tribe of Australian aborigines) state positively that men can bear children themselves as well as women, though of course they do not believe it as a fact. It is just a wish-fantasy.

(2) They create in males, by the operation of sub-incision, a wound in the urethra which they call by their name for the female genital organ.

(3) At certain ceremonials they make this " Aralta-hole " bleed ; but women are carefully excluded from these rites.

(4) They are remarkable among primitive people for having little or no ceremonial in connection with menstruation.

Taking these data in order I infer that (1) is simply a wish-fantasy, that (2) is a make-believe imitation of the female sex carried out as far and as explicitly as word and deed can do. (3) and (4) I regard as complementary. The all but universal horror of menstruation may owe much to man's *envy* (again inverted on the " sour grapes " principle) but this Australian man evades this " envy-disgust " of womanhood, by annexing to himself her most conspicuous functions. Naturally he excludes the " inferior " female even from a spectator's rôle in this jealous ritual. Her intuition might penetrate to its meaning and imperil her gravity along with the dignity and social ascendency of the splendid Freudian male !

For convenience of reference I will call this the *Zeus Jealousy*, because Zeus is depicted as having swallowed his pregnant wife, Mitis, in order to bear her child, Pallas, himself. Other mythic illustrations of masculine child-bearing could easily be given as showing the wide incidence of this wish.

But man's jealousy of the woman with a child is supplemented also by his jealousy of the child who has arrived to take possession of the wife. The advent of the child enriches the woman's love-life ; but, to begin with, impoverishes that of the man. Hence we find what I call the Laios Jealousy, Laios who had his son Oedipus exposed and abandoned at his birth. Many other myths and a great deal of animal behaviour attest the resentment of the father at the child's advent, e.g. Kronos, Ouranos. As this jealousy is directed against boys and girls *alike* we must reject Freud's interpretation of it as merely a " timely provision " against the son's future challenge to the father's sexual possession of the mother.

To summarize, Freud in his social theory has concentrated almost exclusively upon :

(*a*) The son's precocious sexual jealousy of the father's right to the mother—Oedipus Complex.

(*b*) The woman's jealousy of the " superior " male sex organs—Penis Envy.

To each of these jealousies it seems to me there is an equally important complement. Thus, corresponding to (*a*), we have (*c*) the father's regressive jealousy of the child's nurtural possession of the mother—the " Laios " or " Ouranos " Jealousy— and (*d*) corresponding to (*b*) the male jealousy of the woman's power of producing and suckling the baby, i.e. the Zeus Jealousy.

(Incidentally the fable that Pallas sprang full-armed from Zeus' head seems to indicate that she did not *require* suckling, but was endowed from birth with the military and political qualities *of the male*. The complete jealousy is thus indicated as if by saying " Men produce women, not women men.")

(*e*) The fifth form of jealousy, that of Cain for Abel, seems to me by far the most important in the process of socialization, if only because it is biologically inevitable (except perhaps for youngest children) and because it must, under primitive conditions, appear very early in life. The Central Australian mother eats every second child, sharing it with the older baby. Roheim, who reports this as a fact, does not take it into account in explaining the racial character of these peoples. According to him they are " all heroes ", as " happy as wolves ", but he attributed this idyllic character to the fact that they have suffered no weaning trauma and no early sex repression (latency period). Surely the child's secure possession of such " yielding mothers " is in some measure due to this unusual solution of the problem of Cain Jealousy. Not only can the child go on " eating the mother ", but she even lets it *eat the younger baby.*

CHAPTER VIII

ORIGIN AND NATURE OF SOCIETY

WITH such a view of the jealousies obstructing social harmony and of the nature and functions of repression, naturally Freud's conception of the process of socialization of mankind is incoherent and old-fashioned. Setting aside the possibility that our sub-human ancestors were quite as sociable as ourselves (I think it highly probable), we can speculate upon the " origin of society " *as if* this were an historical event. This exercise of fantasy will at all events express and expose our own social and anti-social impulses by displaying how and why *we imagine we would* unite into a group if we were these " mythical monsters ", independent individuals !

In *Totem and Taboo* (1912) Freud infers that the sexual jealousy and suspicion of the patriarch of the horde, directed against the maturing sons, leads him to expel them. Thereupon their unsatisfied sexual needs draw them together as " The Band of Brothers " in a (more or less) " goal-inhibited " homo-sexual community. Subsequently this group encounters the patriarch and, by their united strength, slay and eat him. Thereupon, overcome with remorse, they renounce the incestuous " spoil " (the mothers) which is now under their control, and become a community integrated by their common guilt, superstition, fear and remorse. They are equally bound by and bound together by the taboo of the dead ancestor's prohibition.

Here and there in his writings Freud adds emendations and alternatives to this social theory.

In one place, he casually suggests that it is rational foresight of the practical advantages of co-operation that led man into the social experiment. " Once primitive man had made the discovery that it lay in his own hands (speaking literally) to improve his lot on earth by working, it cannot have been a matter of indifference to him whether another man worked *with* him or against him. The other acquired the value of a fellow-worker, and it was advantageous to live with him." Within a page or so, this discovery of the value of co-operation is represented as dependent upon the primal parricide. " By overpowering the father the sons had discovered that several men united can be stronger than a single man " (*Civilization and its Discontents*, pp. 65, 67). With or without foresight, the socializing motive here depicted is *rational*. On p. 66 the integration of the family itself is attributed to " economic " motives, " the female who wanted not to be separated from her helpless young, in their interests, too, had to stay by the stronger male ".

Besides sexual and rational motives, Freud also refers social tolerance to fear of losing the parental love. Here he is dealing with Cain Jealousy and it is noteworthy that he refers consistently to " parents ", not to the *mother* specifically. " The elder child would certainly like to put its successor jealously aside, to keep it away from the parents, and to rob it of all its privileges ; but in face of the fact that this child (like all that come later) is loved by the parents in just the same way, and in consequence of the impossibility of maintaining its hostile attitude without damaging itself, it is forced *into identifying itself with the other children.* So there grows up in the troop of children a communal or group feeling, which is then further developed at school " (*Group Psychology and the Analysis of the Ego*, p. 86).

E

Self-interest and fear are here presented as the basis of " identification " and hence of " communal or group feeling ". " Esprit de corps ", he says explicitly, is based on " envy ". " Social feeling is based upon the reversal of what was first a hostile feeling into a positively-toned tie of the nature of an identification " (p. 88). " So far as we have hitherto been able to follow the course of events, this reversal appears to be effected under the influence of a common tender tie with a person outside the group. We do not ourselves regard our analysis of identification as exhaustive."

Here again we find Freud employing (illicitly so far as his systematic premises and fundamental conceptions are concerned) the *fact* of tenderness as an *explanation* of the *development* of tenderness.

Group psychology in fact is so obscure to Freud that he has to postulate two kinds of human psychologies, social and individual (p. 92), or rather two kinds of individual—the leader and the *group of followers*. Contradicting his previous paragraph he says : " from the first there were two kinds of psychologies, that of the individual members of the group and that of the father, chief, or leader ". (In the preceding paragraph he had been uneasily half-conscious of having artificially " isolated " " individual psychology ", by neglecting all traces of " the group ". This, of course, is the gravamen of my criticism of Freud.)

Two pages further on, however, he has gone back upon these positions again (i.e. upon the admission that group psychology may be primal or at least coeval with individual psychology). He says (p. 94), " He " (the leader) " forced them, so to speak, into group psychology. His sexual jealousy and intolerance became in the last resort the causes of group psychology." Then, in a footnote, " It may perhaps also be assumed that the sons, when they

were driven out and separated from their *father* "
(my italics) " advanced from identification with one
another to homo-sexual object love, and in this way
won freedom to kill their father."

Though Freud ignores the ethnological fact that
sex jealousy is variable in general and more
pronounced in higher than in lower cultures, he
has one of these twinges of doubt that make him
" hedge " so successfully.   On p. 82 we find " we
must reproach ourselves with having unfairly
emphasized the relation of the leader ", while on
p. 85 he reproaches Trotter for going to the opposite
extreme.

Even allowing for this reasonable (and indeed
radical) retreat, can we make out of all these
scattered and variable conjectures anything
resembling a coherent theory of social life ?   We
have here, pressed into service, such socializing
forces as self-denying pacts, economic purpose,
rational foresight, tenderness, remorse, sex desire,
homo-sexuality, fear and authority, " identification " and " reversal of hostile feeling (envy) "—the
last two themselves being hypothetical processes
more difficult to understand than the phenomena
they purport to explain.   Freud himself at one
point confesses his inability to understand the fact
or even the possibility of social unity.   In *Civilization
and Its Discontents*, p. 102, he says of human
integration, " *Why this has to be done we do not know ;
it is simply the work of Eros.   These masses of men
must be* bound to one another libidinally ; necessity
alone, the advantages of common work, would not
hold them together " (my italics).   Here it is plainly
implied that there *can be no factor* beyond libidinal
desire and other selfish appetites *although these
admittedly do not suffice to explain the phenomena in
question ! ! !*   Two pages later, he professes total
incapacity to explain the relative harmony of

certain animal socïeties, but conjectures that they too *must have* passed through "thousands of centuries" of struggle "before they found the way to those state institutions which we admire them for to-day". That is to say he postulates conflict, struggle and repression as inevitable and indeed as the welder of society.

The nearest approach to a love psychology I can find in his writings is contained in *Group Psychology*, where we find (p. 57), "love alone acts as the civilizing factor in the sense that it brings a change from egoism to altruism. And this is true both of the sexual love, with all the obligation which it involves of sparing what women are fond of, and also of the desexualized, sublimated homo-sexual love for other men, *which springs from work in common*." Here we have one of these astonishing interpolations in which a genial intuition overcomes for a moment his habitual pessimism and narrow outlook. But if love is purely sexual, what obligation does it "involve of sparing", etc. ? Does it not rather, in its original form of pure appetite, involve the necessity of destroying the rival ? And how does homo-sexuality "spring from work in common" ? This idea is a complete reversal of all the conceptions which are articulated together to form the Freudian Theory.

Freud, in fact, is unable to derive love or altruism from the sex-appetite, is unable to see that hate is contingent, not primary and inevitable, and he is unwilling to admit the existence of any positive, primary, "other-regarding" feeling. As a consequence he is unable to explain society, human or animal, in spite of the licence he allows himself in regard to eclecticism, and in spite of his inconsistency and transcendent hypotheses (e.g. "reversal of affect" where the two affects are regarded as fundamentally, genetically, independent). Not

only is he unable to explain " good " conduct
(altruistic or social) by the formula of selfish struggle,
but he even fails to explain badness itself, and so has
to postulate, " ad hoc ", a primal, independent
instinct to destroy for the sake of destruction and
irrespective of provocation or thwarting.   And so
the last state of Freud's social theory is worse than
the first—if this were possible.

I, on the other hand, see the germ of society in
the " band of brothers " *and sisters* which is formed
under each mother, independently of expulsion or
otherwise by the father, *who may even in these early
times have been an absentee from the family except at the
mating season.*   The first operative jealousy, then, to
be overcome is the nurtural or " Cain " jealousy,
and the first " moralizer " is the mother.   For
Freud (as already quoted), *the parents together*
overcame this by threatening withdrawal of love
from the jealous elder and so compelling him to
" identification " and " reversal " of hate into love
for the younger.

An interesting comparison suggests itself with
animals born in a litter.   They start life partially
socialized, since "the other" puppies serve each other
partially in lieu of mother while she is absent.   Man
by contrast goes through a period of sole ownership
of the mother herself which he is forced to renounce,
and so his moral and anti-social feelings remain far
more conscious, more plastic and precarious, and
undergo much further elaboration.

When the mothers have enforced and encouraged
mutual tolerance among " the young ", the latter's
own associative need and plastic interest establishes
the play-relationship from which culture develops,
and also a *social habituation* which is never
completely superseded by the subsequent mating of
all the members.   The females certainly "drop out"
of society more completely than the males, since the

family life affords *to them* a more complete satisfaction of the social need ; but, broadly speaking, sex and reproductive unions never completely supplant the associative activities and companionships of interest to which individuals have become accustomed during the long interval between infantile dependency and sexual maturity.

It should also be noted (see Chapter VII) that the prospect of bearing and nurturing children—the future rôle in life—must have a profoundly differentiating effect upon the characters of girls as distinct from boys. The fashion is to regard this as due to chemical differences in the body ; but however it originates it will tend to mitigate the tenderness-taboo in girls and so to alter their social needs and drives. This in turn is probably a factor of great importance in the origin of society, inasmuch as mental sex-differentiation could not have proceeded far at that epoch.

The regulation of sexual jealousy is thus not the crux of socialization but a secondary matter. It is probable in the first place that this particular " greed " is less monopolistic, less focussed upon individual personalities in these primitive (hypothetical) ancestors of ours, than in our own, high, cultures with their intense individuations of character, temperament, etc. In the second place, it is probable, I think, that with the simplicity and freedom of life, the absence of sex taboos (owing to the effectiveness of the " endogenous " or maternal repression of incest wishes) will prevent any neurotic distortion of the sex impulses. This, in turn, will obviate the neurotic (and hence unsatisfactory) choice of mate and, further, freeing the sexual impulse, will lead to its complete detensioning or satiety in marital intercourse. *Given* " its place ", I believe sex would " Keep its place ". Mating under these circumstances would be satisfactory, and man would have a natural tendency towards monogamy like so many other animals. That being so, social reinforcement of monogamy and suppression of behaviour likely to lead to disruptive sex jealousy, would be less necessary than in our own neurotic cultures, of which impotence and Don Juanism are admittedly two artifacts.

Sex jealousy, I suggest, is largely based on an anxious, infantile, exclusive possessiveness and is aggravated socially by the unbounded greediness of this type of mind which is a product of patriarchal culture. If we could exclude Don Juanism and the morbid anxiety about sole possession, the social *occasions* for sex jealousy as well as its psychological motivations would be much reduced. Sexual jealousy cannot then be regarded as the crucial factor in the establishment of society ; though by mistaking the products of our modes of upbringing for human nature itself, we tend to reconstruct the remote past on lines that would hold good for the present. At any rate we do know,

(1) That " Don Juanism " is an infantility (mother-fixation and incest quest) on the authority of psycho-analytic investigation. In this case, as usual, Freudian *Theory* has failed to " digest " inconvenient discoveries of Freudian *Method*.

(2) That much supposed sex-jealousy in animals is not *really aimed* at and *does not attain* exclusive possession of the desired mate. For example the jealous intolerance of one queen bee for another has been shown elsewhere by me to have a nurtural and not a sexual reference.

(3) That sex-jealousy can have definitely morbid exacerbations (i.e. the delusions of unfaithfulness of the chronic alcoholic) and that psychotherapy can do a very great deal to reduce jealousy *even where good cause exists.*

(4) That individuals and cultures vary very greatly between themselves in regard to sex jealousy —which apparently may be almost zero—and that in matriarchal cultures this jealousy is characteristically and substantially less than under patriarchal conditions of rearing.

From these facts and the preceding arguments I reject the Freudian conception of the establishment of human society as being essentially identical with the overcoming of sexual jealousy. This jealousy appears for the first time as an important social factor with the advent of the Primal Father, of whom Freud is so fond, but society reaches back before his time. Only if we postulate him " a priori " as the centre and pillar of all social life, are we compelled to reckon sexual jealousy as the principal disruptor of society.

Of course a truly matriarchal *society* is an abnormality or theoretical " possibility " which hardly, if ever, can exist. When I talk of matriarchy, I mean a state of society where the woman is the effective head of the household *so far as the young children are concerned*, and where, consequently, the matriarchal family organization affects the character and maturity of the adults as well as, to some extent (a less important matter), the formal structure of society.

We have, then, the germ of society, with all its needs and capacities, its dissatisfactions and jealousies, in the *group of children* each of whom has to accept the " others " (i.e. the group) to some extent in lieu of the lost mother as the sole available antidote to the separation-anxiety. The individuals of this group are truly social in so far as they have acquired social tolerance and social needs *not concerned with organic* (bodily) *cravings and satisfactions*.

From this matrix I imagine social evolution as not proceeding in a single line, nor even as branching out in different directions in the manner of organic evolution. The social organism is so plastic that its structure (in the course of many generations) will reflect the general conditions of life, adapting to them now in this way, now in that, with a " lag " at the very most, of a few centuries. Thus it is conceivable that society might become matriarchal and patriarchal *by turns* tending always purposefully *towards* that point where, (*a*) the *maximum* amount of tradition and continuity is retained with the *minimum* prejudice to the adaptability of the social structure ; and

(*b*) the *minimum* restriction indispensable to social life is placed upon individual, natural, impulse and is enforced with the *maximum* effectiveness as either social taboo or endopsychic " repression ".

(*c*) the maximum of institutional expression of human impulses is allowed—included Sublimation and Cultural interests.

These are the conditions reconciling internal stability with adaptability ; but where a state of struggle or competition between societies obtains, the unbalanced societies will more readily divert their attention from the process of " living " and of cultural pursuit to predatory and aggressive action. Thus there arises a tendency to the *survival of the unfit*, or of those *whose fitness is only for struggle—a selection of the " unfit " in the struggle for elimination !* This point will be considered further in the next chapter.

The factors affecting social evolution have now become so complex and delicately balanced that their results are very difficult to evaluate. Where the woman is an important food-producer she tends to preserve a high social and domestic status—to maintain her dignity and authority over her children and her relative independence of them as the sole source of love and interest for her. Under these

E*

circumstances she has the power and the will to terminate their dependency (" psychic weaning "), that is to say, she can and will repel and repress infantile sensuality and incest-wishes in a permanently and completely effective manner. Their repression and renunciation will be complete, and the child, finding adequate substitutes, will truly grow up. Otherwise the mother, being dependent upon the child, will cling to it and cultivate its dependency upon herself, with contrary effects upon the Oedipus Wishes.

On the other hand food-production by women tends to free the man from this labour, and so the companionship of childhood among the men is continued in the form of a purely masculine society or " club ". The Band of Brothers, in reality, is the association of husbands whose wives are occupied with *their* domestic affairs. This contains the germ of sex solidarity and opens the way to concerted action for the subjugation of women. In general, however, woman's economic importance swings the balance in the direction of a matriarchy-of-the-Household (*Note on Pseudo-matriarchies and Grandmother Rule*) in some such way as this.

In hunting, and in all modes of livelihood demanding or rewarding the exercise of supreme effort or of constant application, man's superior physical organization, and his freedom from the demands of child-bearing and rearing, confers on him an advantage over women. Indeed this is one of the biological values of sex-specialization. On the other hand, as I have said, if " interest " does not follow the lines of natural capacity, but covets a rôle for which the subject is functionally unfitted, the possibility of disharmony arises. In mankind this actually occurs owing to masculine envy of woman's monopoly of rearing-functions. Under these circumstances man's economic superiority

becomes an instrument of his Laios, Zeus and Cain
jealousies, and he uses his " ownership " of the food
he has won to establish *proprietary rights* over his
women and children.   (For a study of the relationships of property and power see Ref. G.)   Hunting
tribes, and indeed all nomadic peoples (where
flocks and herds require the constant tending that
only males, unburdened by children, can give),
are therefore, highly patriarchal—the women being,
in the main, " camp-followers "—objects of desire
—*rather than companions in life.*

When the development of agriculture made it
possible for communities to settle in one place
without exhausting its food resources, a remarkable
change occurred.   The home became an institution
of comfort and importance, and in its establishment,
women played a leading part.   In primitive
agriculture, too, it seems probable that women
were the pioneers ;   they certainly, in extant
communities of this type, work and own their
gardens ;   property is entailed in the female line,
sometimes *by ultimo-geniture.*   The male is now to
some extent a drone—a sojourner in the house of his
wife or his wife's mother.   Sometimes he does a
little mild warring or at least " sports " his weapons.
In more fortunate communities he does the heavier
work in jungle-clearing, house-building, fishing, etc.,
and co-operates in the domestic (and feminine) arts
of weaving and pottery.   He cannot, in this
civilization, establish any proprietary rights in
women and children ;   *he himself belongs to his
mother's clan while the products of his industry in some
cases belong to his wife.*   In this matriarchal civilization arise the great mother-cults and the ethical
ideals and racial character which belong to this
mode of upbringing.   This civilization is essentially
peaceful.   Dynastic wars are unknown ;   though
certain natural causes (independent of psychology),

leading to the migration of peoples, produce social upheavals on a vast scale.

The gradual evolution of this peasant culture (which at one time spread from Spain to North China), where fertile soil, good climate and means of communication permitted a dense population, once again threw women into the economic background. The village grew into the " city state " ; agriculture was carried on at a distance from the home ; ploughs, drawn by domestic animals, replaced the hoeing sticks of women, and agriculture fell into the hands of men. At the same time arts and crafts became highly specialized " whole-time " jobs, incompatible with motherhood. Man once more was economically dominant ; and property was inherited *in the male line and by primo-geniture*. Once again man could gratify reproductive and Cain jealousy by asserting his ownership of women and children.

Now the cult of the fruitful " food-giving " Earth-Mother begins to be replaced by that of the disciplinary Sky-Father. The feeling of guilt is displaced from regression to precocity—from Cain jealousy to Oedipus jealousy. " Sacrifice " changes its meaning accordingly, as mentioned in next chapter ; and the myths of jealousy and ambition reflect this change in the child's outlook on life. The priest-king is no longer the Earth's baby, but the representative—son and " alter ego " of the Sky-Father. His annual sacrifice and substitution by another becomes a mere formality—someone else is sacrificed by proxy—or he submits to a ceremonial degradation which does not affect his real power. He becomes King-for-life, not king-for-a-year ; and his son—not his sister's son—reigns after him. Dynasties are established and the history of the world as we know it begins. At the same time the domestication of the horse and the building (in the Mediterranean) of boats capable of carrying large crews a long way, make organized mass-warfare and a predatory mode of existence possible and profitable, so that society is militaristic and commercial and hence patriarchal *almost from the beginning of written records.*

I cannot here work out further the economic and other factors moulding society. It is not our purpose ; I wish merely to show that love, not " selfish appetite ", is the mainspring of social life and that the very jealousies which are its main disruptors are produced not by sexual desire so much as by frustrations of love itself and by unbalanced and violent efforts to overcome these.

The family, like society, is a very delicately balanced system of forces. Love must, at every turn of individual maturation and adjustment, be forced into new channels, and this is inevitably attended by tensions and stresses of all kinds. Primarily, however, all jealousies centre round the mother, and she alone can control them by repressing the wishes concerned. The conditions under which alone she has the power and the will to do so have been indicated. When children get out of hand, and in turn control " the mothers " themselves, violent results ensue, and defects of repression and renunciation have to be made good by excess of social and superstitious coercion. Social evolution has then inclined in the patriarchal direction.

Broadly speaking we conclude that the abiding problem and central task of mankind has been maturation and the harmonization of his love-needs with his appetite-needs and the attaining of maximal satisfaction in both. It is a task which must be pursued simultaneously in the developing, adapting, *individual*, and in the ever-changing *community*, culture and tradition. Repression can be practised by the individual and, " in a complementary manner ", suppression by the group. This negative solution, however, is impermanent and precarious in both cases, and what is really required is a double process of adjustment, i.e. the individual to society and society to the need of the individual. One might even define the ideal culture and social organization as that which gives the maximum socially permissible freedom of expression and development to human nature (the minimum restriction and coercion) along with the most effective substitution and suppressions *where this is inevitable.*

CHAPTER IX

RELIGION. IS IT A DISEASE OR A CURE?

IF we conclude that all " Good " and Human Happiness depend upon personal relationships of a harmoniously responsive character and that all Evil and Unhappiness spring from the inadequacy of these relations, we must ask ourselves—is this a discovery of modern science, and is our psycho-therapy the only agency from which we can expect help in the improvement of the lot and destinies of our species ? The answer is in the negative. The intuition of the past has grasped this truth in both a practical and a mystical manner, though the thinkers had not the knowledge (or, for that matter, the interest) to work out its biological, ethnological and psychopathological implications. Broadly speaking, *religion*, which, like mental illness, springs from dis-satisfactions of development and par-ticularly from the surrender of infancy, is mainly concerned in its higher forms to better our affective relationships with each other (i.e. is ethical). Unlike mental illness proper, it is a social not an individual and selfish attempt, and hence differs also in that it expresses itself in social institutions rather than in misery, alienation and dementia.

We are apt to be prejudiced nowadays against religion by reason of two things besides the general antipathy to sentiment (tenderness-taboo). First, most of its organized expressions exercise powerful social influence, and so affect—even where they do not express—selfish interests. Secondly, most religions lay great stress on a body of tradition handed down from a pre-scientific age, when historic accuracy was as little prized as in a modern press-bureau in time of war.　We ourselves would regard as monstrous certain interpolations and embroideries of tradition that are known to have occurred, but the chroniclers and transcribers responsible for the forgeries would be astonished at our point of view ; and would have regarded it as mere pedantry to sacrifice " spiritual truth " for the petty scruples of the historian of mere earthly events.　" Superstition " and even " rascality " are normative judgments, inimical to psychopathological insight, which depends to a great extent upon our power to " put ourselves in the other fellow's place ", and in this manner to understand *why* he performed the acts in question.

Turning then to the origin and evolution of religion, the earliest historical records we possess of it in the civilizations which did not use writings are found in burial remains.　From the customs they indicate, we can infer only the existence of a regard for the dead, probably ambivalent and possibly implying a belief in a future or " spirit " life.　Such customs go back at least 50,000 years.

The art of pottery, however, leaves imperishable records and we find what are called Painted Pottery Cultures extending at a remote period from Spain to North China.　From the glimpses we get we can infer the existence of a peasant culture, organized in villages round a Temple, having no organization for warfare, probably no hereditary leadership and possibly no individual hereditary ownership of land. These cultures in many respects seem similar to later ones, known to us in fuller detail.　In the latter we find a matriarchy, at least of the household, matrilineal inheritance of property and " dignity " (even if social functions are exercised through the husband or brother), and a quite distinctive socio-religious mental life.　Myth and religion, ritual and

festival and, above all, sacrifice, portray or " *project* "
a certain phase or attitude of child-mind. This
phase is still discoverable by us in analytic studies,
though it no longer determines these features of
our culture.

You might say that the ethical, religious and
sociable practices of these peoples express and refer
to psycho-social problems and interests different
from those inspiring our own. The deity they
worship is not the Sky Father but the Earth Mother,
and this indicates that the mind of the "worshipper"
has a different balance of devotion to the earthly
(actual) father and mother, from that of the Father-
worshipper. Naturally therefore the crimes the
Mother-Goddess punishes are *offences against mothers
and against babies, not* precocious sexual jealousy of
the father's privileges and rebellion against *his*
authority. Her moralizing and punitive functions
are altogether less conspicuous than those of the
Father God whose worship comes to succeed hers.
She is in fact regarded far more as Providence than
as Policeman ; and " fertility " rituals accordingly
are more in evidence than the later expiatory rites
and sin-offerings which assuage the father's wrath
vicariously.

True, if offended, the Mother-Goddess punishes
inexorably. Indeed her implacability is as distinctive as the simplicity and tolerance of her ethical
and ritual demands. She does not fill life with a
network of neurotic taboos each with its appropriate
punishments and techniques of expiation ; but
where her law *is* broken, that is death. She listens
to no excuses ; she is Atropos, " The Unturnable ",
Fate, Urth, who dooms the gods themselves, who
will listen to no plea for Balder and before whom the
souls of the dead are dumb, unable to defend themselves—*like infants.* Plainly this theology embodies
or projects the pre-oedipal (*infantile*), ambivalent,

conception of the mother who appears to the young child both unboundedly good and utterly terrible, whose displeasure is the end of all good things and of life itself.

What are the ethical exactions of such a Mother-Goddess ? We find they are all directed against *regression* rather than against *precocity*, therein differing from Patriarchal Ethical-sentiment. Further, the jealousy which must be renounced on pain of her displeasure is that of Cain for his younger brother Abel, whose " offerings " were more acceptable to the parent Gods, i.e. who seemed better loved—the baby. It is not the sin of Oedipus against his Father Laios that must be eschewed. " Sin ", for these people does not concern sex at all, but the jealousies centreing round nurtural needs and favours. Incidentally, while Oedipus' punishment was symbolic castration, Cain's was *expulsion from the home and the refusal of the earth to yield her fruits*. Earth (Mother) indeed was the instigator of his punishment, while Jehovah (Father) continued to afford his protection to the sinner—a most significant circumstance, psychologically, as showing the relative resentment of the two parents at the offence of infanticide. The mother protects and avenges *the baby*, the father sides with the older child who, *like himself, has been supplanted*. (Incidentally this suggests an explana-tion of the puzzling problem of Primo-geniture and Ultimo-geniture.)

Sacrifice is peculiarly interesting to psycho-pathologists since it frequently combines in one act the gratification of the guilty wish and its expiation and renunciation, like a neurotic symptom. In strict accordance with what has just been said about the difference in ethical attitude between matriarchy and patriarchy we find sacrifice in the Mother-cults sharply contrasted with that in patriarchal religion.

The victim in the former case is an " innocent "
one, and is held in high honour ; further it may be a
woman. He or she has been allowed every favour,
freedom and privilege *since election the previous year*
(a custom which persists into recent history under
the figure of " The Lord of Misrule "). He has
been regarded explicitly as the Earth's Child and
has enjoyed all the love and central importance
which regressive longing and envy considers is
enjoyed by the baby. At the end of the year,
however, the sacrificial victim, the Dying God, is
due to be supplanted like a mere human child.
His dignity and his life are forfeit to a fickle mother,
whose nature is always to produce new babies.

The sacrifice gratifies a variety of motives. First
it appeases our own sense of the injustice of *our*
being supplanted and gratifies us by the view of
another undergoing this privation. Second, in
killing this baby, which we have envied for a year,
we satisfy our direct jealousy of the favours he has
been enjoying since he supplanted us. Third, by
electing a new baby we enjoy (by identification) a
fantasy of re-birth—resumption of infantile privilege.
[This " theme " of re-birth as the all-important
baby is widespread in myth and ritual and of the
greatest psychological importance.] Fourth, by
allowing the Earth Mother to have her new baby
we have renounced our guilty, regressive " Cain
jealousy". We have propitiated her and ensured
the continuance of her nurtural favours to ourselves
—the (now) " good " older children—for the
ensuing year. This is the essence of the " fertility
ritual ", which is not so much concerned with the
production of *babies* as with the production of *food*.
The worshippers, being now, in a ritual sense,
" grown up ", conclude the proceedings with a
feast and an orgy of sexual licence. The genital
activities are not therefore the fundamental idea

of such rituals. (This idea, that fertility ritual is primarily sexual, appears to me a misinterpretation due to patriarchal incest-suspicion or a corruption of custom due to the activity of the incest wish itself.)

The mythology bears out the view here put forward of two contrasting forms of cults and cultures. In matriarchal cultures jealousy-myths are concerned with the struggles of brothers and sisters for *nurtural objectives mainly*, rather than with the struggles of fathers and sons for the possession of the mothers. In European folk-lore we are dealing with a body of tradition that comes into direct contact with our own children in the nursery. Cinderella and her type reject the " faithless mother " and *younger* sisters (newcomers) as merely step-relations, i.e. chosen by father, but treacherously alienating him too. Innumerable tales illustrate on the other hand the younger child's struggle with the elders. Significantly enough in the latter type of tale the younger rival achieves his end by fair competition rather than by murderous rivalry, and proves more magnanimous than does the supplanted *elder* in the former group of jealousy-tales. Matriarchal mythology, then, like " sacrifice " in these cults, is largely concerned with the (" projected ") struggles between the children themselves for nurtural objectives. Further, in so far as the incest-motif enters this form of myth, it concerns brother and sister, not parent and child ; showing a deflecting of interest from parent to playmate.

The mother-cults readily develop into polytheisms, which of course contain father-gods conceived in the image of the father as known to the minds which fashioned these religions. The attributes of these father-gods should indicate to us, then, the attitude prevalent towards "fathers" *at the phase of culture and development* in which these ideas (of god) originated. In other words, at the pre-oedipal phase of development and in the matriarchal nursery, the father presents a very different figure to the child mind from what he does in the household of say an East European Jew, and consequently his divine representation will have qualities very different from those of Jehovah. He is less authoritative and less responsible.

Our expectations are abundantly confirmed. The gods of the primitive polytheisms are leaders, helpers, and (occasionally) providers. While they may take personal offence and revenge themselves, and even, in special cases, be the *guardians of the higher social obligations* such as the sanctity of oaths and treaties or the duty of hospitality, they have no *general* moral functions in these religions. These law-giving and law-enforcing functions are attributed to women, along with the functions of healing and of presiding over growth and over the forces of nature which regulate this. *Goddesses* are both punishers and providers, Gods are instructors and defenders in accordance with the actual domestic status of mother and father as known to the mythmaking child-mind.

We find then a systematic difference in myth, theology, ritual and sacrifice, ethics and other mental characters between matriarchal and patriarchal peoples, which seems to me to indicate that the two cultures respectively *derive their inspiration from and appeal to different levels of psychic development*.

If matriarchal cult, myth, theology, initiation ritual and sacrifice deal with and give expression predominantly to *regressive* longings and jealousies, the patriarchal equivalents deal mainly with *precocity* and its repression. Initiation ritual in the former insists in effect " now you are a man " (or woman as the case may be), " put away childish longings and the jealousies which they inspire ".

Under patriarchal conditions, however, it says, "you are only a child ; see that you do not disobey or infringe the privileges of the old men ".   While, however, patriarchal initiation ritual is dealing with the precocious (supposedly sexual) jealousy of the son, Oedipus, it is doing this *in the interests of* Laios the father.   Now the father's jealousy of the son is not merely (as Freud appears to assume) a legitimate and necessary defence of his *rights* against the (potential) encroachments of the son.   Biology suggests the existence of a violent jealousy in the male of the female's monopoly of (organic) child-bearing and rearing functions.   Ethnology amply confirms this with evidence of widespread rituals which represent an *imitation by males of the female functions of child-bearing and menstruation.*   Psychology has revealed that the unconscious infantility of adults may be so strong as to make the mother hate her own child and see in it a supplanter ousting her from the childhood rôle she has never truly surrendered.   " A fortiori ", then, the father finds his child, son *or* daughter, come between him and his wife—who is unconsciously regarded by him as *his* mother.   His own child then supplants him in precisely the same way as a younger brother or sister would have done in *his* childhood, and so far as unconscious regressive longings are concerned jealousy must be felt.   Thus he will transfer his Cain jealousy to his own offspring.

Laios jealousy, i.e. of father for child, is thus very complex and powerful, as the Grecian mythology clearly teaches us.   Ouranos, the Sky Father, will not allow sons *or daughters* to be born to Mother Earth.   (Not sexual jealousy here, surely !)   Kronos in turn swallows them alive, *again irrespective of sex.* Zeus went one better and swallowed his pregnant wife, Mitis, so that *he bore Pallas (Athene) himself and thus monopolized parenthood.*   Finally in the famous

Oedipus myth itself, *the hero is not the original trans-gressor*. *Before he was born* his father, Laios, had "forebodings" about being supplanted *in his kingdom*. Consulting the oracle (? his own infantile, unconscious suspicion of the coming of a younger baby) he was well assured that this would be so, and accordingly he got rid of the rival (baby ?) at birth, i.e. separated it from the mother. That is an interpretation that Freud never considers.

It is clear then that at all times the male has a natural "drive" to usurp maternal functions and so to redress the unfairness of evolution in this respect. Further any immaturity in his own character will intensify his nurtural-tenderness-jealousy of his child's relationship to his own wife (his mother). On the one hand therefore he tends to displace the mother "vis-a-vis" the baby ; on the other to displace the baby with the mother. Like a child he seeks the undivided attentions of each.

Under conditions of culture and rearing which do not mature the males but leave them with selfish (i.e. anxious) infantile longings, there will then be a strong drive on the part of fathers to intervene between mothers and babies and assert authority and proprietorship over both. Wherever, in addition to this, social and economic circumstances vest all power and property in the males, then their jealous aggressiveness and possessiveness towards women and children is unchecked and a patriarchal society and home-life is established. This form of upbringing intensifies infantility *and* precocity in a self-perpetuating and even self-intensifying circle ("vicious" or "benignant" according to our point of view) and the whole mental life and character of the folk reflects the change.

Concurrently the Sky Father displaces the Earth Mother as supreme deity and usurps her attributes one by one, until her cult is banned as a pagan (and incestuous) fiction. (It does become Oedipus-haunted, superstitious and sensual in the transition stage—as witness the Castration of her priests, mythologically done by the Goddess herself.)   The " priest-for-a-year " becomes " King for life " by finding a substitute victim, and represents the earth's " Consort ", not her baby.   The office becomes hereditary in the male line and the dynastic " motif " appears for the first time in human history.   The king now becomes the earthly representative of the Sky Father himself.   The sacrificial victim on the other hand, *from being a God dying for his people* and thus highly honoured, becomes a *criminal*, or *a scapegoat* loaded with the *sins* of the people.[1]   The act of sacrifice is no longer regarded as one of symbolic renunciation of regressive jealousy in submission to the will of the food-giving and pregnant mother—it is no longer a symbolic " making way " for the newcomer.   It has become a killing of the precocious child to satiate the wrath and Laios jealousy of the Sky Father.   A variety of jealousies are still appeased, but, in the main, *sacrifice has now become a sin offering*. The problem of " guilt ", not that of " providence ", becomes the mainspring of religious interest, and this change is reflected in the mythology (by now verging on theology) which depicts the *struggle of discipline versus disobedience between father and sons* and no longer that between the children themselves as the main jealousy theme.   The jealousies unconsciously *gratified* in sacrifice become parricidal rather than infanticidal.   Mother-cults must now be *renounced as the acme of irreligion*, since devotion to mother has become suspect of incestuous intention. *Sin is now virtually identified with sexuality not with greed*, jealousy and other actually antisocial behaviour.

---

[1] Christ fulfils both rôles according to point of view.

Goodness is now submission to authority, observance of a multitude of taboos, cultivation of a sense of unworthiness and the practice of asceticism, none of which ethical activities were regarded with the least esteem under the matriarchal culture and upbringing. If matriarchal religious ritual and fantasy represent the projection of *pre-oedipal* (*psychotic*) *wishes*, dreads and conflicts, the corresponding factors in patriarchal religious thought and feeling represent those of *Oedipal " levels " and neurotic conflicts*.

We are now in a position to understand why Freud, from *his* starting point and pre-occupation, concludes that religion is a neurosis, an illusion and a product of primitive, unreal, thinking. Freud has interpreted all religion through the medium of the Oedipus principle and his mind fastens upon and selects examples of its working and regards these as the essence of the whole phenomenon. Facts that do not fit into this scheme of things are just put to one side to await future consideration ; problems are adjourned " sine die " ; Freud dismisses the great and mysterious Mother-cults of antiquity with two brief references in *Group Psychology and the Analysis of the Ego*. " But it is only ", he says, " with the elevation of the never forgotten primal father that the deity acquires the features that we still recognize in him to-day." True enough—for patriarchal religions of historical times ; but why neglect their precursors ? Roheim goes even further in applying the oedipus "blinkers" to research, where he says, " We are human beings because we have an Oedipus Complex " and I suppose he would add, " and we are religious because of the necessity of defending ourselves from its disturbing influences ". The facts just glanced at show, however, that a wider view of the social and therapeutic functions of religion is necessary and that the range of its variety cannot be understood on an exclusively " Oedipus " formula.

We must remember that neuroses and psychoses are not wholly morbid processes any more than are bodily illnesses.   Like the latter they may embody undesirable elements in themselves, as pus may contain the germs of disease.   They would be of no value if they did *not* deal with evil, and it would indeed be strange if they never got distorted in the struggle, thus becoming compromises and maladaptations which may even have less than no social value.   We must therefore study religion without making up our minds that it is either a disease or a cure, a psychopathy or a psychotherapy.

I have presented two sharply contrasted outlines of religion under its extreme matriarchal and extreme patriarchal forms respectively, and suggested the conditions which determine the prevalent form at any time and with any given people.   The truly pathological conditions of religion (I repeat) appear to me to arise from *transition phases* where there is neither the " stability " of childish wish freely expressed in ritual nor the " control " of organized repression, submission to authority and the *cultivation and* expiation of the sense of guilt.   Nevertheless the interesting question arises, has religion, regarded purely as a psycho-social therapy, reached its most effective expression ?   Is it possible in some way not yet practised to combine the simplicity and stability of matriarchal cults with the regulation and stimulus of those of a patriarchal character ? The attempt seems actually to have been made by Christianity, and both the successes and the failures of this religion seem to me to have been due to this circumstance.

In approaching our own religious feelings, beliefs and practices with so appraising an interest we must be on guard against two opposite prejudices. I have already " entered a caveat " on the one hand against a scientific distaste for examining what might be regarded as a tissue of old wives' tales, full of superstition and sentimental illusion, based upon the credulity of anonymous recorders of remote antiquity—in places manifestly a compilation of folk lore. The subject matter of religion has a primal interest for psychology ; and a measure of sympathy is as necessary for understanding this as " objectivity " itself. A negative attitude is bad science and bad citizenship. On the other hand I would deprecate religious enthusiasms or suspicion of science. The enquiry into the social character and functions of Christianity can and ought to be carried out without any metaphysical implications whatsoever.

Thus the historicity of Jesus[1] is a problem that does not arise in our enquiry and is not affected by our conclusions ; but, as much of the evidence is of a " miraculous " character, we must consider how this is to be interpreted from a psychological point of view.

We are able to consider that a miracle, like any other act, real or phantasied, has both a mechanism and a motive. With the former we are not concerned, but an analysis of the " motive " underlying the " canonical " miracles yields psychological conclusions surprisingly in harmony with those drawn from a study of the reputed life and death of Jesus, the " temptations ", the parables and teachings, and the personality depicted.

It is indisputable of course that the human mind has an insatiable and infantile craving for wonders, and for the favour of an all-powerful protector and provider. Miracles have been posthumously

---

[1] His reputed date and birthplace however would bring him in touch with the opposite religious thought of Greeks and Jews.

attributed to Christ from the time of Paul to this day. A great deal of this was frankly written and regarded as fiction, e.g. Ernest Bramah wrote a detective story introducing the miraculous virtue of a bit of the true cross. Many " Miracles ", then, have as their central motive the *demonstration of mysterious power*, and others have the kindred purpose of showing that the doer *must be* " good " in his life and " right " in his opinions. A whole group of miracles then are concerned mainly with raising the miracle-worker in the esteem of his fellows. These I would call miracles of power and prestige ; but it is noteworthy that while they are conspicuous in the Old Testament, the Gnostic Gospels, the Hagiology and even in the Acts, *they are insignificant in the Canonical Gospels*. In fact Christ is reported to have refused explicitly to demonstrate the *truth and value* of his teachings and " ethical laws " by his *power* to interfere with the " laws of nature "—" there shall be no sign given them ".

While, then, we can dismiss the miracles of power and prestige as evidence of the validity of *other*, collateral, teachings, we must not be prejudiced against the latter because of the way the medieval mind thought fit to buttress its beliefs ; the " purpose " of the miracles *might* carry a meaning more important than that of silencing objection and dispelling doubt. Further consideration of the various classes of miracles must, however, be deferred until after observation of the general tone and tendency of the Gospel stories and teachings.

Psychologically, the essential features of the Christian teachings and its main departure from preceding ethical thought appear to me to be twofold. First it offers the conception of social life as based upon Love rather than upon authority, and so tends to substitute a conception of the Deity as a *free-giver and " forgiver "*, rather than as with-holder and rewarder, compellor and punisher. Secondly they appear to uphold the notion of religious behaviour as concerned with good social relationships *between men* rather than with the individual duty of every man towards God. This general view can be applied, by analogy at least, to the child's relationships to its parents. When this is done we see that the Christian innovation in theology and social theory (ethics) is closely parallel to a certain transition-phase of childish development. Prior to this transition the child's relation to parents has been jealously exclusive ; (in the analogy Christ condemns the Pharisaic " monopoly." of God's favour). Until this transition the child's affective attitude (to parents) has been anxious, abject, and guilt-ridden, but un-consciously hating and aggressive (Original Sin). *After* the transition, however, the child is reconciled with the parents *whom he has forgiven* or, rather, recognized to be " good " and " kind ". Simul-taneously the " Cain jealousy " which separated him from other children is overcome and he " finds himself " in the society of playmates. Both *apprehension* and *expectation* from the parents are diminished, but the child's love and confidence have gained, not lost by its socialization ; and the total happiness of " the family " is much increased. *Only* the anxious, jealous, regressive child clings to its dependency with a mixture of querulousness and assiduity—an ambivalent love for the parents which quite overshadow any friendly interest in the other children.

We must now see whether the parallel between religious teachings and the affective (social) development of the child throws any light on the meaning of the " supernatural " parts of our religious tradition. The recorded life of Jesus and the parables (i.e. those which are admitted to be such) require no interpretation, but appear manifestly as a systematic exposition and practical demonstration of the nature and significance of love. The personality that is depicted is psychologically remarkable as combining serenity with compassion in a theoretically ideal way. The emotional attitude of Christ presented to us by tradition is just what is needed alike by the child and by the neurotic ; the confidence never suggests indifference while on the other hand the sympathy never appears as agitation. The parent must be *moved* by the child's dislike, but must not be " upset " by it. " Mutatis mutandis " with analyst and patient.

In 1932 I came to the conclusion that the Last Supper dramatized and illustrated *free giving*. Even the body is given as food, as the mother gives it. Further, the whole story of the crucifixion seemed to illustrate free " forgiving " on the understanding that hate and evil *have no independent existence* but are merely the frustration-forms of love itself, distorted as protest, reproach and that kind of aggression which is originally intended to *compel* attention. (See Chapter I, Note A.) The last prayer, " forgive them, for they know not what they do ", seems to imply that forgiveness is not a condescension to an unworthy object, but a recognition (on somewhat Socratic lines) that evil is merely error, not to be met by retributive error. The whole of this story illustrates non-retaliation— even non-resistance—to the very utmost limit.

About a year later, in formulating the classification of psychopathies I will outline later, I was suddenly struck with the analogy between the three main " wish-psychoses " and the three traditional " Temptations ". Dementia Precox is a tendency towards self-sufficiency and consequent isolation, and it seemed curiously related to the notion of living in the wilderness and using the stones as bread, by means of a magical power-fantasy that makes its possessor independent of his fellows and hence a-social. The morbid, deliberate, dependency of hysteria again, seems to be illustrated in the notion that whatever the subject does " angels will bear " him " up ". The third temptation appears obviously to depict the paranoid goal of world-mastery by *power* through the worship of power. Each of the three temptations then appeared to me to be a parable illustrating and " exposing " a corresponding morbid social goal, though hitherto I had always accepted them as illustrating the rational and conscious adult snares of vanity and self interest. It is abundantly clear, however, that there is a systematic refusal to seek or to exercise power, as has already been said.

This refusal is explicit in the statement " there shall be no sign given them ", meaning by " signs ", as by " wonders ", a demonstration of the importance of the miracle worker and a bid for the submission and admiration of his fellows—indicating his own false social attitude. The only occasions on which Christ seems to exercise miraculous *will* are where he " casts out devils " or raises the dead or stills the storm. Psychologically, exorcism (the first of these) corresponds to the function the child longs for the parents to exercise, namely the control of *its own* dangerous impulses—" making it good " *independently of its own efforts* and mental conflicts. Raising the dead is emotionally identical with the parent overcoming the separation-anxiety, unaided by the child. Saving and protecting are of course further extensions of nurtural demands. With these exceptions, Christ, according to the canonical gospels, performed very little of what might be called *ostentatious magic* or a demonstration of power qua power.

This restraint, of course, frustrated not only the need for thrill and amusement but also the profound infantile craving for the comforting belief in parental omnipotence. Later tradition amply remedied this omission ; but without entering into controversial matters I might remind you of the supernaturalism of the Gnostic Gospels which attributed all sorts of " useless " miracles to Christ. I understand that the selection of " our " four Gospels (Canonical) was based not merely on expediency but upon various distinctive characters they possessed in common. Perhaps an intuition of the ego-centricity of the power-miracle and of its " moral " incongruity with the general tone of the " Life " and " Teachings " aided in this discrimination. I shall have to show elsewhere that there are religions from which the " motif " of the " omnipotent will " of the parent is totally absent—here I will only suggest that the *appeal* of the idea of power seems to me to be to a level of maturation of character *below that to which the ethical teachings were directed*, i.e. as mentioned above, to the *child* whose attention as yet is wholly occupied by the parent *to the exclusion of the playmates*.

The second type of miracle to which I want to draw your attention, concerns the parental function of punishment. This, so far as I know, Christ is not recorded (in the Canonical Gospels) to have employed. When he had occasion to punish (i.e. the money-changers) he used the physical means of human indignation, which, after all, if not friendly, is at least sportsmanlike. The threats to Chorazin, etc., could I think be read as a dispassionate warning rather than an operative curse. The monstrous fantasies of Revelation supply the need for power-manifestation and retributive justice on the " *other* " " bad " children, which Christ himself so *culpably* neglected ! The need of *rescue and control*, as we shall see, were gradually met by the developing Christian theology.

There are, however, other early needs which one might call nurtural and these seem to find expression in certain healing and "provident" miracles. There are three "techniques" used in "healing" miracles, namely, to do something *to* the patient, (service), to encourage him to do something for *himself* (re-assurance), and to say "Thy sins are forgiven thee" (Absolution). These functions also are very closely paralleled in the mother's relations to the infant. They meet respectively the needs of the helpless infant, of the timid child, and of the older child who is dealing with the sense of guilt. "Provident" miracles are illustrated by the feeding of the multitude, turning the water into wine, etc.—a miracle that seems to me to indicate the most delicate social sensibility of the lot.

We have then found that the recorded miracles illustrate a number of childish needs and longings— "Providence" (food-providing) before all, healing and strengthening, serving, saving and protecting, helping, encouraging and forgiving or even *making* a person good (by casting out "devils" who represent uncontrollable childish impulses) *in spite of himself*. It may turn out to be a fact that certain epilepsies are nothing but a masked and chaotic expression of such impulses. One might add rescuing from death and danger to complete the list of parental or psychotherapeutic functions. But the list is not *quite* complete, as I have said. Punishment and the demonstration of superiority are poorly represented in this list of miracles which are otherwise so *coherent in their social intention* or motive and so consistent with the recorded life, death and teachings, as an illustration of the amiable and moralizing functions of the "good" parent.

F

The social psychology corresponding to the aim and affection which is so constant and characteristic throughout the miracles, parables and teachings and life and death stories, does seem to have been a radical innovation in human thought. Neither the mystic Philosophy of Buddha nor the practical and rational Civics of Socrates seem really to have anticipated this theory of social motive and behaviour to any substantial extent. Unfortunately however the Christian Philosophy of Life never secured a psychological formulation before the Christian tradition had been transmitted through emotionally distorted minds. On the assumption here put forward that Christianity was primarily a system of psychotherapy, we would expect to find that it appealed to those in most need of this help (" salvation ", " at-one-ment ", etc.). Though it is hardly correct to say that religion is a neurosis (unless we remember that neurosis itself represents an attempt at cure), it is true from the nature of the case that religion tends to fall into the hands of neurotics.

In the course of its transmission, therefore, it is only natural that wherever it has failed to *cure* the neurosis of its practitioners, this neurosis in turn should make its mark upon religious teaching. The history of Christianity affords abundant evidence that this is true.

From the point of view of mental health I imagine the original Christian ideal as implying (1) confidence in God (i.e. reconciliation with the " imperfect " parent so that the faults of the latter, jealousy, vindictiveness, tyranny, etc., are not introduced into our idea of God). (2) good-fellowship with man. The former involves getting rid on the one hand of a sense of guilt and inferiority on the part of the believer, and, at the same time, aims at expunging unconscious grievance, fear and hostility against the parent. This purpose, expressed as worship or glorification of good, seems to be mainly a characteristic of patriarchal cults. Good-fellowship implies the renunciation of infantile (Cain) jealousies, and this can only come about through the surrender of all regressive infantile wishes, i.e. by maturation of character. It is thus the salient characteristic of matriarchal cults. It also implies the abjuration of morbid infantile ambitions and idealisms aiming at power and privilege, dominance, dependency, or isolation which I will describe in the chapter upon Psychopathy. The humility it advocates is *not based on guilt or a sense of abject permanent unworthiness*, the service towards man it enjoins is not patronage, its " propaganda " was neither subversive nor coercive, its faith was not arrogant nor contemptuous of " paganism ". This is why I suggest that Christianity represented an attempt to integrate the ethical attitudes and other advantages of the two types of cult.

In fact Christianity idealized the Kingdom of Heaven on Earth—a human fraternity not dependent upon authority (human or divine), for its solidity and stability, not regulated by competition and not troubled with neurotic guilt and aggressiveness.

The appeal of such an evangel or salvation-doctrine to neurotic anxiety is easily intelligible, likewise the antagonism with which rival psycho-therapies would greet it—with their precarious repression-defences against neurotic wishes and their own particular compromises with guilt, dependency, jealousy, etc. (It is what we have renounced through fear, repressed, but still long for and envy in others, that arouses our greatest reprobation of indulgence and even apparently evokes genuine loathing and indignation.) Whatever the suggestions raised by the paucity of contemporary historical evidence and by the resemblance of the crucifixion story to the sacrifice of the King-for-a-year, it must be admitted that crucifixion is just the sort of thing that *would occur* to *any teacher who challenges the beliefs and rituals connected with defence against the neurotic sense of guilt.* Further, in the story, the tolerant attitude of pagan Rome (impersonated by Pilate) and the emotion of a priesthood guilt-ridden towards God yet jealous of their loyalty to and favoured position with him are represented in a manner that is psycho-socially true. In any case we see from the first public promulgation of Christianity three different reactions to it, first, a *welcome* proceeding from a great need to overcome the isolating, depressing effect of unconscious guilt, anxiety and hate ; second, an anxious *resentment* on the part of those whose " working defences" are weakened, rivalled, questioned or slighted by the new ideals of freedom ; third, an attitude of genial *tolerance*, characteristic of the practical, guilt-free pagan mind, which, by its apparent unconcern, earns the liveliest resentment from all who are of the first two ways of thinking.

Immediately, then, we can observe divergencies in the therapeutic needs and preferences of different individuals and of *different cultures*. One of Peter's first miracles is one of punishment. By power of " will " he kills Ananias and Sapphira for their childish compromise of seeking to win acceptance and approbation while secretly and selfishly retaining for their own private enjoyment and security a portion of their wealth. Here already we see (in Peter's act) an intolerance of privilege. Peter was a practising communist ; he could give up privilege himself—possibly—but could not bear that others should enjoy any advantage. (Curiously enough, in a novel called *Here Comes an Old Sailor*, the medieval theme of Christ and his disciples wandering about the world doing miracles is employed. Here Peter is displayed as ostentatious and aggressive while Christ is content with a " back seat " unless anything special has to be done.) It is important to notice the character of the minds which were the only channels through which the Christian teaching and tradition has reached us, for, lacking radical analysis, their neurosis (which itself is a defence-compromise) is *not abolished* by the therapy of Christianity, but *forms a further compromise with it,* thus contributing a neurotic character to the " tradition". Peter's personal character is depicted as essentially childish, emulous, impulsive, exhibitionistic and unstable. To call him a " rock " may represent the form of therapy known as suggestion and encouragement, but it certainly is not in agreement with the " record ".

Paul, on the other hand, first appears in history as already a fanatic, with all the scrupulosity which a fanatic combines with ethical insensitiveness (e.g. martyrdom of Stephen for " Hellenizing "). The better side of his nature breaks through the taboo-on-tenderness here and there, and may be said to find its culminating expression in the famous poem on love, which might be called an ecstatic definition of social feeling. Nevertheless the breaking through of infantile tenderness in a badly synthetized personality produced the usual results—intense anxiety, guilt on account of pre-oedipal regressiveness, coupled with the anti-feminism which represents revenge on mother and the representation of *her* as the temptress. The duality of Paul's nature was not overcome ; he never became a synthetized personality, but retained a defensive pride and aggressiveness to the end. Under such circumstances it is natural that his teachings should be pre-occupied with the problem of guilt and

atonement, and that he should be deeply offended
at the Hellenistic calm of the Laodiceans.

Contrasting with Pauline Christianity, which is
so largely a reversion to its Judaic original, we find
that the leading psychological characteristic of the
Grecian Churches appears to be a more philosophic
interest in the relationship of God, Christ and man,
their essential nature and vital purposes.

We thus find a rough differentiation of religious
interest even in the New Testament. Certain
writers are evidently dominated by an intense sense
of separation, with consequent guilt and anxiety,
which pre-occupies them with the problem of sin
and redemption and elaborates propitiatory ritual,
aims above all at atonement and conceives God as
terrible, man as vile. To this temperament appeal,
in particular, miracles of punishment such as abound
in the Old Testament (e.g. Elisha's treatment of his
servant) and the post-Christian era. The supreme
miracle of forgiveness is only credible to such minds
as an adjunct to vicarious vengeance, and even so
can only be enjoyed under precarious conditions
or as an act of pre-destination of an entirely
autocratic nature. Miracles of healing have to such
believers no meaning beyond the demonstration
of power involved.

Other writers seem less obsessed with the problems
of guilt and other sources of the separation anxiety.
As it were, these have taken " salvation " for granted
or as something that can be, and has to be, earned ;
and, from this more assured standpoint, they spread
the " good news " without assuming that the " fear
of the Lord " and the " conviction of sin " are the
only possible starting-point and foundation for
secure and friendly relationships with the Heavenly
father. My suggestion, I repeat, is that this
difference in religious temperament and attitude is
correlated with a corresponding difference in the

childish attitude to the Earthly father (and mother), and that this in turn is determined by cultural circumstances affecting the character and domestic status of the mother. These circumstances operate by affecting her will and capacity to wean the child and to repress and deflect its wishes for herself. Where this deflection has not been satisfactorily achieved, regressiveness and Oedipus Wish dominate character and arouse a sense of guilt which calls for propitiatory rituals and cults.

Naturally, also, to the guilt-ridden mind, enjoyment of life is impossible. Pleasure even increases the pathological sense of unworthiness and thus the " need for punishment ". The world appears evil ; " a snare " to " the good " and source of pleasure to the " bad ", so that the whole attitude of life becomes ascetic and, towards others of a different way of thinking, misanthropic. Happiness to such minds appears as a proof of irreverence and " paganism " —a danger-signal in the self and a " mark of the beast " in others. Origen literally made himself a eunuch for the " Kingdom of Heaven ". Augustine condemns unbaptized infants to everlasting torments for the sin of Adam and Eve and the wrath of a just God. Naturally the saving of souls justifies (to such thinkers) the slaying of bodies, and Augustine appeals to the " lay arm " of the Emperor of Rome to crush the Pelagians who disputed his views of the means of attaining salvation. Persecutions and inquisitions, religious wars and crusades, take origin from this violent guilt-anxiety with its need (1) to propitiate God by the conquest of " the infidel ", (2) to maintain precarious repressions, (3) its underlying separation privation-rage against the mother (hence anti-feminism), and (4) its jealousy of the free, " self-indulgent " pagan who psychologically represents the younger baby.

My point at present is that this anti-social
behaviour and misanthropic attitude of mind is
determined by neurotic privations, anxieties and
resentments, and that these intensify the sufferers'
need for religion and the appeal (to them) of a
particular brand of religion.   My view is that the
" psychotherapy " of religion, in so far as it is only
partially effective in "curing" the neurosis, becomes
coloured by this when, in turn, *the former sufferer
becomes the psychotherapist to the next " generation " of
neurotics.*   The originally psychotherapeutic *intention*
and inspiration of religion thus becomes distorted
by the neurotic medium (succession of neurotic
minds) through which it is transmitted.   The
testimony of the enthusiastic patient who *feels*
himself relieved of all sufferings does not necessarily
represent what the treatment actually *did* for him—
still less does it show what it was *intended to do*.   Thus
religion tends to degenerate and to develop these
neuropathic traits which to psycho-analysis appear
to be its very essence.

The fact that religions do develop on lines which
show significant psychological divergencies and that
they appeal to a very different extent to different
temperaments appears to me to justify this view.
Further, it seems to me that the type of religion
which prevails at any given time and place is
related to the prevalent culture and racial character;
modification in either implies change in the other.
The trends of religion just discussed, with its
associated character-traits, developed from Egypt,
along the North Coast of Africa and so from
Carthage to Rome.   A sharply contrasting trend of
religious sentiment originated in the Hellenistic
colonies of Asia Minor, and its influence penetrated
as far west as Ireland.   There we find, as early as the
fifth century, a critical attitude towards superstition
and a tolerance of opinion that moderns might envy.

For example, professed witches were excluded from church not so much because witch-craft was unholy as because it was a cheat.   More than a thousand years later witches were being " smelt out " and burnt alive in enlightened England. Again Pelagius, who resisted the Augustinian doctrine of eternal damnation of unbaptized infants, was an Irish monk.   Duns Scotus, who later upheld similar views, was, as his name indicates, a Scotsman. The spread of Christianity in these regions and early times was by persuasion (i.e. mission work) rather than by conquest and coercive " conversion ". The tolerance of this strain of Christianity was further indicated by their treatment of pagan myth and festivals—new saints borrowing the harmless celebrations (and sometimes even the names) of old deities, e.g. St Cuthbert and St Gertrude.

The attitude to paganism of this branch of developing Christianity was not one of loathing and abhorrence, as it was with the " African " Augustinian variety.   The Hellenistic transmitters of Christianity conceived that they had something so good that it was their duty to share it ; the Augustinian felt that to save his own soul he had to " conquer " others " for God ".   To the former there was no irreverence in borrowing the Feast-day of Diana for the Virgin-Mother or, for that matter, the name of Easter.   To the Hellenist it appeared merely as a practical concession to established custom.   The desire not to disappoint the people of their seasonal holiday was a sufficient reason for the concession. The " European " branch of Christianity was not so much interested as the " African " in sin, punishment and the conditions of forgiveness, that is to say in the neurotic problem of guilt.   It was mainly interested in the meaning of life and the relationship of Creator (parent) and created (child). It even introduced a maternal principle into the

F*

God-head. (For the effects of this in inducing a long period of instability in the Catholic Church and a mass-neurosis in Europe, see Ref. J.) Its ethical problems were those of practical good-fellowship, not that of the expunging of involuntary and unconscious guilt of a sexual nature. It conceived of man as the potential ally of God rather than the innate and irreconcilable *rebel* against him. Its conception of religious life might be represented thus —"God and Man versus Evil", whereas Augustine's was " God versus Man and Evil ".

In all this I am not concerned to show which of the differentiations of primitive Christianity has the most claim to meta-physical truth nor which is the most authentic representative of Christ's actual teaching. I do not even base any argument upon the respective outcome of the two doctrines in regard to ethical behaviour and tolerance of opinion in particular, though I have not troubled to conceal my bias in this or any other direction. I am only concerned with the fact of the peculiar tendency of the Christian religion to schism, antipathy and intolerance, a tendency which only recently seems to have become reversed. I suggest that this tendency to violent schism is characteristic of psychotherapeutic systems *as such*, in so far as, appealing to, and propagated through neurotic minds, they tend to express the anxious aggressive individuality of the psychopathic temperament.

In the study of religion, then, we have found the main concern of the Christian teachings to be the cultivation of " love " as the basis of happiness, mental stability and social harmony. We have found that this makes a dynamic appeal to two different neurotic character-traits ; firstly, that dominated by *guilt* and separation-anxiety, and, second. that dominated by regressive infantile dependency. The former seeks to *restore* a state of love with parents existing before " *The Fall* " ; the latter seeks *to maintain* a state of love with parents and, if relieved, to cultivate a fellowship rapport with playmates. All are alike in the quest for love (which supports the general thesis of this book). They *differ in regard to the precise obstacles to love which they set themselves to overcome.* That is to say they differ in regard to the infantile wishes they seek to satisfy and the guilty jealousies they attempt to control.

A third attitude has been glanced at, namely paganism. This is characterized by a lofty standard of *practical* ethics linked to an extreme tolerance of theological *opinion*. Psychologically one might describe " the pagan " as taking parental love for granted. He is willing, therefore, on the one hand, to surrender the privileges of infancy for the responsibilities of adulthood, while unafraid, on the other, to take and enjoy the pleasure and privileges of the latter state. He has steered his development between the Charybdis of infantile regression and the Scylla of Oedipus-precocity, and so he is left without distrust in himself or unconscious fear of incurring parental wrath and separation. To the guilt-ridden mind such an attitude as this is a blasphemous presumption, and the cults which embody it appear as a standing threat to " the true believer ". The orthodox unconsciously envy the pagan cults they hate, and easily destroy them, for Paganism has no common purpose to unite it in defence or aggression. It never persecuted Christianity except when its sentiments were exploited for imperialistic or other non-religious purposes as under Domitian in Rome or Hitler in Berlin. (Curiously enough if Hitler could restore the ancient Teutonic character to the highly feudalized German mind, he would destroy the urge to persecute non-conformity of all kinds.) It lacks the drive of the guilt sense—the need to coerce others A.M.D.G., and to remove temptation or doubt from ourselves (i.e. reinforce repression). Thus Paganisms of the Greek or Teutonic type, besides appearing to the zealot irreligious (or, better, a-religious), have no unifying, driving, social, force, beyond a sort of conservative sentiment, and so cannot make head against proselytizing religions like Christianity or Mahommedanism. Of course many paganisms are full of superstitious anxiety (neurotic guilt) like the degenerate form of Buddhism and like many primitive cults of the animistic and early theistic types. But the cults found in any society where there is a good domestic relationship between men and women consist rather of social festivals than of sin-purgation techniques.

Broadly speaking it can be shown that romantic and tolerant paganisms are found wherever the rearing of children is matriarchal in character. That is to say wherever the mother is not dominated by the father or by her mother-in-law, or, for that matter, *by her own mother*, as often happens in societies that are matriarchal *in form*. The general character and culture associated with a truly matriarchal upbringing is dealt with elsewhere, but here we may say that the quest for love under such conditions is directed upon the *real social environment*. Consequently these people find " worldly " life " good " and turn less in childhood to regressive longings (which also are more firmly, because maternally or " endogenously ", repressed), or precocious expectations. They have therefore less need of dependency fantasies on the one hand or of (guilt) propitiatory techniques on the other. Nurtural deities are less necessary, punitive ones less dreaded than is the case with patriarchal upbringing.

NOTE C.

THE MOTHER CULTS IN CHRISTIANITY

While the cult of the Virgin Mother appears to have risen to importance relatively late in the development of Christian thought, it is noteworthy that maternal functions are ascribed to the Holy Ghost from the very beginning. The miracles of tongues (teaching to speak) and the title The Comforter, along with the idea of omnipresence are psychologically of this character. Presumably the amelioration of the conception of God and the lightening of the sense of sin (resulting from Christ's teaching) permitted this development of religious thought.

Summarizing my conception of the psycho-social innovation represented by the Canonical Gospels, I would say the Christian message is addressed to, and meets the needs of, more developed minds than those to which the older Father-cult appeals. In fact if we might say that the Old Testament is concerned with the moral equivalents of the cleanliness training and weaning, we could say that the Christian teachings are concerned with the actual process of socialization—namely the transition from an *exclusive rapport with the parent to an all-embracing rapport with fellows.* Pursuing the analogy (or homology) between the religious needs of the adult and the love needs of the child, we recognize that the condition of renouncing the exclusive rapport with the parent is the *assurance of its security.* That is to say, we must be convinced that the parent is " provident " even without continuous solicitation. (Even Old Testament writers knew this.) Even more, we must be assured of our acceptability to the parent ; that is to say we must be able to expunge the sense of guilt (original sin). Once we feel sure of our " base of supplies " (of encouragement and of love) we can adventure into fellowship. The attainment of salvation, atonement, is the *beginning* of religious or social life, not the *end* or aim of it.

Hence Christ's insistence that we will *accept* forgiveness, and get on with the business of social living. Hence also the apparent switch of devotion from God to mankind, so unacceptable to the guilt-ridden and anxious child-mind.

CHAPTER X

HEALING CULTS AND PRACTICES

In last Chapter I referred to the psychological " appeal " of the Healing Miracle, and we shall see that there is a whole class of illnesses which results from unsatisfactory relations with other people. In our survey of the functions of love, therefore, it seems worth while to glance at *the psychology of some " Healing Cults " and medical " Heresies ", to see whether here (as in religion) the therapeutic factor is not indeed love in some disguise or other.*

Histories of medicine seem to confine themselves too strictly to the orthogenesis of the Art, and to deplore, rather than to study, the great heresies and " Healing Cults ", which represent deviations from the lines of development which have led up to the scientific medicine of to-day. But no system of medicine can long maintain itself far in advance of the culture of its patients. If the public were so ill-educated as to be wholly out of sympathy with, and to have no confidence in, a " scientific " medicine, the development and practice of the latter would be seriously retarded. The people *pay* for the medicine they *want* and for that alone, and so a process of *cultural* and *economic selection* or pressure is brought to bear on the development of medical practice, just as happens in the case of religion. For this reason the theories of disease and the " practices " by which this is treated throw a light upon certain aspects of the culture and character of their exponents second only (and related) to that afforded by religious belief and ritual.

It is therefore worth while to study the human appeal of medical theories over and above their validity as methods of understanding and curing organic disease.   Besides, even in our own culture, many patients seek relief from suffering and distress which is not directly produced by *any bodily ailment*. It has been estimated that thirty per cent. of invalids are suffering from some form of " nervous " trouble. Indeed, nearly all of our patients require from us something over and above *technical* services.   " Bed-side manner " *does* count for much, except perhaps in extremely accurate and objective *techniques* like dentistry and refraction work, where, moreover, the patient's sense-of-illness is not great and his contact with the specialist is brief and " to the point ".   The *subjective factor* not only produces symptoms of its own, but even plays an important part in the production or removal of physical disease-processes themselves.

The technical advances in the science of medicine over the last half-century have been so enormous, that we might reasonably have expected orthodox medicine to triumph conclusively over all " quackeries ".   Moreover the scientific education of the people—or *at least* the popular prestige of science—has made corresponding advances.   On all these grounds we might have expected the virtual extinction of quackeries ; but the very opposite has happened ; they thrive and multiply as never before.   What is the reason for this ?   I suggest that, in their enthusiasm for effective and direct interference with the physical process of disease, physicians have rather neglected the task the patient actually demands of them—namely the relief of his *suffering*.   True, they accomplish this *finally* by the removal of its causes (if these are physical) ; but his demand is for *immediate comfort*, if not cure.   Disease—in the sense of a lowering of efficiency, an incapacity for enjoyment and general malaise—is something more than its ultimate physical causes, and its *subjective* aspects and developments necessarily and closely concern the practising physician.

It is undeniable that our medical teaching is *more objective and impersonal than formerly.* Series of "Cases", illustrating " Stages " and " Forms " of this or that " Disease ", are demonstrated to the cramming student, whose attention is naturally directed to the common factor—the *essential disease entity*—underlying all *cases* in a given group and not to the personal, human, *factors in the individual patients themselves.* We fail therefore to give the public all it really wants, and these wants are naturally supplied elsewhere. We ought therefore to take account of a source of suffering whose very existence was not taught us as students.

There is one great but obscure source of suffering which finds frequent expression in appeals for medical help. To the normal person the causes of this suffering are not appreciable, because the need it represents has been forgotten by him and seems therefore meaningless to him. Often this discomfort is not accompanied by any physical disturbance, the removal of which might bring relief to these patients. In fact their appeal for medical help seems (to " normal " people) to be a somewhat emotional and egoistic one, and, as such, it excites in us rather *less than none* of the sympathy which, unconsciously, it was intended to evoke, and which we as physicians are ready to offer to bodily distress. Yet certain of the great " quackeries " can handle such cases with considerable success, and *from the nature of the cure we may infer the nature of the disease.* For this purpose I have chosen to study Homœopathy and Christian Science—devotees of which cults frequently declare themselves to be cured "whereas the Doctors had all failed". After all—with a disease which we declare is *fictitious* or *factitious*—our object must be to make the patient *feel and believe himself well* and return to the enjoyments and avocations of everyday life, accepting these as adequate recompense for the effort and responsibility they impose. If (as is the fact) our reproaches to the patient regarding the unreality of his illness do *not* remove the unhappiness he mistakes for illness, have we not failed in our purpose of making him well? Is it of any practical use to throw the responsibility for the continuance of the trouble upon his "will" or lack of it? Apparently these cults succeed in removing such troubles ; and, though we consider that they cure an unreal disease by unreal means, still, the phenomena as a whole are of great theoretical and practical interest. Why *do* some people suffer all the inconvenience and disabilities of a physical disease when this is absent, and why does not the *conviction* of its absence serve to relieve them of its symptoms? Perhaps an examination of Homœopathy and Christian Science can help us to answer these questions.

Now the starting point of Hahnemann's doctrines was a belief in the *subjective* nature of disease. He refused to admit the existence of the " Humours ", " Morbi ", etc., and all the other hypothetical entities which traditional medicine imagined to lie behind the patient's disabilities and feelings of illness. Naturally he concentrated his attention upon *symptoms* and so the patient's own story came to have paramount importance for Hahnemann. He urged upon his followers an unwearied interest in the patient's past history and present experience, and an expectant attitude towards all *new* subjective developments. Hahnemann viewed disease entirely as a non-material " need for assistance "—and regarded each case as being as unique as the personality of the sufferer himself.

This, it will be observed, accords exactly with our modern view of the individuality of every case of neurosis and psychosis, and affords us a first hint of the nature of the " appeal " his *system* of healing makes to the public. Hahnemann was indeed a most earnest symptom-hunter, his zeal would have satisfied most hysterics. The patient's circumstances and personality were examined by him as a matter of course, and, moreover, *new* symptoms were earnestly inquired for. Even *latent* symptoms are inferred to exist, though quite inconsistently with his own fundamental tenet that the disease *is* the symptom-complex and nothing else. Hahnemann is very insistent upon the " receptivity " of the physician, who must avoid alike leading questions and any *interruptions* of the informant's story. In fact an extremely " analytic attitude " is enjoined upon his followers. In one paragraph even, he is strongly in favour of yielding to the patient wherever possible, and in paragraph 198, he insists upon a friendly, sympathetic, confident, demeanour in mental illness. Even " imbecile chattering " must not be received " with inattention ". " Contradiction, eager explanations, violent correction and harshness are disastrous to the mind. Contempt, deceit and fraud exasperate these patients and aggravate their condition. A semblance must always be maintained of treating them as reasonable beings." Here Hahnemann is in line with the best modern teaching and considerably in advance of the average *practice* of to-day.

In paragraph 196 he recognizes the existence of psychogenic mental disease as distinct from that which results from bodily disorder and notes the amenability of the former to personal influence, i.e. he tacitly recognizes the possibility of psychotherapy. He also recognizes that emotional disturbances have grave repercussions upon bodily symptoms (197). He says of mental symptoms that "They are the characteristics which the observant physician can *least* afford to overlook."

In all this Hahnemann clearly advocates treating patients first and foremost as *human beings in trouble* and insists that it is essential to establish friendly relations with them.· He deprecates cruelty to lunatics in the same way as he deprecates the treatment of physical ailments in an entirely technical, impersonal way. His remedy is kindness to the mentally troubled ; and, where there is *bodily* disease, this sympathy takes the form *of infinite patience and interest in the patient's feelings.*

At certain levels of development and in certain forms of nervousness, the patient's greatest need is for someone to listen and to understand. To these, the most helpful attention we can offer seems to be genuine interest as shown by the physician's willingness to study thoroughly their problems and perplexities. Hahnemann's clinical method therefore meets the needs of these patients exactly. He also preaches indulgence and non-retaliation as emphatically as Adler does to-day ; and, from a psychological point of view, his regime might be called one of psychotherapeutic kindness and consideration. That he is well aware of the value of suggestion is shown by his remarks on the necessary " psychical demeanour " of the physician and " mind regimen ". But he deprecates rushing at the patient with suggestions before the latter is allowed time to unburden himself.

His knowledge of human nature shows itself clearly again in his remarks upon the administration of hospitals and upon the conditions of employment for nurses and attendants. Hahnemann's whole attitude to the sick was one of solicitude and benevolence, and this, with his mystical, subjective, conception of disease, must at once have put him on good terms with all patients in whose illness neurosis played an important part.

Ultimately Homœopathy developed a theory attributing the majority of diseases to *itch*. Syphilis and " venereal warts " were also mentioned. Such views would have been unpopular and were not obtruded, but they indicate the mystical association of the ideas of disease, dirt and sin in the minds of the Homœopathists—an association which appeals very much to the neurotic sense of guilt.

This theory of course is the oldest and most widespread view of disease. Indeed, some languages have no words which distinguish between disease and sin, and our own religions for long regarded the former as the direct consequence of the latter and still constantly employ the symbolisms. The nature of the sin to which homœopathic theory referred most chronic disease is obviously sexual. This is indicated in many ways. Itch was not regarded in those days as a parasitic invasion, but as a " voluptuous tingling and itching ". Sexual abstinence was enjoined during the " proving " of medicine just as it is at all critical times among many savage peoples. Hahnemann was as keenly aware of the pathogenic significance of the sense of guilt as any pre-Freudian observer, and like Freud he kept his eye lifting for the sexual factor. This must undoubtedly have impressed many neurotic guilt-ridden patients with a regard for his insight.

The original Homœopathic system had many other striking features, impressive to the public, linking it up with " folk belief " and appealing to the mystic and the neurotic.[1] It had moreover the

---

[1] The unconscious sexual associations of the ideas of infinitesimal doses and of *increasing their potency by shaking* need no emphasis.

practical advantage. of dispensing with the harmful doses prescribed by pre-scientific medicine. But Homœopathy established itself with the public principally on the strength of two characteristics : (1) the interest and kindness it showed to the patient as a *suffering human being*, and, (2) the development of a powerful indirect *suggestion of cure* under cover of this close rapport of *confidence* on the patient's side and consideration on the physician's. The "system" and its mysteries enabled the homœopathic physician to establish a relationship with his patient both intimate and influential, instead of the domineering and aloof attitude demanded by the orthodox professional dignity of these times. In this way, and by paying due attention to the patient's affective and guilt-involving problems, Homœopathy probably met the need, as common then as it is now, of many patients for *understanding and protective care*. This need, as I will try to show, is the result of an anxious childhood and one expression of that sense of loneliness which is all but universal among psychopathic patients.

We may turn now to Christian Science, not with a view to following the bewildering mental gymnastics it performs in the vain attempt to avoid self-contradiction in its metaphysics, but to discover the reason for the impression it makes upon the public and for the strength of its hold upon its devotees. We find that it addresses itself really to three *things*—loneliness, sin and suffering. All these are declared to be illusions of the " mortal mind " which itself in turn has no real existence according to these Deistic Solipsists. The soul itself is held to be an emanation of God, never separated from Him, and so, it is argued, *isolation and loneliness* are " proved " to be quite impossible. Mankind, further, is an inseparable brotherhood by reason of this virtual identity of each member with God.

Next, as God is "all love" and "perfect", He cannot have created evil or even have any knowledge of it. Therefore, since He is all-knowing, evil itself cannot exist in any form. This revelation of Christian Science admits of no argument since logic itself, they declare, is invalid—the creation of mortal mind ; it follows also that sin and suffering are as non-existent as loneliness and so we have merely to shift our attention from them to God's goodness to realize that they are nonentities. The problems of illness, of suffering and of sin are thus solved at one stroke, yet without reproach to those involved in these illusions. Hahnemann declared that God *must have provided a remedy* for each disease, thus nullifying it, and encouraged us to believe that the disease is no more than the sum of its symptoms (i.e. is merely subjective) ; Christian Science goes one better in denying the very existence of disease and every other unpleasantness. This is at once a weakness and a strength, so far as its popular appeal is concerned.

The attempt is then made by Christian Science to establish a metaphysical dualism. On the one hand we are to believe that there is the immutable world of perfect love, wherein nothing can ever happen, not even creation, because change implies two states, one before and one after, and these *could not both be perfect*. In this world there is no "separation", no possibility of bewilderment, doubt, antagonism, competition, or of surprises ; *nothing in fact is admitted to exist which could disturb the small child's need for security and comprehension.* The infant in its mother's arms must in fact experience a universe very much like the " reality " admitted by Christian Science to exist, and its objection to change in any form is well known.

On the other hand, there is for them the non-existent world of " mortal mind " wherein evil desires, dangerous competitors, jealousy, hate, cruelty, sin and the perpetual struggle for survival threaten and disturb. In this sphere the individual must depend upon himself and upon his power of pleasing or influencing other people. He is exposed to accidents, hardships and the injustice of others and above all to anxiety about his own powers. But the Christian Scientist can sweep this world out of existence—so far as his own mind is concerned —and can retire to his imagined world of love and security, by simply denying the reality of everything he doesn't like, and by surrounding himself, in fantasy, with the fictions he desires. But this is exactly what the Dementia Precox does for *himself individually* (see later) and the directing and driving motives are the same in both cases, namely, the quest for the security and care required and experienced in infancy. How then is it that the life of the Christian Science convert does not have the same stormy onset, fantastic course and demented termination as that of the Schizophrenic ?

The answer is quite clear. In the first place the Christian Scientist seeks shelter from the world ; and, that desired asylum once obtained in fantasy, he is quite willing to go on *playing with the world* with the mental reservation that it is unreal—a familiar childish state of make-believe and one retained in hysteric invalidism. In the second place, he has the support and guidance of a fellowship which, by helping him towards his conclusions, saves him from conflict, bewilderment and anxiety, and, by retaining him in social relationship, forbids him to regress towards the asylum end—" dirty, degraded and demented ".

Now making allowance for the fact that Homœopathy is an affair of " Doctor and Patient ", while Christian Science works with the ideas of " God and ' the fellowship ' " (i.e. a number of

" patients "), there is a most significant identity betwcen the two *systems of " comfort "*. Both psychologically reinstate the relationship of parent and child. Both insist emphatically, if tacitly, upon the necessity for human relationships of a friendly, protective, character. They differ in their mystico-delusional *backgrounds for suggestion*, but both agree in treating subjective distress by establishing pleasant, confident, affective relationships with the patient. In this way, they restore the lost sense of security and abolish that feeling of loneliness and isolation which owes so much to a neurotic sense of guilt and to a childish sense of incapacity. Psychologically speaking, the vestigial child-self within the patient's mind is taken back into its mother's arms and is reassured, " loved " and comforted.

Whatever the objective suffering that has to be endured thereafter loses, under these comforting circumstances, *its agitating and depressing character*, and even the physical powers of resistance are increased, or, at least, are no longer dissipated in the endocrine turmoil of anxiety and panic. The sufferer has gained a quiet mind and that is a substantial advance. The baby within him has cried for help and has been comforted.

A large section of the population has never outgrown childish dependency, but has merely covered this up. Under stresses like illness, misfortune, anxiety, overwork, neglect, etc., a partial regression occurs to the childish craving-for-protection and for the assurance of being personally cared for and *wanted*. Bodily illness for such individuals, is, firstly, *of use* as constituting a claim for the attentions of nursing ; secondly, actual suffering constitutes a special danger and discouragement to these people ; it throws them back more and more upon infancy and consequently into invalidism. They are therefore " bad " patients and lack the will-to-be-well, they harbour " the need to fall ill ".

Such patients require not only to be *cured* of their disease (if any), but also to be persuaded to take up the burdens and responsibilities of health. It is in the latter part of this healing task that I consider our ultra-technical, wholly objective, modern medicine fails. This failure on our part constitutes a standing invitation to every mystic and neurotic to set up a healing system of his own. We cannot reasonably object if others supply a want whose existence we contemptuously ignore.

We say, in effect, that the patients *ought not* to feel this need for " petting " and tacitly reprove them for doing so. If there is an organic factor in their trouble we concentrate our whole attention upon that, and up to a point this attentiveness succeeds in appeasing the patient's need to feel—as the Adlerians say—" of consequence " to others. The patient, however, cannot forego the disease even when its physical basis is cured. Consequently, it reappears in new and elusive forms. After referring him or her to specialists, and after invoking the aid of surgery, our impatience evokes in us an intuitive awareness of a fictitious, " self-indulgent ", element in the case. We may even—erroneously— regard the symptoms as fraudulent (malingered) ; almost certainly we will feel that the patient is " *weak* ". And so, insensibly, we adopt a *hardening* treatment—a withdrawal of sympathy and patience which amounts to a scolding and to the threat : " If you don't give up this selfish pretence, we will have nothing more to do with you." Our own " tenderness taboo " is rejecting the patient's appeal and repressing impulses of a similar infantile character in ourselves.

Now, is this in actual fact the best way to deal with these regressive appeals for affective comfort ?

In my opinion, it is not. Just as checking a child's genuine crying is the greatest shock to its sense of security, and increases, consequently, the reflex impulse to cry, so the rejection of the appeal for sympathy (which underlies so much neurotic illness), increases the need which is the " mainspring " of the *unconscious* malingering which we are required to " cure ". Indeed the word malingering implies that the patient seeks some material advantage—which these patients *do not*. They need parental love, and its denial aggravates the need and its symptoms. As I have pointed out elsewhere much overt and foolish delinquency has precisely the same motivation as the childish trick of " being hurt to be made well ". There is a pretty general agreement that coercion in these cases is futile as a means of cure or reform. But in the case of adult neurotics (who are aiming at a similar goal-of-illness), are we not pursuing this *admittedly useless* coercive technique when we seek to *shame* the patient by saying " there is nothing wrong with you " ? So far as curing the patient goes I think we might as well add to this imaginary statement the words *"in order that others also may have a chance to forget you"*. The purpose of the illness is to gain attention and sympathy, and its underlying need will not be satisfied by a tacit expression of dislike and contempt ; it will rather be intensified. A display of impatience and disapproval aggravates the unconscious need for security (in the liking of others) which is the main drive towards illness. Only when the patient has discovered *within himself* the meaning and factitious origin of his symptoms, can such an appeal for adult co-operation be made without doing harm. Otherwise the physician is merely another edition of the " bad " unwelcoming parent who (probably) caused the disease.

The point is, I think, well illustrated by the history of the famous Weir-Mitchell treatment for hysteria. This regime virtually surrounded the patient *with the environment appropriate to the infant.* Food was good and abundant ; silence and darkness encouraged unbroken rest ; attendance was unremitting ; but conversation was discouraged except during the daily visit of the physician, which—I understand—lasted an hour. No one has been able to repeat Weir-Mitchell's results ; and why ? I have read the suggestion that it is because we cannot afford the expense of his type of establishment. This is sheer nonsense. I consider myself that our failure to get his results *with his* treatment is entirely owing to our total misconception of the " modus operandi " of his regime. From our materialistic point of view, we usually try to interpret his cures as bodily responses to *material* treatment (over-feeding) ; but over-feeding, " per se ", does not cure hysteria. The giving of food is, however, for the child, a sign of love, so that over-feeding will have incidental psychological effects. So far as we admit a psychic factor in Weir-Mitchell's success, we tend to regard this as due to the *coercion* of the patient by *privation* of adult interests and pleasures. I would suggest that, on the contrary, the Weir-Mitchell treatment represents a gigantic *indulgence* (and thus a reassurance) offered to the *unconscious baby-self* of the patient. It is a reinstatement of the friendly " nursery " environment. That it is disagreeable to the adult personality is merely incidental and immaterial, as also is the fact that it *reinforces* adult desires and wishes by inforced abstinence. By taking the illness seriously Weir-Mitchell won his patient's confidence and was able to ask him—without words, but effectively—" is this what you really want ? " The Baby-Self, if I can personify it, was satisfied and reassured by interest and attention and became willing to leave mothers' lap and recommence its *play*. The adult self could heartily answer " No ". The need-for-illness was here, as by the therapeutic systems of Homœopathy and Christian Science, appeased by kindness—but by a *kindness addressed to the regressive infantile longings. Once confidence is restored at this level, the need for " nursing " is appeased and the natural attractiveness of adult life returns.*

I submit, then, that a very common factor in ill-health is a regressive need for a quasi-parental care ; a need which expresses a childish lack of self-confidence. Disapproval, ridicule and neglect increase this anxiety and so *intensify* the need to fall ill. This need we may obstruct along one line or along many ; but it is hopeless to attempt to check *all* regressive (infantile or flight) tendencies. Psychic dependency of one sort or another is a feature of everyone's character—if only in the form of a craving for popularity and power. When this dependency assumes the infantile form of seeking to be *nurtured* by others, it should be taken very seriously but sympathetically by relatives and by our profession. The encouragement required by the patient may be afforded to him (as by the Homœopathists) by the serious and assiduous treatment of factitious symptoms. The feeling of isolation (neurotic loneliness) may be mitigated by Christian Science delusions *or* by friendly suggestion and by the provision of a satisfactory environment. It can, however, only be *cured* when the patient acquires insight into his condition and accepts the responsibilities and *privileges* of adult life. This insight, in turn, cannot be given by critical precepts but must be led up to in friendly and confidential conversation. The patient, in fact, must be encouraged towards self-*discovery*, and towards the simultaneous discovery of a fellowship relation with other people.

I suggest, therefore, that the prevalence and success of " healing cults " argues a widespread need for love—a need which results from our method of psychic weaning and which is a correlative of the taboo on tenderness.   The need for love as seen in neurotic illness and the repudiation of love as seen in neurotic normality are, as it were, equal and opposite reactions to the denial of love by a mother who either, herself love-starved, cannot bear to replace, gradually and at the proper time, the tender relationship with the infant by the companionship of interest, or else, having repressed her love need, cannot respond to the infant's legitimate claims and rejects them too early and too abruptly.   In any case we see in the need for illness a substitute for the crying of the child for its mother and yet another demonstration of the importance of the love quest and of its independence of bodily needs ; for after all the incidence and importance of the " nervous factor " in illness is, if anything, less in the poor than in the rich.

CHAPTER XI

PSYCHOPATHOLOGY

It was in this field that Modern Psychology took its origin and where, for the first time, we were able to form a conception of mind as a real, living organism. Naturally therefore the views it still affords us of minds developing, adapting and disintegrating are of vital consequence to psychology. Before studying these aberrations from a psychological point of view, and regarding them as faulty responses to abnormal life-history, we must deal with a fallacy which is still prevalent, namely that mental disease is always and merely the result of *brain* disease. If it were so then any attempt to explain mental disease as mere maladaptation (or " psychogenic ") would be absurd. What follows is quoted from an article in *Probation*, by kind permission of the Editor.

Mental Disorder without Brain Disease. " Thanks to the advance of scientific medicine, it was realized that disordered behaviour *can* be produced by bodily disease. Unfortunately, the enthusiasm of doctors carried them too far along this line, and they jumped to the conclusion that *all* morbid behaviour is due to malnutrition, intoxication, injury or faulty development of the brain or of the nervous systems in connection with the brain.

This materialistic view of all mental abnormality prevailed in medical circles until Charcot suggested that the disease known as hysteria might be caused by *ideas*. It was quickly seen that in this illness, at least, the symptoms may be produced, removed, or altered at the will of the doctor, and sometimes at the convenience of the patient. This fact forbade us to believe that this disease was really caused by any definite lesion of the brain. The shell-shock blindness, for example, that was present at one moment and disappeared the next, or a paralysis that might come on because the patient was told he would become paralysed—such symptoms as these and a host of others could not conceivably be caused by any damaged brain cells.

It was then realized that in some way, without such damage being present, mind, the brain function, could be deranged ; and the term 'functional mental disease' was introduced, although at first it had a very indefinite meaning which served to cover up the uncertainty of our ideas. Illogically enough, however, the idea still persists, that if mind, the function of brain, is diseased, then there must be some corresponding derangement in the brain itself. Of course it is generally accepted by scientific men that for every act or feature of mind there is some corresponding brain process ; so it is loosely argued that disease of one means disease of the other.

However, this argument is just a play upon two meanings of the word disease. We call certain *conduct* 'morbid' or diseased, *by analogy* with disease of bodily organs, but it is not necessarily more than an analogy—a deceptive resemblance.

Every peculiarity of mind or conduct must have a corresponding brain process. Thus the set forms of thought and activity which we call 'speaking English' must have a brain process different from that which lies behind the activities we call 'speaking French'; but no one would suggest that speaking English or French, as the case may be, depends upon the way the brain is endowed, nourished, injured, or poisoned, or what not. It is clear, therefore, that *brains* themselves *may vary without being diseased, and it follows also that minds may vary without disease of brain.* Now the question arises, whether *some* of the conditions that we call mental disease do or do not depend upon upbringing, even as language depends on upbringing. This seems to many people an absurd question. They are quite sure that mental disease does not depend on upbringing, although the same people are often confident that it depends upon heredity. It is obvious, however, that we cannot rule out the *possibility* that *some* disorders of conduct which we call mental disease may be the consequence of experiences that the patient has undergone without the health of his brain being in any way actually impaired. Mental disease on this supposition could be present in a physiologically healthy brain.

A child may be taught to steal. Well ! stealing is supposed to be 'bad', not 'mad'; but at least it is abnormal conduct. A child may be taught to be afraid of ghosts. Ghosts do not exist, or at least are not an element of most people's experience so that this child might be said to entertain a delusion—a belief that is contrary to experience and contrary to what he is later taught to consider true and reasonable. He may himself *not believe* in ghosts, and yet *be afraid* of them ! Surely we are here approaching what we might call mental symptoms, yet the peculiarities of the child's brain which lie at the back of the inconsistency between his belief and his feeling are incontestably laid down *by the child's experience and not by any infection or other cause* particularly affecting *the health* of his brain.

A certain course of upbringing may impress upon the child his own incapacity and the critical, unsympathetic, attitude of other people. He may become shy, nervous, retiring, isolated. He may lose interest in things and fail to develop his cultural

G

energy and capacities.   In his own defence he may become suspicious, resentful and hostile.

This condition may go on increasing itself in a vicious cycle of suspicious isolation and corresponding impoverishment of mental activity.   Occasional small but real slights, misfortunes, or unfair dealing may lead the person, now a young adult, to feel that the world is hostile and contemptuous and to re-act against this imagined hostility and contempt with a hatred and a readiness to put the very worst construction upon any mishap, however trivial or accidental it may be—attributing all these misfortunes to somebody or other.

Here, plainly, we are dealing with a character-distortion which may amount to a full-blown mental illness, and it is equally plain that it may have arisen without any ill-health or malnutrition of the patient's *brain*—arisen purely by an accidental miscarriage of the normal processes of social development.   That is to say, it is originally merely a disturbance in the relationships between the individual and his fellows, due to causes incidental to his daily life which affect him disagreeably, but without damaging his brain in any way.

Now, it is true that his brain has been *affected*, inasmuch as the memories of these slights and the suspicious thoughts that he has entertained about them must be stored up in his mind, and consequently, in some unimaginable way, ' photographed ' on his brain ; but the point to believe is that this has not been brought about by any process of infective or other *disease* of brain, but merely as a result of an accidental abnormality in his relationship to his environment, i.e. in his *experiences*.

I have said that we cannot imagine in what form these injurious *memories* are stored up in the brain and, as psychologists, we do not find it necessary to imagine them or think about them, and we see no hope whatever of discovering what they are. It is even possible that at the instant of death every trace of memory is wiped out of the brain (by autolysis) so that study of the dead brain, even if it could be examined molecule by molecule, would yield no clue to the former content of the living mind. The physiology of memory therefore may very likely prove for ever a sealed book to man's knowledge. Fortunately, however, the psychopathologist, while admitting in purely metaphysical discussions that these memory traces *must* exist in some form or another, sees the possibility of advancing his understanding of mental illness *without engaging in such a hopeless investigation of brain cells.* Psychopathology investigates, on the one hand, the behaviour and feelings of the patient, and on the other, the life history of the patient. The present actual behaviour and feelings of the patient are then interpreted in terms of his life history *without making any assumptions as to the manner in which the life history is, as it were, ' stored up ' in the brain.* It is easy to say that a person who speaks English was brought up among English people, it is by no means so certain that a thief was brought up among thieves. It is not at all certain that a hysteric was brought up among hysterics. Indeed, it is on the whole improbable. Nevertheless, we are beginning to learn that certain subtle factors in upbringing affect the patient severely in after life, and do produce characteristic morbid effects upon his behaviour. That is to say, we are beginning to be able to explain any given mental illness as due to some particular abnormality in the patient's upbringing."

Since it seems permissible, then, to assume the existence of " psychogenic " mental disorders we must examine the conditions supposed to be of this nature in order to discover what part (if any) is played in these phenomena by love-privation and the love-quest. How is mental abnormality related to the stresses of development and socialization, and what light do its manifestations throw on the nature, aims and origin of love and hate ?

The most definite and important symptoms of mental trouble are these :

(*a*) *Loss of interest in people*, or its conversion into shyness, seclusiveness, suspicion and aversion.

(*b*) *Loss of interest in things*, " affairs ", cultural pursuits, etc.

(*a*) and (*b*) are closely associated and together produce what we call " dementia " or, in less degree, apathy.

(*c*) Depreciation of self, always depressive (shyness, guilt, etc., sense of inferiority).

(*d*) Over-estimation of self, generally involving excitement and elation (exaltation, dominance, delusions of grandeur).

(*e*) Anxiety—apprehension of trouble and loss, often referred to bodily functions, (e.g. hypochondria).

(*f*) Despair, which is accompanied by depression of all interests ; (*a*), (*b*) and (*c*).

(*g*) Anger, generally unconscious or else actually provoked, often expressed as suspicions of others, (perhaps delusional) and aggression.

(*h*) Regressiveness—a return to dependency and other infantile characteristics.

All these symptoms (even (*e*) when closely examined) are found to refer in some way or other to the patient's relationship to other people—his social environment. They could not exist in a " solitary " animal, since *they mean nothing but a disturbed social rapport*. But besides these disturbances of the social disposition there are a number of symptoms affecting the individual functions of knowing, feeling and acting. As already seen,

PSYCHOPATHOLOGY 181

these may be produced either by (a) disease, defect, malnutrition or intoxication of the brain, etc., or (b) by mental conflict (endopsychic conflict) or the struggle of two incompatible motives for expression, one of which is usually social, i.e. super-ego. Symptoms produced in the former (" organic ") manner are usually easily distinguished as such, since they involve *destruction* or *impairment* of functions, such as hallucination and confusion (delirium), actual *loss* of memory, failures of attention amounting to incoherence or failures of interest amounting to apathy or stupor. In such cases the symptoms have no *meaning* or relation to environment or to the patient's life and purposes. They represent the *dissolution* of mind—temporary or final. With these symptoms we are not concerned. In other cases, however, the false perceptions (e.g. bodily feelings), blocking of memory, inattention (inability to " concentrate "), depressions and excitements, or compulsive acts and thoughts are found to have a *reason of their own* and to be related to the patient's (perhaps unconscious) life and social purposes. These do not represent the dissolution of mind into chaos, anarchy and inertia, but are the expression of a *conflict between more or less clear-cut and definite ideals and purposes*. They are found to have some positive aim and underlying method, which it is the task of psychopathology to discover.

All those symptoms are combined in endless different ways so that no two cases are alike. Mental illnesses are the forms of individuality and the expression of the patient's unique life-history. First or last, as I will show presently, a mental illness is a reaction to social-cultural environment and, to begin with, differs only in degree from abnormalities of personality and character. There is, therefore, no clear boundary-line between mental health and disease, though an appearance of such a line is produced in the following way.

When the individual peculiarities of social feeling, interest, temperament, etc., becomes so extreme that harmonious mental co-operation with others becomes impossible, then a profound change occurs, sometimes quite suddenly. This social *crisis* results in what we call " alienation ". It is as if the balance of an object had been upset and it had taken up a new position of equilibrium. To carry the analogy further, if the object had been a cylinder on end, then when upset, it remained out of equilibrium and easily rolls about. Mind is so intimately and constantly dependent upon interplay with other minds that any disturbance of its *interpsychic* relationships *further* alters the affected mind in a " vicious circle ". The loss of touch with others produces a vast number of secondary symptoms, reparative, compensatory, defensive, defiant, etc., and produces *in the observer's mind* the illusion that the patient's trouble is of relatively recent, definite and sudden onset, whereas in reality much of the disturbance and distress is due to emotions evoked by the impairment of companionship (of love and of interest) in the distant past. Further, every lapse from sociability on the part of the patient produces an *antipathetic response from his social environment*, which in turn has its repercussions upon himself. Thus a vicious circle of protest and counter-protest and misunderstanding is set up. In consequence the patient is alienated not so much of his own accord as by a sort of *emotional ostracism* on the part of others. He did not intend to become isolated, even unconsciously. He was forced into it.

We must understand then, that mental trouble is fundamentally merely an abnormality of social feeling and interest adjustment—*which exceeds either the tolerance of the community or the patient's power of endurance.* The alleged increase of insanity in recent years is merely an index of the increasing exactions and intolerance of our social-economic system, not of a depreciation of the mental stability of the race. Mental or nervous breakdown is merely the culmination of social strains which have existed since early childhood, and the secondary consequences of the re-adjustment or mal-adjustment which ensue are usually more conspicuous than the disease itself. Clearly then we can only speak of mental " diseases " metaphorically, since their nature and causes have nothing in common with, for example, a bacterial infection of a bodily organ.

Logically, since these so-called mental diseases are really failures or distortions of social development, they should fall into the " province " of the educator, or the priest. A curious combination of circumstances, however, and particularly the failure to distinguish the symptoms of brain disease from the symptoms and consequence of social and interest disturbances, left the study and treatment of mental " diseases " in the hands of the medical profession. While our materialistic training and bias retarded the appearance of a psychological medicine by nearly a century, the *medical* conception of " insanity " dispelled much prejudice and opened the way for a study of the subject. Our mistaken approach was still a scientific approach. Relatively unburdened by traditional theory or method, and free from the ethical urge to reprehend what appears *wrong*, we were able to study aberrant behaviour in a way the churches had neglected.

Yet a study of desocialized individuals (in asylums) has yielded little more in a century than a descriptive classification of " syndromes " and a recognition of the fact of the infinite variability of mental disease (i.e. that they are not distinct " diseases " as just said). It was a study of the less profound disorders (i.e. hysteria and neurasthenia) that yielded a clue to the " method " which is now believed to underlie all "madness". Even yet the application of these psychopathological theories to the graver forms of mental disease is a matter of great uncertainty, not only because of the relative inaccessibility of the individual patients of the latter kinds, but also because of the fact already mentioned that there are no clear-cut mental " diseases ". Such conditions as scarlet fever, gastric ulcer or appendicitis offer to research a group of comparable cases facilitating the discovery of a common cause. Mental diseases, however, cannot be distinguished from each other in this way, and the more closely they are studied the more conspicuous their *affinities* appear. Indeed a great psychiatrist of the past declared that there was only one form of mental disease, "Vesania Typica" ; and, while this represents merely the despair of the pure *naturalist* who finds that the infinite variability of his data defies classification, it does express also a half-truth. All mental diseases are related to each other inasmuch as they are merely different reactions to the difficulties of social adaptation. All " typical " mental diseases are " connected to " each other by *continuous chains* of cases between which the difference is infinitesimal.

Nevertheless there is general agreement that certain groups of symptoms (syndromes) have a tendency to appear all *together* with greater frequency than chance incidence would account for. These " typical " conditions occur with fair frequency and constancy, and so we can employ them as " *nuclear concepts* ". An analogy may make this vital point clearer. If a number of shot-gun barrels were fixed in such positions as to bear upon *adjoining* spots of a target so as to cover its surface fairly evenly and were then fired a number of times, the target would be covered with shot-marks, but *not quite uniformly*. Near the axis of each barrel there would be a slightly greater concentration of shot-marks than over the general surface. From these " nuclear " concentrations it would be possible to infer the axes, etc., of the barrels. In a similar manner, from the typical forms or nuclear concepts of psychiatry we may be able to infer and discriminate the causes of mental disorder.

These nuclear concepts may be briefly enumerated and characterized here, though later certain of their differences and affinities must receive closer study as also certain intermediate forms.

(*a*) *Dementia Precox or Schizophrenia* is fundamentally characterized by the loss of interest in people and its diversion to fantasy. Consequently there is ultimately a desocialization and loss of cultural tastes and standards. We call this " dementia " though intellect may be relatively unaffected—the loss being chiefly of " common sense ", feeling, interest and purpose in life. This results in inattention, indifference and ultimately in " silly " confusion of thought and speech. Nothing matters to these patients, and coherence of thought and action suffer (inattention).

(*b*) *Melancholia* is essentially a depression with loss of the joy of living and of all sense of its worthwhileness. Very constantly, in its severer forms, there emerges a great sense of personal unworthiness with delusions of guilt. Reactions from melancholic depression into shorter or longer periods of excitement and exhilaration are so usual that *mania* (as this reaction is called) is associated with its opposite (melancholia) under the name cyclothymia (circle in feeling).

(*c*) *Paranoia or Systematized Delusional Insanity* is distinguished by the retention of logical and intellectual faculties and of great force of personality.

G*

The sufferer takes an impossibly egoistic view of life and develops corresponding delusions (a) that he is great, important, able, attractive, etc., (b) that other people are jealous and unfair and keep him out of his rights ; and sometimes (c) that a love relationship, usually of an idealistic character, exists between himself and some member of the opposite sex (e.g. Don Quixote and Dulcinea del Toboso).

Excluding cases of brain disease and senility these three conditions make up the bulk of the mental hospital population, and must number many hundreds of thousands of victims who never " alienate " completely and therefore never appear in mental hospitals. They are called " psychoses " in distinction to the next group, the " neuroses ", though the difference between the groups is obscure and perhaps somewhat artificial.

(d) *Obsessional Neurosis* includes many cases where there is a recurring compulsion to think, say or do some particular thing (in minor forms this is very common and relatively harmless) and certain obsessive fears (phobias) and other emotionally unpleasant ideas. These conditions obstruct and inconvenience the patient very severely and may even paralyse his will.

(e) *Hysteria* is a disease which produces dramatic effects upon the social environment. It is fundamentally demonstrative, either as expressing the patient's unconscious wishes, dislikes, or anxieties, as evading difficulties or unpleasantness, compromising conflicts or dramatizing " repressed " ideas. It is too variable (more so even than precox) to be characterized briefly here, but a very general feature of hysteria is the existence of some marked disability if not of general invalidism itself. It thus produces dependency and secures attention.

(f) *Anxiety Neurosis* is sharply contrasted with Hysterical Invalidism though here again there is an

intermediate group of Anxiety-Hysteria. In
Anxiety Neuroses proper there is dread of something
unspecified (unlike phobias, though the distinction is
not radical). The patient does not know what he
dreads, but he has vague apprehension and
uneasiness and sometimes an agitation in which the
bodily symptoms of terror are extremely conspicuous.
[This classification includes only the commonest
and best defined syndromes and excludes (*a*)
Sexual Disturbances and (*b*) Delinquency.]

This is a widely accepted description and
arrangement of the more common and typical
mental illnesses. It has the further advantage of
grading them very roughly in the order of the
severity with which " the disease " attacks the
personality or social disposition of the sufferer. In
the precox this is wholly lost and the patient
becomes " dirty, degraded and demented "—wholly
isolated from his social environment. During
attacks of melancholia also this sense of isolation
becomes extreme and the patient is unable to
respond, though here he knows and *regrets* this
isolation with the full strength of his feeling.
Further, complete intermissions occur in this
disease, so we cannot suppose that the social
disposition has been lost (as in precox) or distorted
(as in paranoia). The Paranoiac readily becomes
an Ishmael—anti-social, distrustful, incredibly
egoistic with delusions of grandeur that set him
immeasurably above his fellows and delusions of
persecution which make every man a potential
enemy.

In contrast to these three conditions, sufferers
from the so-called neuroses are hardly ever so
affected as to necessitate certification and control.
The obsessional knows and deplores his disease.
The hysteric is usually amiable and (consciously)
anxious for help, though often convinced that the

trouble is bodily rather than mental. The sufferer
from Anxiety Neurosis (like the obsessional and
phobic) recognizes the "absurdity" of his illness
as well as we do, and *we feel* him to be a normal
fellow-citizen apart from his affliction. We say
that his personality has been preserved intact.

Sensible and useful as this classification is,
however, and though the psycho-analysts have a
plausible theory to show that these different
illnesses are due to fixations of libido at different
levels of development, I would ask you to consider
a "rearrangement" of these illnesses which lays
emphasis upon *resemblances* [rather than upon
distinctions between syndromes] which appear more
important from the point of view we are trying out.
The full technical reasons for this rearrangement
cannot be gone into here, but two points at least
can be appreciated by the lay reader. Firstly, the
melancholic *at intervals* rises to the highest levels of
social and cultural capacity, which is quite un-
intelligible if we imagine him as fixated at a
primitive level. Secondly, the hysteric, though
amiable and intelligent, is less really co-operative
and conscientious than the melancholic who is placed
so far below her in this "classical" classification of
psychopathy.

The purposefulness (Krankheits-gewinn or "gain-
of-illness") of much mental illness was in fact first
recognized in the case of Hysteria (by Freud) and
is often so apparent to the onlooker as to lead to its
being mistaken for malingering. The exact gain
or aim achieved by the illness varies, of course,
endlessly with the circumstances and character of
the sufferer ; but broadly speaking they get her
out of difficulties, unpleasantness or responsibility.
That is to say they restore the security, freedom
and comfort of dependent childhood ; they give
her back as an *invalid* what time deprived her

of as an infant, namely attention, sympathy and protection.

On the other hand no illness is more distressing than melancholia, which is characterized by complete frustration and the depths of despair, total isolation from people (loneliness) and consequent loss of interest—absolute boredom. Even its temporary maniacal reactions are uneasy in their excitement, and in many ways suggestive of a child escaping for a few minutes to play. The Melancholic has little resemblance to the grandiose, self-important Paranoiac or to the infantile self-sufficiency and freedom from restraint or obligation of the (terminal) Dement. Yet the classification places melancholia *between* the two latter syndromes.

If we remove it and replace it by Hysteria a remarkable change comes over our classification. We see that the three first syndromes on our new list express predominantly some infantile (and hence psychopathic or socially ill-adjusted) aim. The Precox returns to infancy after struggle. The Hysteric accepts invalidism in lieu of this, while the Paranoiac grasps at the illimitable power and irresponsible privilege which the young child attributes to its parents. The whole group is expressive of the various infantile wishes and of the (anti-social) protests connected with their denial.

The other group, which now contains Melancholia, *now shows an equal homogeneity* ; but on its part, instead of expressing infantile *wish* and *protest* against *social frustration*, its chief syndromes and symptoms are indicative of *self-frustration*. Depression, discomfort, paralysis and conflict are the dominant characters of these three diseases, Melancholia, Obsessional Neurosis and Anxiety Neurosis *taken as a whole*. The following table will indicate briefly the general characteristics of each group (i.e. its homogeneity) and the general contrast between the two.

The characteristics of the two hypothetical groups of psychopathy, the " aim " and the " frustration " syndromes respectively, may be reviewed and compared thus.

Wish or Aim Syndromes	*Self-Frustration Syndromes*
Correspond to the three (or four) envied " rôles " known to the child ; but widely and fantastically variable.	Inhibition, Anxiety, Guilt, and Depression, generally.
Show self-complacency and lack of (critical or effective) insight. *Enjoy* illness even while they deny its existence.	Show depression, inhibition, anxiety, i.e. generally unpleasant ; seem to have *no worthwhile " gain-of-illness "*, the existence of which they admit and deplore.
Tend to dementia : invalidism and alienation, i.e. surrender of social functions. Chronic psychic immaturity or deterioration.	Social functions well developed and maintained. Tend to spontaneous recovery. Maturity of Personality, and no dementia.
Recovery rates low.	Recovery rates high.
Rarely sincerely suicidal.	Often commit suicide.
Distorted person-interest and ill-developed " thing-interest " (culture).	*Normal transference easily* formed, normal high cultural attainments. " Companionship of Interest " is satisfying.
Extravagant, unco-operative or anti-social behaviour.	Ultra-scrupulous with strong sense of guilt.
Sex-interest is labile.	Normal, but inhibited.
General tendency to be only superficially co-operative but uninhibited.	Are co-operative but inhibited under examination.

Allowing for the fact that there is a good deal of frustration in *early* precox and paranoia we can say

that patients belonging to the second or
" frustration " group are more unhappy, have
more insight and more tendency to get well.   Their
characters are better matured and they have a
much better developed interest *in things* than
sufferers from the " aim " psychopathies.   They
may put themselves out of the world by suicide;
but they do not (unlike the other group) drift
complacently out of touch with social life into dementia,
invalidism or a world of delusions of suspicion and,
grandeur.   They supply most of the suicides and
most of the spontaneous and conclusive recoveries.
The resemblances, then, between the three
frustration syndromes are not only numerous and
striking in themselves, but they concern all the most
important functions of mind, namely feeling, interest
and social attitude.   (Sex is not typically affected
in these conditions, though naturally inhibited by
the general state of depression.)

It is impossible here to go into the clinical details
which justify this classification ; but, over and above
the rather striking differentiation into two groups,
a significant fact emerges.   As I have said, the
trouble with all classifications of so-called mental
diseases is that intermediate forms are so numerous
as to form continuous series between one syndrome
and another.   Under these circumstances, diagnosis
was usually highly arbitrary and disagreement was
common.   This very fact, however—the continuous
variability of cases and even the changes occurring
in one and the same case—seems to offer confirma-
tory evidence of the validity of the classification
here offered, namely that of " purpose and
frustration ".   The principal continuous series of
cases which caused such difficulty in diagnosis, are,
in my suggested classification, *found to lie between*
" *diseases* " *which are placed next to each other* ; and,
further, they offer a distinct suggestion that the

syndromes of the " frustration " group are each (in a sense) *the counterpart of its " opposite number " in the " aim " group*. If we include mania as a fourth member of the " wish " or " aim " group its relationship to its " opposite number " melancholia would be incontestable. My classification therefore *is quite as much by " series " as by " nuclear " concepts*.

The most notable *series* between two " nuclear concepts " is that connecting Dementia Precox and Paranoia. These two related diseases develop in many respects distinctive types of social attitude— the former retreating into self-sufficient, infantile, fantasy, the latter advancing upon the real world with boundless ambition and bitter aggressivity. Yet between these diseases the older classification thrusts Melancholia, which has less affinity for either of them than each has for the other. Again, on this old classification, hysteria is far removed from Dementia Precox and Paranoia, indeed it is put in a different class—" neurosis ", not " psychosis ". Yet there are groups of diseases intermediate between (i.e. connecting) Hysteria and Precox where diagnosis is actually extremely difficult, and between the former and Paranoia comes Erotomania which might be classed with either. So far as annectant series go, Hysteria " belongs with " Precox and Paranoia, while Melancholia does not.

The homogeneity of the frustration group is evidenced in the same way (i.e. by " annectant series "). Melancholia has one symptom, retardation, which links it to Obsessional Neurosis (from which, in the old classification, it was widely separated). It has another, " apprehension ", which, in extreme cases, presents us with " Agitated Melancholia "—a condition in many respects suggesting " Anxiety neurosis ". Anxiety neurosis, in turn, has close relationship with Obsessional

Neurosis, and, in the Phobias, we find indeed intermediary conditions.

Of course there are other morbid states intermediary between a "wish" syndrome and its "frustrated" counterpart. For example, Anxiety Hysteria. Further, Obsessional Neurosis has close relationships to Paranoia *and to the early stages of Dementia Precox* (Katatonia). These, however, do not invalidate the classification here offered. Indeed the latter fact tells strongly against the older classification which separated Obsessional Neurosis widely from Precox. While then we find " annectant series " connecting members of the wish group with their "opposite numbers" in the frustration group, these series *are by no means so striking as those connecting syndromes within the same group to each other.* The connections *between the groups* are indicated rather by changes and alternations *occurring in one and the same case* [as in the Manic-Depressive phases and in the striking contrast between the stormy obsessional onset of Katatonia and its demented termination] than by " annectant series ".

These groupings and the intermediate series can be represented conveniently on a two-dimensional diagram. (See page 194.)

The central spot represents the starting point of normal infancy, and normal development (not represented in the diagram) can be imagined as a straight line vertical to the paper. The inner ring then represents the nearest approaches to the normal where the psychopathic aims have either been frustrated or where the attractions of normal life, interests and social relationships have prevented too great a psychotic divergence. The outer ring represents the extreme forms of social alienation.

Starting clockwise we find at 12 o'clock on the outer ring Dementia Precox, at 3 o'clock is Paranoia,

DIAGRAM INDICATING CLINICAL AFFINITIES BETWEEN THE
RECOGNIZED "TYPICAL FORMS" OF MENTAL AND NERVOUS
DISORDER BY SPATIAL PROXIMITY.

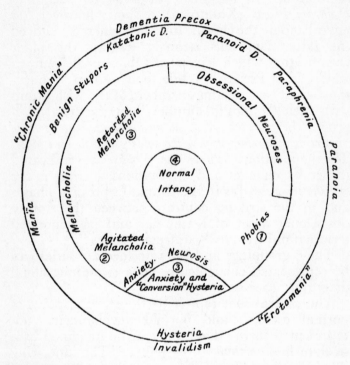

(1) Phobias.
(2) Agitated Melancholia.
(3) Retardation, Inhibition, Blocking of thought, Negativism, Compulsion. All symptoms rather than syndromes.
(4) Normal Infancy.

and between the two, Dementia Paranoides and Paraphrenia are indicated inside. On the corresponding sector of the inner ring we have the heterogeneous collection of Obsessional Neuroses. Moving round the outer ring we find at 6 o'clock Hysterical Invalidism opposite the Anxiety States (neurosis) at the same point on the inner ring. The Phobias, between Obsessional and Anxiety Neurosis (inner ring), Erotomania, between Paranoia and Hysteria on the outer ring and Anxiety Hysteria at 6 o'clock between the rings are indicated by numbers for clarity. Following round the outer ring to 9 o'clock we come through emotionalism and states of shallowness of affect, etc., to Mania, sharply contrasted with its opposite number, Melancholia, on the inner ring. Completing the outer circle we arrive through Chronic Mania (the conception is disused) back to Dementia Precox, while again (as said above) Melancholia and Obsessional Neurosis have a large element of inhibition or blocking of thought in common. Even in this non-technical sketch it may, however, be remarked that the conditions placed towards the left hand side of the diagram (Hysteria="belle indifference"; Mania="flight of ideas" or of attention; Dementia Precox="affective deterioration or apathy") have a common tendency *to a superficiality, insincerity or frivolity of interest in things.* This aspect of companionship (interest) is not well developed in these cases.

This diagram and suggested classification cannot be justified here in detail as scientifically valid; but it will serve the double purpose of (*a*) a mnemonic to bring the confusing pictures of mental illness into one perspective and (*b*) to show how far the differentiations of these "clinical pictures" turns upon the *social disposition* of sufferers. Before passing on, however, we might glance at the outstanding interpretations of the facts of mental disease, to discover whether they give any support to the view here advocated, namely that psychopathy is due to and results in privations, inhibitions and distortions of the social (love) disposition.

The non-Freudian interpretations of these syndromes may by briefly dismissed. Myers characterizes mental disease generally as mal adjustment (i.e. to *social* environment and life generally). While accepting this conception, I object (*a*) that it does not go far enough in offering an explanation for *each of the various clinical forms* assumed by psychopathy and (*b*) that it tacitly suggests that maladaptation is merely an inadequacy or *failure* of adaptive effort, and hence is merely negative, whereas there is reason to believe that the various psychotic lines of development represent *positive but misdirected adaptive efforts* which are in no way lacking in vigour or social intention.

The Adlerian interpretation of Psychopathy demands more consideration, although it also treats details in a rather airy manner. Wexburg for example regards the Psychoses as merely " severer " forms of the neuroses. I have already allowed that the distinction between the two classes of syndromes may be somewhat " practical " and artificial ; but certainly, so far as clinical resemblances go, it is impossible to regard Hysteria, Anxiety and Obsessional Neuroses as merely early or milder forms of Dementia Precox, Melancholia and Paranoia. There are differences of *character* between all the syndromes which cannot be dismissed as insignificant, —differences whose origin we require to know, both for practical and theoretical reasons. For example, differences in prognosis and amenability to treatment and differences in age of onset are of the utmost importance. Like Myers', Adler's Theory of the Psychoses concerns itself very little with these

differences. It seems to care little for exact,
inductive knowledge ; and even its practice seems
affected by a tendency to be satisfied with very
general and " practical " (even ambiguous) conceptions, which admittedly do not supply the
necessary basis for further inductive study.

The Freudian conception of the relationship of
the various forms of mental disease has been
gradually changing. In the very early days, when
psychopathological thought was still dominated
by the newly discovered process of repression
(dissociation), hopes were entertained that analysis
might be so developed as to discover the cause and
cure of the Psychoses—Dementia Precox, Melancholia and Paranoia. These were not realized.
The idea of libido-development was next worked
out to show how each different form of mental
disorder was the reflection and expression of the
" fixation " of a certain volume of libido at some
particular level of its organization.   The series of
" diseases " then (it was supposed) corresponded to
a series of arrests of development at critical stages.
The symptoms of each disease were regarded as the
distorted ebullitions of vestigial childish wishes
struggling through the repressions to attain symbolic
gratification. This conception, however, was
qualified and complicated by the notion of the
cathexis (or investment) of Libido and Destructive
Instinct in various ways, from primary narcissism
and masochism (where this impulse-desire is directed
upon the self) up to object love and hate, with
correlative variations in the goal-inhibited variants,
tenderness and sublimated interest.

Even this rather complex conception has not
proved adequate, however, and the third form of
Freudian Psychology, that of ego-organization
[admittedly difficult to relate to the Repression
Psychology and the Libido Theory] has been

applied to the Problem of the Psychoses—still with unsatisfactory results in two respects.

1st.   An enormous elaboration of very onerous hypotheses has proved necessary. The analysts have had to introduce such ideas as that narcissism itself, in its turn, is the product of "introjection", and that repression may be spontaneous (i.e. not enforced by environment through frustration or fear !) and could therefore occur at birth, automatically and in spite of ideal handling![1]   Further they have still to refer their problems back to the misty regions of race-history and to invoke that good old prop to a lame theory—the notion of psychopathic heredity.   I consider that this false line of theory elaboration is due to their false starting point, which denies the existence of a social purpose and regards all impulse and wish as purely egoistic and "detensioning" rather than as designed to evoke response.   This view has led Freud to the fallacious postulate of a primary, independent, instinct of destruction—a hatred stimulated from within like hunger, and having no reference to external provocation or purpose.   From this standpoint all other errors flow, and, while Freud has *lost his original grasp* of the purposefulness of mental disease (since he will not recognize *social* purpose), he is forced more and more, but always reluctantly and surreptitiously, *to re-introduce the social factor* in the form of Super-ego and Ego-ideal. But in the heavily disguised form of an Archaic Super-ego, this concession to social psychology has not been sufficient to reveal to Psycho-analysis the adaptive, social (though primitive) intention of Psychotic Development.

2nd.   For the same reason (the reluctance to admit a social factor in human nature), Psychoanalysis has never considered the *possibility* that the

[1] p. 24.

phenomenon of libido-fixation, "object choice" and "cathexis" may be *secondary to social adaptive necessities* [that is to say enforced by love and the separation-anxiety] though the facts strongly suggest that this is so and that the libido theory of the psychoses puts the cart before the horse (Reference M.). This libido theory fails conspicuously to account for the continuous *series of cases* (e.g. that from Precox to Paranoia) and has to postulate *multiple fixations at different levels as producing composite diseases*. [Of course, we have to remember that, from the nature of psycho-analytic practice—the amount of time devoted to each case—it is difficult for these observers to come into contact with an *extensive and representative* sample of the graver (i.e. more socially alienated) mental disturbances.]

We are not called upon here to pursue to a conclusion this critique of the Freudian conception of the psychoses. We have merely to observe that it is full of contradictions and inadequacies, thinly concealed by mountains of abstract supplementary hypotheses of a very onerous nature. Further it is in a state of flux, and (largely owing to the more social methods of investigation and treatment pursued by the child analysts) its general trend is towards an increasing recognition of the central importance of the social factor (represented on their theory by the concepts of Separation-Anxiety, Ego-ideal and Super-ego).

In my view this approach to a social theory of the psychoses (Ref. M.) by Psycho-analysis has failed because it is half-hearted (see Chapter XIII). Adler's far more social conception of mental trouble falls short, first, because of the weakness of the inductive, scientific, interest of this school and its contentment with superficial and general formulae (which, it must be acknowledged, are, so far as they go, true and "wise"). He fails, secondly, because he also has accepted struggle and competition as fundamental. Myers, as I have said, while recognizing that mental health and disease have to do with *social* adaptation, has not discerned (as Adler has done) *the positive, adaptive intention* underlying maladaptation, and so has regarded the latter as due to *mere weakness* of a developmental impulse.

It remains true, however, that all these views, each in its way, recognize psychopathy as a disturbance of the social disposition. On my conception of the latter, then, psychopathy is to be regarded as due to the frustrations, distortions and reactions of the *love* disposition in its first adjustments to family life. I would suggest that the psychoses are to be regarded as the vestiges (and their results) of the child's attempt to find a secure " niche " for itself in the family circle. There is a phase of anxiety, and sometimes of jealousy, which appears in the child's life, as, one by one, the attentions it has enjoyed " from time immemorial " are withdrawn from it. It is not merely forbidden adult gratifications (precocity) ; it is deprived of infantile sources of comfort and assurance. It has a sense of insecurity—even, perhaps, of loneliness. It becomes self-conscious and self-critical. The rage and anxiety evoked by thwarting is inhibited and goes to build up a sense of guilt. Idealisms are born of its discontent with itself and its rôle. It strives to increase its consequence to other people (Adler), in so far as it feels it has no one upon whom it can *safely* depend. It wants to be something other than it is, and *what* precisely it *wants to be* depends upon its experience of other people and its conception of their powers and privileges. Its idealism can only be derived from its environment, and its ambitions must be formed by emulation and imitation of some (envied and) outstanding figure within this environment. If this is so we must regard psychopathy as an archaic and (in adult environment) inept attempt to improve love relationships. Correspondingly, Psychotherapy would appear fundamentally as an attempt to assist the patient in his love-quest and to set this upon lines more likely to achieve the desired results. As Psychotherapy is an intuitive art rather than an acquired science it is not too paradoxical to expect that the " rationale " of the " cure " may throw light on the nature of the disease.

CHAPTER XII

PSYCHOTHERAPY

OUR methods of psychotherapy should logically depend upon the opinion we hold of the nature of the illnesses concerned and of the "modus operandi" of the therapeutic process. Our advance in knowledge of mental "disease" is gradually revealing that this term is only a figure of speech, and that these morbid conditions are really distortions and dissatisfactions of the love life (i.e. social maladaptations which in severe cases involve failure of Interest). Experience of the War Neuroses created a widespread impression that hysterical conversion-symptoms and anxiety were due to more or less definite environmental traumata —shocks. It was then supposed that these painful and terrifying memories, as it were, became " encapsulated " in the mind by repressions, and that the task of the physician was merely to uncover and discharge the feeling attached to these psychic " foreign bodies " (complexes). Such a conception attributed prime importance to the *physician's knowledge of the patient's unconscious thought.* Logically then, it encouraged the hope that by improved means of *investigation*, whether by symbol-interpretation or by induction of specially responsive states of mind in the patient (e.g. hypnotism or even drugs), or by surprising or " tricking " the defences by word-association, the skilled physician could accelerate the therapeutic process indefinitely. Such a hope has proved illusory. The progress of psycho-pathology has revealed that the psychopathies of War-time differ from those we meet in peace, among other ways, in one vitally significant circumstance. In war the traumatic factor was *adult* fear of death and injury, and perhaps horror and discomfort at the conditions of life. In peace the " traumata " are infantile anxieties and resentments, whose nature and origin have been completely repressed. Both types of neuroses alike have the function of defence or escape, but the latter represents a complete, life-long, mal-adjustment to life *which has been able, however, to fulfil* important defensive and compensatory functions in the patient's life. As we see it now, the social separation-anxiety, which is the main drive alike of psychopathy and of culture-evolution, forced the hysteric soldier *back to the trenches* in Flanders, while the very same factor pins the hysteric invalid to her bed. This predominant factor in pathogenesis (i.e. separation-anxiety, which is displacing sex traumata even in the psycho-analytic etiologies) was our main *ally* in treating the war neuroses but it is our main *enemy* in the treatment of those of peace. In the former case the separation-anxiety helped us to overcome the *pathogenically* insignificant fear of bodily death ; in the latter, our task is to induce the patient to lay aside her age-old defences against the infantile dread of isolation, and to find an adequate substitute in adult love and interest-companionship.

Perhaps I appear to state dogmatically what should be supported by argument ; but an examination of the various extinct and extant theories of psychotherapy will show that the trend and present consensus of opinion supports the view that psychopathy is a disturbance in the love life. There are some nine or ten theories of therapy that are worth considering. Most of these represent an aspect of the truth, and their changing vogue will perhaps help us to discover the essential process which all are trying to achieve.

We can dismiss at the very beginning such static and intellectual conceptions of *cure* as a process of "increase of insight", "removal of gaps in memory", etc., or even "reintegration", if the latter conception is intended in a structural or intellectual sense. Therapy deals not with ideas and their logical arrangement, but with *free emotion* of an unpleasant character or with its inhibition-effects such as loss of interest, seclusiveness, substitution of fantasy-gratification for reality, paralysis, etc. Although I have suggested a classification of psychopathy into two groups, one predominantly expressing morbid (socially unsuitable) wishes or ideals and another representing their corresponding frustrations, I regard frustration, with its consequent anxiety and hate, as the root cause of both alike. Reintegration therefore means no more than the removal of anxiety barriers, and so does not well express the essence of psychotherapy.

The earliest psycho-analytic conceptions of the mechanism of cure, that of Catharsis or Abreaction, was that already referred to as dominating our treatment of the War neuroses, namely the uncovering of a traumatic, unconscious memory or fantasy and the discharge of the affect of this "Complex", which was imagined to be pent up by repressive fear. Somewhat akin to this mechanistic conception of psychic illness and its "cure" is the idea that we must increase the patient's *tolerance* or diminish his censorship of the evil, sexual, impulses which were at one time imagined as the main content of the unconscious system. The neurotic was held to be morally hyper-aesthetic, and contact with the broadminded analysts de-sensitized, or, as many disapproving lay writers held, *demoralized* him to the required extent. Needless to say such a theory of therapy was never approved by serious analysts, though it

was popular with rebel temperaments who
embraced analysis for anti-social reasons—conscious
and unconscious.

There is enough truth in the idea, however, to
warrant closer examination, for the reduction of the
patient's intolerance could be construed in either
of two ways. Firstly, the aim of cathartic treatment
might be expressed by this imaginary verbal
reassurance by the physician to patient, " these evil
thoughts and wishes are not really bad after all.
Sex is only bad *for children* ; that is why it is hidden
by adults from them. Now you are grown up and
permitted to wish these things." We might name
this type of therapy, initiation. On the other hand
the physician's attitude might be represented by
this imaginary speech. " Of course you (patient)
are bad—if you call sex bad ; we *all are* bad in this
sense. We are merely hypocrites ; and goodness
is an illusion." This might be called *Disillusionment
Therapy*, yet, even here, in practice we establish a
fellowship of sorts with the patient. This latter
(alternative) meaning of analytic " demoralization "
is implicit in Freud's Metapsychology and in his
social and ethnological writings, such as " The
Future of an Illusion " and his recent letter to
Einstein on " Why War ? " We see it again in
Dr Eder's dictum " We are born mad. We acquire
morality and become stupid and unhappy. Then
we die." As I will try to show in a later chapter,
this Freudian pessimism and aggressiveness has its
roots in the author's pre-oedipal separation—
anxiety and rage, and has no real relationship to his
clinical work On this supposition only, it appears
to me, can we account for the unscientific nature
and development of the Freudian General Theory
of Mind and for the curious fact that psycho-
analytic theory and practice are so far divorced
from each other that not only does theory not

influence therapy but it is even unable to explain it. [See Chapter XIV.]

We reject then [in common with all Psycho-analysts] the idea that a mere counter-attack upon social restrictions, idealisms and censorships, and the demonstration of the " hypocrisy " of our traditional convention really relieves neurosis except by substituting for it cynicism and revolt. The rebel is not " free " ; it does the patient no good to bring others down to his level, since it leaves him still without any sense of belonging *to and with* others—without any sense of " acceptance " or common purpose in life ; in other words it leaves him as lonely and aimless as before. Even on the first interpretation of " demoralization " (namely as the demonstration of a dual idealism, one for adults and one for children respectively) we do not get very far. " Enlightenment " and " initiation " have, however, a *momentary* good effect, and as this element of treatment promises quick results (as well as for unconscious reasons) a theory of cure and a corresponding technique of this sort makes a wide appeal.

It is apparently related also to two other conceptions of the rationale of psychotherapy, namely that of " confession and absolution " and that of " the mitigation of the severity of the super-ego ". An actual case may best illustrate the therapeutic limitations of " enlightenment ", " re-education ", " explanation ", etc. Some years ago I treated a woman aged thirty-seven years, for extreme nervousness, seclusiveness, loss of all interest and " weariness of life ". Home was intolerable to her as was the sight of men, and for the same reason she was cut off from religion and all cultural pursuits. She was obsessed by the idea of male excretory organs and her mind was made up to suicide. She still entertained the biblical theory of birth as a curse inflicted upon all women for the sin of one, and was convinced that contact with men, or even close association with them, could produce that greatest of all shames, *even to married women*, impregnation. She interpreted the Garden of Eden story as meaning that God was disgusted with Adam and Eve's *almost* naked bodies ; no other attitude on the part of an ideal parent *was conceivable* to her. The common picture of Christ, " Behold I stand at the door and knock ", meant for her that *God could not bear to let him back into Heaven after he had been seen naked on the Cross*. At five she had a profound pity for little boys who had to wear trousers and thought they must be terribly ashamed. Women, she felt, were nicer, but Christ and the disciples nicest of all because they wore such long clothes.

Surely here is a case where enlightenment, initiation into the meaning of life and the beauty and significance of the more highly evolved modes of reproduction should have done much good. And so it did—*so long as I was with her or at least seeing her every day*. That is to say, so long as the view was backed by my *personal* assurance. Otherwise the feeling of isolation, the sense of unreality, the longing for death and even the umbilical theory of birth (which she still entertained at her age) returned in full force. It was only as a result of two years of subsequent analysis that this monstrous, prudish, obsessional anxiety was dispelled. Only when its *purpose* became clear, namely to propitiate and find acceptance with her mother (who was dead), to recapture her love by the renunciation of all (supposedly) " disgusting " bodily interests and gratifications, did this gigantic *apology for existence* lose its obsessive hold over the patient. This revelation involved the uncovering of the fundamental separation-anxiety and correlative hatred of mother and their dissipation. Only when this is done is a true reconciliation possible ; and the process takes time, because it involves the overcoming the anxiety-buttressed resistances. Well might the Freudians discard the crude Abreaction Theory and even that of " Interpretation " in favour of the view that the virtue of psycho-analysis lies, *not in the discharge of effect*, but in the process which brings this about, namely the *overcoming of resistances*, and that this process cannot be regarded as dependent upon the skill and intellectual *insight* of the physician so much as upon the willingness of the patient and his emboldenment to relax his defences *against expressing his hate and so running a risk of being hated*. This willingness or *trust* is a function of transference (positive) or love so that the original ambivalent attachment to mother is " played off " upon the physician. The love-factor in treatment (or "transference ") *emboldens* the patient to display a protest and reproach against the loved object [personated by the therapist], and the discovery of grievances against it proceeds until the quarrel is " thrashed out " and the difference composed. Cure consists in the removal of frustration, whereupon hate is not " *overcome by love* ", but, *having no more reason for existence*, is reconverted into love. Reductive therapy therefore can be imagined as *reducing* old quarrels by trying them out in the Transference Neurosis ; while non-reductive forms of Therapy such as persuasion, suggestion, hypnosis, etc., could be expressed in the phrase, " Let bygones be bygones ". In this way the latter represent a *strengthening of repression* by the intensification of love, while the former or Reductive (Analytic) therapy aims to discover and eradicate the quarrels that necessitated repression.

Of the theories of therapy, that of Confession and Absolution is important on account of its alliance with the religious theory of guilt and atonement.

These theories of therapy tacitly accept the view that the child (patient) is bad and the parent-analyst is good. They imply that there was a real sin in childish disobedience, namely ambivalence and hatred of a benefactor, and that this sin is annulled *conditionally* by the analyst-parent. The badness is cancelled out by having so much parental mercy or love attached to it, whereupon it can be overlooked and never brought up again. Forgiveness is not only conditional ; it is even regarded as a condescension !

Absolution, in this popular and theological sense, achieves, if effective, two important results. The parent is acquitted of all fault and declared to be " good " now. Instead of saying, " I am bad " to excuse the parents (dissolve the ambivalence), he can say, " I *have been* bad ". It is possible to go on loving, though oneself unworthy, but not to love an unworthy object. Hence the former belief (" I am bad ") is preferable to continued rage at the loved object.

The result of the absolution technique is thus that, having induced an ecstatic love for the parent by contemplating his overwhelming goodness in forgiving the miserable sinner, the latter now feels " good ", i.e. saved. He has renewed the primitive rapport with the mother *and in so doing has gratified the expurgated* regressive wishes. His righteousness is no longer " filthy rags " (i.e. soiled napkins), but is that of the sucking lamb, the innocent infant *which is felt by itself to be acceptable* to the mother.

But we cannot leave our patients in the status of " good children ", especially if there is any chance of their having the charge of actual children in later life. In spite of the economy of the therapists' time offered by techniques of Confession, Punishment and Absolution (which are inseparably connected with each other), and the advantage they possess in

H

the way of wholesale application, we cannot suppose that the higher developments of psycho-therapy will be found to lie along this line. Two reasons have led us to this conclusion : (1) The possible results of Confession and Absolution Therapy are necessarily limited by the *quality* of the social adjustment they offer and by the degree of maturation attainable by them ; and (2) the patients with whom we deal are frequently unable to *accept* absolution, however convincingly offered, by reason of the intensity of their anxiety and consequent aggressiveness and guilt.

Summing up these earlier ideas about psycho-therapy, we can distinguish :

1. Those methods which, broadly speaking, represent a *flight from feeling* into intellectual or philosophical " solutions ". " Explanations ", " insight ", " recovery of memories ", " occupation and distraction ", etc., all work in this manner, as also do the very popular and prevalent theories which assure us that the trouble is all due to some morbid *bodily* condition. The advantage (?) of all these methods is that they save the therapist from the difficulty of understanding his patient and spare him the pain of sympathizing with the patient's distress. They preserve *his* tenderness taboo.

2. If the therapist's own security does not depend on neurotic " flight " from feeling and he is therefore not impelled to an " affective " *flight from the patient*, he may approach the latter in the role of parent armed with *authority and a " patronizing " love*. On this line a whole range of techniques is open, called " persuasion ", suggestion, hypnosis, " confession and absolution ", etc., all aiming at the encouragement or moral coercion of the patient into " normal " ways of thinking and acting. By such methods we disregard the illness, repress its symptoms and seek to reassure the patient. These

methods are criticized on the ground of their ineffectiveness in dealing with the deeper sources of guilt and anxiety and because they do not assist the patient to grow up.

3. From the beginning the Freudian approach showed more interest in and sympathy with the patient than either of the above, and more curiosity about what was actually wrong with him. The earlier analytic theories of therapy, such as " catharsis ", " freeing of the libido ", etc., along with the outlook upon life characteristic of the metapsychology and the social philosophy of psycho-analysis, seem to me to present the therapist as " siding with " the patient's desire for freedom and enjoyment against the tyranny of social environment and the cruelty of life generally. The *effect* of such an approach is tacitly to offer the patient the sympathy and companionship of joint revolt and suffering, and of course this is to some extent reassuring to him. To the love-shy and love-starved patient a systematic denial of the existence of any love but bodily gratification must be comforting. We cannot wish for the non-existent, so that here again the analyst's tenderness-taboo is preserved.

The latest theories and techniques of analysis represent, however, a franker approach to fellowship and the therapeutic employment of love. The play-analysis of children combines the companionship of a friendly playfellow with the insight, equanimity, wisdom and strength of a parent, giving to the child at one and the same time a sense of freedom and sense of security. Even the reductive method of analysis, as will be seen, " exhibits " far more love than is usually admitted, in the sense of a *responsiveness* which is unwearying, tolerant and even appreciative, insighted and alert. A true and full companionship of interest is offered to the patient, which in all therapeutically essential respects reconstitutes the primary interest-relationship of mother and baby in baby and its affairs. (See Chapter II, in which this early rapport is correlated with the Freudian conception of Narcissism.)

Though the physician may not actually respond emotionally to the patient's *emotions* in unison or in harmony (Chapter IV), he shows by his *understanding* and insight that he too has suffered these experiences, so that there is a " fellowship of suffering " established. Ferenczi's " Active-therapy " represents a protest against the more extreme ideals of " passive " technique, and Barbara Low apparently refers to these errors in speaking of the analyst's dangerous attempt " to maintain the fiction of immunity from emotion ". A one-sided, unresponsive, love-relationship must evoke anxiety and cannot be curative. I suggest that the patient is entangled into this dependency by the analyst's insight and sympathetic interest, which seem to promise real (parental) love : and that the physician's subsequent reserve and aloofness forces the love-needing patient into an abject surrender, pleading, protesting, and self-revealing. This is utilized for the exhaustive examination of ancient grievances, anxieties and rages connected with frustrated social needs of childhood. I further suggest that the " *overcoming of resistances* " is therapeutically effective not because of the wishes so released for future gratification, but *because of the removal of the threats and sanctions which had inhibited them* and which continue to produce anxiety and resentment ; that is to say recovery is essentially a *social reconciliation*. This appears to me to be the *use* of anxiety.

I fully accept Ferenczi's dictum " The physician's love heals the patient ", the nature of the love being understood as a *feeling-interest responsiveness—not a goal-inhibited sexuality.* The cure would then appear to be *restoration of that social confidence which is the basis of interest and the removal of the privation-anxiety which is the main disturber of the sex appetite.* If tenderness or love were goal-inhibited sexuality as Freud holds, *then it should itself be anxiety-ridden* and could not therefore form a therapeutic agent. Further, as I have pointed out, it is itself rigorously inhibited although it is not offensive to social feeling as are jealousy, incest-guilt, etc. So I conclude that the essential process in psychotherapy is to offer the patient the means of re-establishing free " feeling-interest " relationships with his social environment in the person of the analyst (to begin with). The latter thus re-plays the original rôle of the mother in becoming the starting-point of a broadening circle of anxiety-free relationships—that is to say of relationships where feelings need not be inhibited or repelled (this does not refer to conscious control) and where interest responses are equally free. This is the foundation of companionship, so that the role of psychotherapy appears to be the restoration of the patient to full membership of society, to a feeling-interest integration with other minds, a rapport in which the patient can express himself in the confidence of evoking agreeable response and in which he feels himself able to respond agreeably to the overtures of others. *Expression*, as I have said, is not merely evacuation or " detensioning ", though Freud often speaks of it in this sense. I regard it as complete only when a response has been evoked and appreciated. Of course the patient, by degrees and according to his capacity, must be led out of the companionship of expressed emotion to that of Interest and Speech. He must grow up and, so, some response must be given to him in psychotherapy or anxiety and not cure will result, as actually happens occasionally.

If I am right in the above representation of Psychotherapeutic processes, then we can discern the factor common to them all—*the quest for a basis of companionship with the patient*. Even in the first group—the flight from feeling—the therapist seeks to share with the patient *his own neurotic* defences, and establishes a fellowship of interest (meanings, ideas, etc.) in lieu of that of " feeling " which neither can tolerate. The second aims at the secure, authoritative, rapport of parent and child ; the third mode of therapy establishes a conspiracy or fellowship of suffering while the later analytic group of " techniques " almost explicitly " *exhibit* " love, *even while theoretically denying its existence*. Here is a progressive approach to the position upheld in this book, but how is it that the social nature of the process is not more frankly admitted, cultivated and studied ?

In the first place we must recognize some non-psychological factors at work, falsifying and disguising what should be a love-interest-relationship. Economic circumstances demand that the therapist should support himself upon fees, and, though this itself ultimately comes to be regarded as an economic co-operation between patient and analyst, it introduces *at first* an appearance of divergent interest and even of selling love. The labourer may be " worthy of his hire " but this does not apply to " a labour of love ".

Further, the patient cannot actually leave his own circle of friends and relations and adopt that of the therapist, while the latter cannot really assume the full functions of parenthood to an adult or a child with parents of his own. For the patient's own sake also it is necessary to abbreviate treatment as much as possible, so that the drive towards " psychic weaning " must be *even more urgent* in the psychotherapeutic relationship than in the original one of child and mother.   The relationship is *formed with the intention of severance.*

All these circumstances (beyond our control) militate against the naturalness of the love-relationship of physician and patient and tend to make both regard it (in spite of the unconscious needs of the latter) as a purely technical one of " service and reward ".   Thus the psychotherapist tends to become less of a Healer than a *Consultant in the Art of Living.*

In the second place, the physician himself is a product of our culture, and, as such, equipped, not only with the prejudices and inhibitions which psycho-analysis originally dealt with, but also *defended from his own love-needs, anxieties and hates* by the tenderness-taboo. When the patient's " transfer " demands to him which the mothers of patient and of analyst alike had left unsatisfied, the physician uses his own defences and at least " maintains the fiction of immunity from emotion " or even dissociates himself from the patient affectively in an ultra-passive, ultra-objective, *technique,* which is really a flight to preserve his own defences.   The therapist literally *dare not* exhibit compassion [i.e. be a man of sorrows], and this, in my opinion, is responsible for our failure to recognize or admit that *love is the effective agent in psychotherapy; and* it is responsible also for the variety of evasions of this truth and for the substitutions for this simple relationship that are produced by our craving for techniques of psychotherapy. All theoretical attempts to establish a therapeutic mastery over the patient appear about to be swept away—significantly enough—*by the example of the child-analysts.*   In the Passive Techniques such interchanges as must take place between patient and analyst exhibit on the side of the latter only qualities such as patience, interest and tolerance which do *not ostensibly* imply sympathy, i.e. an emotional response. Further the patient's own love-memories are discussed and considered (analysed) *in terms of their various bodily expressions and desires*—the *associative craving* being neglected and attention being directed exclusively to the sexual-sensual wishes and satisfactions which served to express it (as well as to satisfy organic needs and cravings). The anxieties, rages and griefs of the past were represented either as due to the privation of bodily pleasures or to the operation of an appetite for destruction (" a primal, independent, instinct ") which arises spontaneously, i.e. independently of any external provocation such as neglect, " snub ", love-privation, etc. The possibility of anxiety and aggression referring to associative and expressive needs and *their* frustrations is beginning to be recognized, but with manifest reluctance. Finally the patient's tender feelings for the analyst were *repelled* by being discounted as " mere transference " ; as if every love relationship except the primary one of child towards the mother was not also transference and were any the less genuine on this account. The analyst thus successfully extricates himself from the love relationship *by which alone he had done* such good as he achieved, and at the same time he had denied, discounted or explained away the agency by which, unknown to himself, he did it. The day of mere " technique " is over.

The whole of the development of Psycho-analysis seems then to have been dominated by the unconscious purpose of utilizing love (in the sense here used) *in practice*, while repudiating any such activity *in theory*. The development of their " technique " ; the emphasis they placed on the various *mechanical* features of this ; their blindness to the secondary and unintentional meaning (for the patient) of the analyst's interest in and mental play with the patient's memories and fantasies ; all these seem to denote an unconscious attempt to evolve an (impossible) *onesided* love relationship. The failure of this quest is marked by the gradual and surreptitious introduction of the social factor into both theory and practice. The " overcoming of resistances " might almost be paraphrased as the development of a *trust* in the analyst-parent *which will be capable of surviving* the reproaches arising from repressed anxiety and rage and which therefore makes repression (and its secondary bitterness, instability and other bad consequences) *unnecessary*.[1] Under cover of the love-relationship of trust, the essence of the neurosis is expressed and re-enacted (Transference Neurosis), and the discovery is made by the patient that there is no real occasion for anxiety and hatred. It is as if the Analyst had said with a sincerity indubitable by the patient, " You think I am a bad parent ; I don't mean to be ; tell me why you think so and give me another chance." Thus, as the analysts say, we " master anxiety " or " overcome hate with love " or, in yet other phraseology, we " mitigate the severity of the super-ego ".

The later teachings *re* therapy insist on the physician's responsiveness ; which indeed is the objective of the training-analysis. The ideal attitude is very like that of Christ (as pointed out in Chapter IX), serene without being aloof, sympathetic without being disturbed : exactly what the child desires in the parent.

In spite of the complex and abstract evasions (by certain psycho-analytic teachers) of the issue which Ferenczi put in a nutshell, we conclude that the development of psychotherapy is demonstrating in ever clearer fashion the reality and importance of that " love " whose nature and origin this book is intended to explore.

---

[1] From this point of view the recovery of repressed traumatic memories is the *sign* of recovery, not its *cause* ; recovery being reconciliation.

CHAPTER XIII

FREUDIAN THEORY IS ITSELF A DISEASE

A Study in the Unconscious Motivations of Psycho-analysis

In the present Chapter I intend to maintain that the *theory* of Psycho-analysis has sprung from an entirely different interest from that which inspired the development of its *practice*. In fact, the meta-psychology appears to me an expression of unconscious hate and anxiety while the practice of psycho-analysis represents a struggle to express love in spite of various inhibitions. Psycho-analytic theory and practice are thus subjectively or mentally complementary to each other and not objectively supplementary as is the case in the " pure " sciences and their " applied " forms. This, I maintain, is the reason why theoretical developments in psycho-analysis have not been reflected in technical advances, and it also accounts for the rather astonishing fact that theory is even unable to explain the rationale of " cure ".

In order to establish this thesis I shall pursue two lines of argument.

(A) I shall show that all the errors and shortcomings of theory *have one and the same general tendency*. Wherever an error has had to be retracted, where there is disagreement in well-informed opinion, where the theory has had to be over-elaborated or is self-contradictory, or where there are gaps, or conflicts of evidence, or where whole ranges of facts resist interpretation—in all these cases the failure of theory seems to be due to its

218

denial of the existence of love and to its depreciation of the social significance of the mother. In biology, as in ethnology, Freudian interpreters have flagrantly selected and, on occasion, distorted their evidence in this doubly tendentious manner—a bias which obviously has an emotional significance.

(B) In the following Chapter I will attempt to show that the successful developments of treatment and that of the *theory of treatment* have been in the direction of a covert employment and recognition of love in a strictly non-sexual sense. The play analysis of children and the more personal relationship allowed to psychotics[1] are practical intuitive recognitions of the need for love, which find overt expression in Ferenczi's dictum, " The physician's love heals the patient ". The anxious, resentful inhibition of love on the analyst's part is not wholly confined, however, to his theorizing, but finds expression in the advocacy of ultra-passive reductive techniques which owe such success as they enjoy to the induction of anxiety (inhibited " *affection* ", not goal-inhibited sexuality). They represent a restricted tolerance by the physician of the patient's love-appeals and love-offerings, conditional upon the patient retaining the rôle of docile, dependent child. Reductive Analysis employs this *anxiety rapport for the* elucidation of infantile *grievances* with a view to their dissipation ; and it is thus the converse of hypnosis which employs a pure love-authority rapport to secure further repression.

A

I. The " best " evidence of Freudian error lies in Freud's own admission. In 1929 Freud wrote in *Civilization and its Discontents*, " a propos " of certain states representing a reinstatement of the infantile feeling for the mother, " I cannot discover this

[1] Paul Federn : " Analysis of Psychotics," *Internat. Jl. of P.A.*, *1934*.

' oceanic ' feeling *in myself* '', and on pp. 20-21 :
" Thus we are entirely willing to acknowledge that
the ' oceanic ' feeling exists in *many people*, and we
are disposed to relate it to an early stage in ego-
feeling ; the further question then arises what claim
this feeling has to be regarded as the source of the
need for religion.

" To me this claim does not seem very forcible.
Surely a feeling can only be a source of energy when
it is itself the expression of a strong need.   The
derivation of a need for religion from the child's
feeling of helplessness and the longing it evokes for
a *father* seems to me incontrovertible, especially
since this feeling is not simply carried on from
childhood days but is kept alive perpetually by the
fear of what the superior power of fate will bring.
I could not point to any need in childhood so strong
as that *for a father's protection*.   Thus the part played
by the ' oceanic ' feeling, which I suppose *seeks to
reinstate limitless narcissism* '' (i.e. love of self, not love
of and need for mother !), " cannot possibly take
the first place.   The derivation of the religious
attitude can be followed back in clear outline as far
as the child's feeling of *helplessness* (for lack of a
father)."   " *There may be something else behind this,
but for the present it is wrapped in obscurity*."   [Inter-
polations and italics mine throughout.]

In these conjectures Freud has dismissed almost
without consideration the possibility that the need
for mother is strong enough to motivate religious
feeling.   He presents the father as almost the only
important object of the child's desires ; while the
child's love—even of the father—is represented as
essentially selfish, the desire for personal security.
He cannot deny, however, that *other people* may have
" oceanic " feelings, etc., but considers them
unsatisfactory data for science (pp. 8, 9).   He also
makes the significant admission that his own

explanations of these data leave the origin of religion " wrapped in obscurity ".

Three years later, in his paper on " Female Sexuality ", we meet, as I think, the same temperamental disability on Freud's part and the same (and related ?) limitation in his vision. " Everything connected with this first mother-attachment has in analysis seemed to me so elusive, lost in a past dim and shadowy, so hard to resuscitate that it seemed as if it had undergone some *specially inexorable repression*. But possibly I have received this impression because, when I have analysed women, they have been able to cling on to that very father-attachment in which they took refuge from the early phase of which I am speaking. It would in fact appear that women analysts—for instances, Jeanne Lampl-de-Groot and Helene Deutsch—had been *able* to apprehend the facts with *greater ease and clearness* because they had the advantage of being suitable *mother-substitutes* in the transference-situation with the patients whom they were studying " [my italics]. Let us notice. " To *me* so elusive ", " whereas women analysts had been able to apprehend *with greater ease and clearness*." Freud suggests that it is the patient's fault for clinging to the father transference, but we have seen that Freud all but deifies the father in his earlier theory and all but ignores the first mother-attachment. Might it not be he himself who " clings to the " father rôle in his practice and who is a victim to that " *specially inexorable* repression " which, I suggest, is responsible alike for his personal inability either (1) to experience the " oceanic " feeling in his life or (2) to admit the significance of the mother and of love in his theory. At any rate, we have an admitted failure in his *practice* and an insensitiveness in his *experience*. If we find in his *theory* too a defect identical in tendency with these two, it is surely an

economy of hypothesis to suppose that all three
related failures are an expression of Freud's own
personality and not a coincidence.

And we do find such an admission of theoretical
oversight in the later paper. The need for " a
father's protection " which in the former was
regarded as the strongest in childhood, is not in
evidence in the latter. It is now found to have
" been preceded by a phase of equally strong and
passionate attachment exclusively to the mother ",
even on the part of the little girl who on Freud's
theory should prefer the father. Further, " the
duration of this attachment to the mother has been
greatly underestimated ". It is now found to last
into the fifth year, occasionally throughout life.
" Actually, during this phase, her father is not much
more to a little girl than a troublesome rival, even
though her hostility towards him never reaches such
a pitch as the boy's." Here the sex attraction does
no more than mitigate jealousy ; but is this a sex
jealousy ? Surely not. Surely we must admit that
it is a jealousy of love, which is thus found in
opposition to sex from the time the child can
distinguish persons. Thus we have a belated
recognition of the significance of the mother and
almost an admission of the existence of a love
independent of and capable of opposing sex
attraction from the very beginning. The first
consequence of this enlightenment is this—" it
seems that we shall have to retract the universality
of the dictum that the Oedipus Complex is the
nucleus of the neurosis. But if anyone feels
reluctant to adopt this correction, he need not do so.
For, on the one hand, we can extend the content
of the Oedipus Complex to include all the child's
relations to *both* parents " (my italics), " or, on the
other, we can give due recognition to our new
findings by saying that women reach a normal

positive Oedipus situation only after surmounting a first phase dominated by the negative complex."

But why, I answer, *should* we be " reluctant " to correct an admitted error ; why should we merely obscure it by making our original propositions all but meaningless (through an indefinite extension of the Oedipus Concept), or maintain the error by piling one abstract hypothesis on the top of another ? Why should we not as analysts ask ourselves what was the reason for the original oversight (i.e. whether we ourselves were biassed), and why, as scientists, not overhaul the whole theory so as to make the correction systematic ?

I suggest that the reason why Freud is reluctant to do any of these things is that he has, as a result of the " specially inexorable repression ", a grudge against mothers and a mind-blindness for love, equal and opposite to the mind-blindness and repugnance that many of his opponents had for sex. The Oedipus dictum was originally applied as an explanation of all social life and culture, and its inadequacy will not be repaired in *these* fields by making it more vague or more complex in that of psychopathology.

II. Another mass of evidence pointing to the conclusion that Freud's theory expresses a personal bias is found in Ethnology. This may be summarized briefly :

(1) Just as the mother attachments of the individual are for Freud " lost in a past so dim and shadowy ", so the great Mother-Cults of antiquity are for him a mystery as repellent as they are insoluble. Though they constitute perhaps the greatest problem for the archaeology of culture and the psychology of religion, he dismisses them in a couple of lines with the most casual and tendentious conjectures. [" Group Psych." postscript.]

(2) The castration of the priests which the Myth imputes to the Goddess-Mother herself is represented by Freudians as done at the instance of the father.

(3) Human sacrifice too, which originally was associated with the problem of fraternal (Cain) jealousy and the propitiation of the nurtural (Earth) Mother, is represented by Freudians either as a ritual killing of the (sexually) jealous father or as the expiatory and vicarious sacrifice (to placate the Father) of the incestuously inclined son. [Money Kyrle : " The Meaning of Sacrifice ".] The sacrifice of women is either discreetly ignored or asserted, again without evidence, to be a substitute for Father-killing. Here again we have the related obsessions with the father and with sex which were noted above.

(4) Freud has assumed that sex jealousy is universal and imperative in man, whereas the evidence is conclusive that it varies widely in intensity as between one culture and another, and so points to it being to some extent a *composite factor*. Indeed the only other jealousy to which Freud pays much attention is also sexual, and antifeminist in accordance with Freud's habit of thought—namely the penis envy. Ethnology teaches us that this is an *artifact of a particular type of culture*, and that, on the contrary, the fundamental jealousy is that of the man for the woman's reproductive and lactational powers. Indeed Patriarchal culture and character are themselves largely expressions of this envy and not that of a natural superiority. Freud's father-worship shows itself again in his overlooking the primal fact in the Oedipus legend itself, namely that the initial aggression came from Laios, the jealous father, himself. [The oracle was Laios' " baby " self.] Yet an impartial study of the *mythology* would have shown the preponderance of the *regressive jealousy* of the father for the baby *as such*, girls and

boys alike, over the *precocious jealousy* in the son of his father's sexual privileges. But it would have shown him that the greatest jealousy of all is that of the older for the younger child (Cain, Cinderella), a point upon which Freud touches very lightly, perhaps because it shows the mother as esteemed otherwise than sexually, perhaps because it shows her as the prime mover in the moralization of mankind. She first created the " band of brothers ", she armed Kronos with the sickle that was to *protect her children against their father's jealousy*. Freud can see none of these things. Why ?

(5) A more flagrant, tendentious, self-contradictory distortion of data could not be found than Röheim's interpretation of certain totemic ritual. The Aranda tribe asserts :

(*a*) that men *can* bear children ;
(*b*) they term the subincised penis a vagina ;
(*c*) they ritually cause it to bleed ;
(*d*) they exclude women rigorously from the ritual ;
(*e*) (unnoted by Röheim) they have little or no taboo on menstruation.

Röheim says they do this to unite fathers and sons by the bond of a common castration-anxiety and homo-sexual love on the basis of the son's renunciation of incestuous wishes for his jealous father's wife. Surely (*a*) is a plain wish-fantasy, (*b*) subincision, etc., implements the wish to *be* a woman as far as act and deed can do. (*c*) seems an imitation of the menstrual function particularly in connection with (*e*) the absence of menstrual taboos in women. The horror of menstruation may be fundamentally envious—sour grapes—and there would of course be no occasion for this among a people where the men have appeased envy by annexing this function to themselves as well as that of child-bearing.

(e) The exclusion of women from this ritual need not be due to incest anxiety, but might simply be an intuitive precaution against their mockery of a feeble, jealous imitation. It might imperil the dignity and authority of the male. At least alternative interpretations are possible though they are never suggested.

(6) In his attempts to account for the fact of social life on the basis of masculine sex jealousy and without admitting love to be a factor—Freud has been driven to offer here and there in his work no less than four mutually incompatible hypotheses. One of these even seems to attribute reason and foresight to a presocial animal (who must have lacked language and conceptual thought), and in addition, to imply the existence in this unsocialized being of moral sentiments such as remorse, good faith, and self-control. This is all the more absurd when we consider that Freud denies the existence of these qualities in his contemporaries. [p. 112ff.]

(7) Any attempt by analysts to supplement or test their social theory by a comparison with the facts of animal behaviour selects facts so as to make the overcoming of masculine sex-jealousy appear the key to the problem of socialization in the race ; that is to say, concentrates attention upon the father and sex, to the exclusion of the mother and love. Further, it makes the *overcoming* of the aggressiveness and selfishness of the individual the key to socialization in individual development. Society is always regarded as a product of compulsion never of mutual attraction. In *Civilization and its Discontents*, p. 104, he confesses himself totally unable to account for the absence of a cultural struggle in animal societies. Yet here, too, he confidently assumes that even insect communities are based upon " restrictions of individuals ", the result of " thousands of centuries " of struggle. The facts

of insect behaviour point conclusively to a general *tendency to socialization inherent in all nurtural practices* and to the evolution of insect societies without either struggle or restriction. Numerous instances of sociability in animals show society unequivocally as a continuous outgrowth from the nurtural association of parents and young, untroubled by the problem of sexual exclusiveness. A good proportion of the jealousies we do find active are in fact themselves *nurtural* even if they *appear* (as e.g. in queen bees) to *have a reproductive reference.*

(8) Finally we can accuse the Freudians of being tendentious in their treatment of matriarchal cultures and religion. These are assumed to be inferior, secondary and transient, though evidence points to their being both more peaceful and more stable than their patriarchal counterpart. They tend to disappear under the aggression and propagandism of the patriarchies which are tacitly assumed by Freud to be the primal, natural and most excellent form of social organization. Freud assumes " inter alia " that man is a fighting animal, and, though he personally deplores the fact, it is not difficult to see that he accepts conquest as evidence of superiority whether this be the conquest of the woman by the man or *of the Jew by the Gentile*, or vice versa. [Vide "Why War?", quoted p. 232 of this work.]

III. Historically and otherwise the point of departure of Freudian Theory from Freudian Practice, lies in the conception of Death Instinct put forward in *Beyond the Pleasure Principle*. Röheim calls it " the Pillar of the Metapsychology " and Dr Brierley regards it as a key or turning point in the development of Psycho-analytic Theory. It is, likewise, from an affective point of view, the supreme expression of hatred, elevating this, as it does, to

the status of a primal, independent, purpose in life—
a separate appetite which like hunger requires no
external provocation and is an end-in-itself.   The
conception therefore supplies good evidence, *unless
objectively justified*, that it is an expression of subjective
antipathy in line with Freud's systematic denial of
love.   Indeed I hold that the theory is not only as
I say an expression of unconscious rage, but what
empirical evidence can be adduced in its support
can only be so interpreted by shutting our eyes to the
existence of love.   It is therefore doubly perverse
since it is scientifically unjustified.

(1) The first point of criticism is the manner and
matter in which the theory originated—a radical
departure from all Freud's previous manner of
working which had been in the highest degree
empirical.   Freud himself apologized for " speculations often far-fetched " ; but a few years later he
refers to the theory as having *insensibly* won such a
hold over him that he is *unable* to think otherwise.
Could there be a more apt description of the
characteristic origin and growth of a delusional
expression of unconscious impulse ?

(2) I do not intend to go into the evidence
logical, biological, psychological and philosophical.
I have marshalled these arguments in H. and F.
Dr Blacker in his book has also made effective
criticisms.   Here I will merely instance one
objection.   The conception of Death Instinct
involves the attribution to the atoms themselves (not
the organic molecules), memory, preference and
purpose—in fact it supposes them to have an
objection to entering into organic compounds or
remaining in them.   While attributing to the atom
this anti-social disposition we are compelled by
this theory to imagine that all the individual
"objections" of the atoms of the body are in some
way organized to secure expression in the attempt

"to pursue the path to death peculiar to the species". Life is thus imagined as forced upon the organism from the outside in spite of its will-to-death. I submit that Freud's adoption of such a supposition in face of the fact of evolution, is evidence of the dominance of personal motive.

(3) It was the Theory of Death Instinct that terminated my own rather blind devotion to Freud and it is upon this theory that most of the internal dissensions of the psychoanalytic party turn. But characteristically the issues are evaded, not by retraction, but either by reducing the whole theory to nebulousness or by piling up supplementary hypothesis. Both of these tactics are frequent in the defence of emotionally held beliefs. I have heard Death Instinct even equated with Katabolism and thus deprived of all positive meaning or justification, besides implying the purposeful attempt by the atoms to free themselves from organic bonds and their "preference" for inorganic combinations. Anabolism and Katabolism are mere abstract aspects of Metabolism (though there may be a quantitative unbalance). There is only the most mystical analogy between them and the " positive independent primary instincts " of love and (as Freud holds) of " Hate " which are expressions of the purposes of the organism *as a whole* and not of isolated atomic attractions and " repulsions ". Some psycho-analysts, however, frankly refuse to follow Freud *in this matter* and I find this cleavage of opinion distinctively suggestive of an affective rather than objective basis of the theory.

(4) We find further grounds for distrusting the origin of the Death-Instinct Theory in its heuristic uselessness. It is supposed to explain (with the help of most elaborate hypotheses) the phenomena of Sadism and Masochism, but the explanation is admitted to be unsatisfactory. Thus : Primary

Narcissism, in its own defence, projects the Death Wish against an external object so that it becomes *death dealing* rather than *dissolution seeking*, i.e. anger rather than desire. At the same time, linking itself with and subserving the erotic impulses, it becomes sadism. Subsequently, in defence of the (ambivalently) loved object, the aggressive-destructive impulses are reflected back against the self in " secondary masochism " In addition a repetition-compulsion has to be postulated. Yet all this elaborate theory has no other clinical application or utility, so that Dr Melanie Klein remarked, when I attacked the validity of the Theory, " What does it matter ? " A theory whose truth *does not matter empirically* has another very significant resemblance to pure fantasy.

To sum up the case against Death Instinct, it was arrived at by fantastic speculation, is intrinsically absurd, has produced acute disagreement except when reduced to meaningless abstraction and accomplishes nothing in the way of explanation though with the help of mountains of onerous hypotheses.

IV. We must now deal with the Freudian conception of love to see whether this also has the same tendency to express a defiant pessimistic antipathetic attitude of mind.

(1) Freud is most insistent upon the sexual origin of love and ultimately of all (sublimated) interest. In *Group Psychology*, etc., on p. 116 we find Freud talking of an " easy *transition* " from a nurtural tie to a sexual tenderness, and, further down the paragraph, of a " complete *fusion* of tender and jealous feelings and of sexual intentions " (my italics). This seems to imply the original independence of nurtural and sexual impulses. On the next page, however, he says that the child's first love is

typically "co-ordinated with the Oedipus Complex". This, however, Freud himself has later found incorrect in any sexual sense though it is the basis of the pan-sexualism we attack.

Under repression, he goes on to say, all that " is left over shows itself as a purely tender emotional tie, no longer to be described as sexual." " It gives us courage to assert that wherever we come across a tender feeling it is the successor to a completely 'sensual' object tie." On the next page he is even more explicit in the matter of the sexual derivation of tenderness. The evidence lies in (a) the erotic behaviour of young children towards their loved objects and (b) the tendency of analytically evoked memories ultimately to find an erotic expression.

It is never denied that love must be expressed somehow through bodily means, and of these the most definite, easily described, and intrinsically interesting (particularly in adults) is sex. The association is in any case close and, as Freud says, the transition is easy, so that the evidence does not prove that sex is the sole root of love—indeed Freud's change of front mentioned above shows that his position *when he formulated* this pan-sexual theory is admitted to have been invalid. The proof is not conclusive, even the theory is not clear, but Freud is insistent nevertheless, and here as elsewhere he goes beyond his evidence *always in the same direction*.

(2) Thus he denies that the infant loves anything *but* itself—narcissism—and thereby minimizes the mother tie. Significantly this theory is *also* coming into question in analytic circles. He attributes much of the mother's own love to narcissism and sex interest in the footnote in *Group Psychology and the Analysis of the Ego*, p. 54. In fact his whole philosophy of life is summed up in the line, " Oh, I care for nobody and nobody cares for me." Such

an attitude to life is of necessity correlated with a pessimism and aggressive attitude which in fact we find in all Freud's writings. The independent "instinct" status he denies to *love* he gives, as we have just seen, to *hate*, while his pessimism is seen not only in accepting death as the purpose of life but throughout *The Future of an Illusion*, and in his letter upon War, which declares this to be " inevitable and indeed biologically useful ", etc., etc.

(3) We find the same tendentious straining of the evidence in his theory of sublimation which starts from the sound assumption that satisfied impulses do not require to seek alternative outlets. Sex is unsatisfied in modern European culture, ergo it is probably the energy source thereof (?). Much culture too has a definite if covert sexual content ; sexual symbolisms in art and religion are indisputable, ergo, the whole thing is a sex substitute (?). Further, savages are " free " sexually (now known to be false) and their culture is *therefore* (?) primitive. The cultural development of children is also most notable during the period when sex is most inhibited, etc. On these facts a complementary relationship between sex and culture is clearly demonstrable—" the more of one the less of the other " in a *very* general way.

This complementarity, however, need not be one of identity as Freud assumes *without question*. There is much reason to believe it to be one of opposition (i.e. indicating two independent sources) ; while it is at least possible that the complementarity is one of function (i.e. sex and culture perform the same integrating function and so overcome the separation anxiety. I have worked this out elsewhere ; but of course Adler must have had long priority—if it matters—in this idea). The significant point is that Freud as usual *does not consider* any alternative interpretations which might imply a non-sexual but social interest (i.e. love) of one individual for another. His conjectures as to the origin of culture imply that it began as a series of sexual symbolic gratifications, e.g. hoeing the ground=incest with the mother. If, as seems likely from available data, we find that agriculture was started *by women*, then of course the formula will be—hoeing the ground= homo-sexual intercourse with the mother via penis envy. The plasticity of the Psycho-analytic Concepts make them an elastic measuring-rod that reduces everything to the form that was "expected". That *form* is not fairly representative of the evidence, hence the suggestion that it accords with pre-suppositions whose nature is revealed from a study of the general trend of the *invalid* portions of Freudian Theory.

It will, of course, be said that this objection arises from Psycho-analysis referring to the *latent* content, while, its criticisms being based on *manifest* content, a systematic opposition is natural. But this is a question to be judged on the facts and the internal consistency of Psycho-analytic Theory itself. This I am attempting to do ; but I would point out that Freud tends to dismiss manifest content as *merely a cover* for latent content, a position that is manifestly impossible. For the *unreal interests could never serve to disguise the real*—the meaningless could not hide meaning any more than a wanted criminal could hope to escape police notice by posing as a centaur or some other unreal creature that has no valid excuse for existence. The manifest content of mind is real and indeed manifestly the dominant factor in life. Its dismissal as a *mere* . disguise to the repressed is manifestly ridiculous.

(4) Where Freud does not attribute culture-civilization to substitute-sexuality he still finds its motivation in the desire for material gratifications. Perhaps his most complete denial of good-will is

contained in *The Future of an Illusion*, pp. 10-13, where he regards all civilization as built upon the selfish coercion of the many by the few for purely material objectives. Thus : " One gets the impression that culture is something which was imposed on a resisting majority by a minority that understood how to possess itself of power and coercion." If we could abandon " coercion and the suppression of the instincts—men might devote themselves to the acquisition of natural resources and to the enjoyment of the same. That would be the golden age." This materialistic paradise, however, Freud despairs of ever attaining. " It seems more probable that every culture *must be* built up on coercion and instinctual renunciation " (my italics). " All men are destructive " and so anti-social tendencies predominate in any society.

" One thought at first that the essence of culture lay in the conquest of nature for the means of supporting life " (Why then should culture have developed so early and favourably in generous climates and soils ?) The three problems of politics appear to Freud to be (1) how to diminish " the burden of the instinctual sacrifices imposed on men ", (2) " in reconciling them to " these inevitable sacrifices and (3) " in compensating them for these ". " *It is just as impossible to do without government of the masses by a minority as it is to dispense with coercion in the work of civilization.*" Leaders " should be independent of the masses by having at their disposal *means of enforcing their authority* " As Freud ranks himself with the moderns, presumably he means machine guns, poison gas and bombing planes. One is almost inclined to assume that Freud also is among the prophets who will be quoted by those who exclaim " Heil Hitler ! " He holds that it is a " fact that the organization of culture can be maintained only by a certain measure

of coercion " and that in regard to Utopias " one
may be appalled at the stupendous amount of
force that will be unavoidable if these idealistic
aims are to be carried out " (p. 14).

The whole social theory is in line with that
propounded in *Group Psychology and the Analysis of
the Ego* and in *Civilization and its Discontents*. The
only need man has for man is (*a*) for his material
services, and (*b*) through a goal-inhibited sexual
attraction (?) Vaguely Freud speaks of an identification by which the other person's advantages are in
fantasy enjoyed. But this seems again just a means
of explaining *away* the fact of organic sympathy and
love. Group psychology, the social tie which binds
men together, is for Freud a common fear of and
subservience to the superman-patriarch, whose
sexual jealousy denies them any other outlets for
genital love. He alone is perfect and natural ;
he alone has not been deformed by coercion.

In this central position Freud's philosophy is
perfectly consistent. His evasions and contradictions, his selection, rejection, and distortion of
evidence, all occur in the attempt to apply this
preconception universally. Though now and again
he lets drop a phrase that appears to regard tenderness as a force in itself or refers to fear of " loss of
love " he returns faithfully to the central position
that (1) ignores the mother for the father ; (2) denies
tenderness—filial or parental—and universalizes
sex ; (3) interprets socialization in man as *merely*
the overcoming of *sex* jealousy by coercion and fear ;
(4) regards hate as a spontaneous, ineradicable
appetite and all motive as egoistic ; (5) regards all
cultural interest as substitute sex gratification and
all else as materialistic utilitarian interest. His
position is consistent subjectively but not objectively.
Therefore it is an expression of temperament not a
conclusion based on empirical study. It is the

personal "scheme of reference" in which he constructs his metaphysic, or as he prefers to call it metapsychology. (See Note D, p. 239.)

V. *Fear and Repression.* We must now consider the Freudian concept of fear and repression, beginning with the theory of anxiety, since the retractation of views long and confidently held in this matter is surely "prima facie" ground for doubting the validity of the whole Freudian approach. It was long and confidently held that Angst was merely converted (sexual) libido which had been denied its genital outlet. This view has been given up, though the mechanism of anxiety is still an unsettled question. Separation Anxiety has been referred back to pre-oedipal times and an explanation has been sought in the organic distress experienced by the child during the process of parturition itself. Significantly enough this reference to a situation not involving the father is not a Freudian contribution to theory. The notion of the Birth Trauma originated (so far as I know) with Rank; for Freud *the* trauma has always been castration. He finds the idea of parturition-distress, however, acceptable; it is egoistic and materialistic, it does not imply the existence of love. In regard to "separation from the mother" (*Inhibition, Symptom and Anxiety*, p. 62), Freud says : "*If the nurseling longs to behold the mother, it is only because it knows from experience* that she satisfies all its requirements without delay." This dictum definitely denies the possibility of the inheritance of a craving for companionship apart from that affording satisfaction to the bodily appetites. According to Freud then the infant *learns* to value the mother as a *utility to itself* ; it is not born with or does not instinctually develop a direct desire for the *presence* of others or a corresponding *direct dread of loneliness*—

(though, apparently, there are many other animals and birds which have their self-preservative instincts adapted to infancy in this way). For Freud all fear is primarily aroused in the mind by a *state of unsatisfaction*, secondarily by its apprehension. This arouses " by analogy " in the infant or child mind the memory of the birth distress and so organizes the " impulse towards self-preservation ". That this origin of the disposition to self-preservation differentiates man radically from other animals— even from mammals—Freud recognizes, but dismisses the " objection " to his theory as " outside the limits between biology and psychology " (op. cit., p. 58), though no one has been more guilty than himself of reckless incursions into these regions. Surely this is a strained, tendentious, theorizing and surely it has the negative aim of *denying* the existence of any natural disposition to love others except in so far as they are objects of bodily appetite.

Freud quickly gets back to his castration-fear from which alone he can admit the development of a moral sense or dread of isolation by the discipline of others. " With the depersonalization of the parental instance, from which one fears the castration, the danger becomes more definite. Castration fear develops into conscience fear and social fear. The formula of separation, exclusion from the herd, applies only to that later portion of the super-ego which has developed from leaning upon social prototypes, and not to the nucleus of the super-ego, which corresponds to an introjected parental instance." In plain English, the child does not love its parents but depends upon them for its gratifications and necessities. It is therefore concerned to maintain good relations with them only for this purpose. Their pleasure and displeasure arouse its fears and affect its happiness only so far as they promise continuance or threaten withdrawal of their nurtural care and/or the infliction of bodily injury. Now it is quite true that mental good relationships (interest and affection) are more necessary and therefore more explicitly cultivated after the loss of the demonstrative fondling child-mother relationships ; but it should be observed here again how extreme and emphatic Freud is in his negation of love for its own sake as an independent reality in life.

Before leaving the subject of fear it may be pointed out that the Freudian conception of the repressing instance is still so unsatisfactory that the suggestion has been put forward that repression occurs *spontaneously* on account of the mere magnitude of the repressed affect threatening the psyche, and irrespective of any social exigencies preventing the overt *expression* of emotion. This implies that the human infant is born unadapted to *any possible* environment and therefore already in a state of conflict to which the only solution is repression. I agree that the two-phase life, involving the later surrender of a parasitic infancy for a free-living maturity, appears to make some stresses of development inevitable ; but these would occur later in development than the hypothetical, spontaneous, *self-adaptive* (as distinct from environmentally adaptive) repressions. I would require a good deal of evidence to believe that any successful species can be born with useless and even self-conflicting dispositions, and the fact that Freudian Theory seems driven to postulate this is to my mind a suggestion of its own inadequacy. [See pp. 24, 198.]

One can say broadly that Freud sees no positive drives whatever in life. Indeed, he regards it as forced to go on by environmental compulsion against its will to death, and all the complications and elaborations we find in biology, ethnology and psychology he regards as due to conflicts and unbalances within the vital urge itself. For him the species is absolutely broken up into individuals each seeking its own ends exclusively. Even sexual union with another in the last resort is understood as a lowering of instinctual tension, a step on the road to inertia and dissolution. " Expression ", for Freud, is merely an evacuation, and does not imply "getting it across" to others or their response.

All social activities are thus defence-reactions, substitute gratifications, guilt-expiations or aggressions. Guilt is an apprehension of personal loss ; grief is its realization ; pity is inconceivable ; love is unreal. Elsewhere I have tried to put the concept of love on a strictly bio-psychological footing, but the argument is too long to summarize here. All I wish to point out is that the consistency of Freud's attitude in these matters is never disturbed by its inconsistency with fact. Where Freud's imagination is free, or where his acquaintance with fact is unsystematic, his pessimistic philosophy of life finds free play. Where, however, he is in close contact with human nature—even with the seamy or latent content sought and displayed in clinical analysis— Freud shows a totally different side of himself. In practice he abandons theory as promptly as the physiological psychiatrist abandons his idea that brain pathology determines thought whenever he comes to reason with patients or opponents.

NOTE D.

THE FREUDIAN ATTITUDE TO SEX

Röheim at the conclusion of his work on Primitive Cultural Types remarks that " the sexual practices of a people are indeed prototypical and that from their posture in coitus their whole psychic attitude

may be inferred ".   This is true only in so far as
from their posture in coitus their *attitude to sex and
social attitude to women* generally may be inferred.
As I have shown elsewhere the social status and
domestic dignity, the cultural and other interest
and companionship resources of women, affect their
emotional relationships to their children and to
boys as distinct from girls.   In particular these
factors influence women's need for their children
as children and hence their will and their power to
effect psychic weaning and the repression of
pre-oedipal (regressive) and oedipal wishes.   Upbringing recreates in the rising generation the
emotional attitudes which determined its own
special features, in an endless chain of reaction with
certain vicious and benignant cycles, and subject to
outside influences, e.g. economic.   But this is not
what Röheim means.

Elsewhere in this work he talks exultantly of
" biological *maleness*, an inheritance from our animal
ancestors " (p. 56).   Coitus is castration of the
woman (p. 51), "beating her into obedience" (p. 43)
" rape "—a pure *evacuation* of seminal products
(detensioning), not an *expression* of feeling whose end
and aim is to evoke *response*.

Yet Röheim oscillates in his beliefs, talking of
" admixtures of tenderness " and makes the
surprising discovery that " the phallic weapon is
not love " (p. 221), and admits by implication that
women have more use for " love poetry " and less
for the " phallic sadism " than men.   Here, as in
Freud's own work, we find the same theoretical
assurance that there is no love apart from genital
desire and its derivatives ; yet here again we find
the same uncertainty when dealing with fact, not
abstract theory, and the same tendency to help out
the description with casual references to the love
and tenderness whose independent existence theory

denies. Surely there is here an emotional over-insistence upon the aggressive, selfish and sensual aspects of *sexuality itself*, and an implied depreciation of all desires that have not an organic appetitive end. Surely also the assumption of a constitutional (" biological ") difference in the sexuality of men and women is " a priori " and proceeds from the same anti-tenderness, anti-feminist, bias.

CHAPTER XIV

FREUDIAN PRACTICE IS "CURE" BY LOVE

THIS is the other side of my argument, that the empirical side of psycho-analytic work was never the source of its metapsychology, never owed anything to it, could never be more than verbally related to it, and that the divergence is increasing so much that an intermediate body of theory has arisen to meet the needs of clinicians. The same bias, however, crops up sporadically even in practice (e.g. the ultra-passive technique) and in certain theories of the "rationale" of cure, so that the metapsychology should not be dropped entirely and tacitly. as some practical analysts do. If there is a delusional element underlying the fundamental conceptions of metapsychology we must trace it right through into clinical practice. If we do this, I maintain, we shall reach the broad but astonishing conclusion that the Freudian Theory is based on Hate—a denial of love—which is naturally and inevitably inapplicable to psychotherapy—the healing of the mind. Hence the reason that it is not employed therein except in the most casual and irrelevant way. In argument with Freudian clinicians I have found again and again that the Death Instinct is " a cock that won't fight ". Conversely Freudian Theory is unable to profit by observation in its own field, unable to direct research or influence technique, unable even to explain the rationale of cure. There is in fact a complete genetic and functional separation of theory and practice except in so far as the latter has developed

242

a very unco-ordinated and changeable theory of its own.

I. The earliest Freudian conceptions of mind already contained the germ of two theories (1) that of the Conscious-Unconscious, separated by a Censorship, and (2) that of libido organization at the Oral, Anal and Phallic level, with the changes involved in the substitution of object-love for narcissism. The former of these theories played a far greater part in the theory of the neuroses and the interpretation of therapy, the latter had more significance for the development of the psycho-analytic theory of the psychoses. The significant point is that the logical relationships of the two theories was never worked out, while the conception of censorship with its two aspects of resistance and repression also remained unsatisfactory. When we consider the enormous difficulty of the problems confronting psycho-analysis and the uncertainty of its data in these early days, this is exactly as it should be. Alternative ideas have to be tried out, and so *consistency in theory is proof merely of disregard for the facts*.

Our philosophical endeavours, however, should be directed towards attaining a consistent, articulated account of the facts. It is therefore with extreme surprise that we find that Freud's acceptance of the Death Wish and Aggressive Instincts as fundamental to human nature is followed by a move of his *clinical* Psychology not towards pessimism (as in the case of his social theory), but towards a recognition of the importance of *social* feeling, i.e. optimism.

It is, of course, extremely rash to judge the evolution of ideas by their date of publication, but, taking this chance, we note that :

(1) The idea of Death-Aggression Instincts appear in 1920 (" Beyond the Pleasure Principle ",

which has all the internal appearances such as
self-contradiction, of a "free association", and
therefore seems to be the starting-point of the new
development).

(2) The notion of Ego-Ideal—what we would
like to be—is first offered in 1921 (*Group Psychology
and the Analysis of the Ego*), and it is already apparent
that Freud realizes that this is conditioned by the
approval or dislike of others.

(3) In 1923 appears *The Ego and the Id* in which
the social instance figures definitely as the Super-Ego
—first identified with the parent (introjected
"imago")—next depersonalized.   It is, however,
impossible to equate this with the "Censorship" of
early Psycho-analytic Theory.

We find here then that the department of
Freudian Theory that deals with the handling of
patients and with the data of analysis steps forward
progressively from a metaphysic of (1) absolutely
a-social egoistic pessimism through (2) a conception of egoistic but socially directed ambition
to (3) one of social compliance and submission.
Whether this is due to the influence of Adler, whose
ideas had been social from the first (e.g. inferiority
to others and its compensation in *power over them*), I
leave to others to decide.   The main point is that
Freud, from the moment he had declared in the
metapsychology that man is radically anti-social,
has had to introduce the social factor into psychology
as an endo-psychic "instance" in the form, first
of the Ego-Ideal, and then of Super-Ego.   The
organization of the super-ego is now a subject of
interest, as the cognate subject of Censorship once
was.   Disturbances arise from its "severity" as
well as from eruptions of Id impulses—the ego being,
as it were, between the "upper and the nether
millstone".   Here we have the original social
situation stated in terms of hypothetical instances

or organization *within the individual mind*. The mind " introjects " the imago of the parents and later social environment and moulds its ego-ideal and to some extent its actual ego accordingly. This is only another way of saying that the child forms an idea of the parent's nature and wishes, and develops a " conscience ", an idealism (more positive) and abstract ethico-aesthetic standards. But the reason for this introjection is still obscure (because love is not recognized), nor is the mechanism rendered any clearer by saying it is founded upon " identification " unless by this is meant that in the very beginning of consciousness there was no discrimination between self and mother and so that the germ of the super-ego was always present. Setting this aside however, why should the infant identify or introject at all ? Obviously for love alone. Sexual-sensual love ? At the very dawn of consciousness ? Freud is no less insistent here than usual.

The point is that in the development of his clinical psychological conception Freud has come so close to dealing with the essentially social nature of mental development and the meaninglessness of the individual in isolation from others, that his abstract formulae can almost be translated into the language of common-sense, *except in so far as the latter assumes the existence of tenderness as such*, and human psychology is practically always dealing, not with the individual, but with his relations to others. Freud himself has admitted " that we take abstractions too rigidly " (Symptom, Hemmung, and Angst, section III) ; but is his drive towards a sort of psychological shorthand *not itself a flight from love* and a refusal to accept it as a scientific concept— a real factor in life ?

II. The trend of Freudian *clinical* theory towards a clearer recognition of social development and activities is even more clearly shown in the history of psycho-analytic attempts to explain the success of their techniques, which after all developed *from a mode of investigation* which *incidentally* proved therapeutic.

Perhaps the earliest of all these theories of therapy was that of catharsis—the evacuation of a pent-up emotional complex. This was almost a pre-analytic theory and is not mentioned by Freud in his résumé in *Beyond the Pleasure Principle*. Nevertheless the idea still holds him in this very book, appearing as the " Economic " or " detensioning " principle of psychic functioning. Needless to say this is an entirely egoistic principle of cure. On this conception, so far as inhibitions are socially established and sanctioned, cure is attained by the demoralization of the individual. [See p. 204 ff.]

The first and most characteristic analytic theory of therapy might be called the Interpretative. Herein it was supposed that the discovery of the content of the unconscious enlarged the power and control of consciousness. Here again we are dealing with a theory that regards the patient as a self-contained psychic entity—as being potentially independent of any particular social contact and whose balance or unbalance lay within himself and not in his relationships to others.

When it appeared, however, that the essence of cure consisted in the *removal of resistances*, a much more social conception of mind was implied. Resistances were *against* the physician—either resentments or suspicion of *his* criticism—while repression appeared very largely as a function of the *social* instance in early childhood.

A further development in the recognition of the social factor occurred when it was realized that cure was effected only by an actual reconstitution of the loves and hates of the past with the person of the physician as their objective. This theory of treatment by "transference neurosis" recognizes at least tacitly that nothing matters—at least nothing is of psychopathological significance—which does not concern the love, hate and anxiety relationships of the subject to other people.

Correlatively with this theory, that of libido-development and the distinction of narcissistic from transference diseases seemed to explain why the psychoses, Dementia Precox, Melancholia and Paranoia, were relatively refractory to the Therapeutic Technique employed. Sufferers from these conditions are unable to form the love-transference which is necessary to cure and indeed to the state of health. From this standpoint we can no longer regard the psyche as a mere "detensioning apparatus" and its fundamental drives as the quest for sense-gratification and self-expression. To be of value, gratification and expression alike *must take place within* a love-rapport, with the partial exception of the simple organic appetites. Otherwise even sex-gratification is only semi-potent as a psychic satisfaction, while masturbation is guilty by reason of its a-social autistic character. Health then is not determined by freedom from restriction and restraint. The internal inhibition represents the condition of *loving* activity as revealed to the patient when a child. The removal of these restrictions is the removal of early social misunderstandings with their correlative grievances and resentments.

The overcoming of anxiety and hate appears as the assurance that *there is no occasion for them*. Reductive analysis itself in the all-important phase of the negative transference acts by displaying the essential lovingness of others and their need for his love, i.e. his own lovability. Finding confidence in himself and trust in others, he finds thereby the

interests whereby mental intercourse—intellectual
or aesthetic—the companionship of speech, is
developed ; and the patient is now " well ".   The
love-interest-rapport between himself and the social
environment—lost in childhood—is restored because
the forgotten quarrels have been explored and
forgiven—threshed out to such an extent that the
patient sees there never was anything to forgive—
never any lack of love on either side.

But this is a very un-Freudian interpretation of
therapy—at least I have carried my explanation far
beyond what Freud allows in his Introductory
Lecture, No. 27.   My account would not square
with the abstract idea of mitigating the severity of
the Super-Ego, or of acquiring a tolerance of Id
impulses.   Yet it squares very well with Ferenczi's
dictum, " The physician's love heals the patient,"
and completes it by asserting that the healing is a
reconciliation of the patient to his social and cultural
environment.   The physician's rôle is not the
technical one of doctor nor even the godlike one of
perfect parent.   It is much more that of sacrificial
victim upon whom all hates, anxieties and distrust
is worked out, so that he is the mediator, the
catalyte—whereby the separated psyche is re-
integrated in its society.

If I have not exaggerated the tendency of the
Freudian Theory of Therapy towards more social
interpretations of the process of cure, I would
suggest that this is significant of a splitting of the
unconscious motivation of practice from that of the
free theorizing seen in the metapsychology. Contact
with concrete people—particularly in the childlike
rôle of dependent helpless sufferers who trust the
physician with their inmost secrets and display
emotion without reserve—overcomes Freud's own
bitterness, and evokes parental love.   In the free
fantasy of the metapsychology, however, his own

childish rage and despair find expression in anti-feminism, the subjection of love to sex, the acclamation of aggression and hate as universal—a complete social pessimism. The thwarted purpose too is (covertly) revealed in the theory of Death Wish, for the dissolution desired is psychic—in fact nothing but a loss of the boundaries which delimit the self from the mother (His personal horror of death is manifestly related to this). Freud's theory is the work of a thwarted infant revenging itself on mother. His practice is that of the ambitious parent who would teach the whole world to grow up—his way. His scientific activities betray tremendous originality and competitiveness, co-operating if at all with the workers *of the past* (patronizing the parents), though accepting the criticism and correction from " followers ". (How far is this due to an emotional reconciliation to women based on their co-operativeness?) I submit therefore that there is much evidence of a systematic difference of interest, attitude and bias as between Freud's theory and his practice and that this is the reason for the extraordinary functional separation of the two. If we find not only that the errors of the theory are derived from the denial of non-sexual love but that the efficacy of the practice is due to the exploitation of this love, I submit that the case is worthy of your serious consideration.

III. We have found now that the conception of mind derived by psycho-analysis from its *clinical practice* recognizes (if only tacitly) man's social nature much more adequately than the meta-psychology, which is derived by speculation from physics and biology. Further, the successive theories of therapy have laid more and more stress upon the significance of the social factor in human life and well-being. Steady—if covert— progress is being made on the clinical side towards the recognition of love as a real factor in mind, although the formula of an introjected super-ego still represents social wishes and feelings as part of the structure of an individual mind and as built up through experience for exclusively selfish gratification and security. We must now examine the techniques of psycho-analysis to see whether, as this paper seeks to prove, they denote a still further departure from the metapsychological view of the individual psyche as an utterly independent unit in the struggle for existence.

There is only one technique officially " recognized " besides that of reductive analysis. It is admitted that the latter is not applicable to children for various reasons which I shall try to show are not the true ones. As you know however—even in the analysis of adults—Ferenczi advocated a more " active " technique, while recently Paul Federn has admitted that the anxiety of psychotics necessitated greater kindness being shown to them by the psychotherapist. He even admitted the giving of food. In regard to this as also to the co-operative play with children there can be no serious dispute that the physician's love is at least an important part in the treatment—in the allaying of anxiety—but in regard to the extremely passive techniques it might be maintained that they *are* techniques and not, as Prinzhorn maintains, " shared social experiences ". We must see whether there is not enough love surreptitiously or unconsciously administered by the physician or imagined by the patient to justify Ferenczi's dictum already quoted. If we can do so I will then be able to ask you to consider the significance of a practice that depends for its effect upon love, having been devised by the author of a theory which denies its existence.

I consider that even in the most " passive " therapy the patient's need for love is met in numerous and devious ways. What are the features common to all analytic treatment? I would characterize them thus. Imperturbability and perfect tolerance on the part of the analyst, his inexhaustible patience and unfailing interest in the patient's mental processes (highly reassuring to infantile anxiety), a ready memory and responsiveness of mind that makes the patient feel at one with the therapist and valued by him and an unerring insight that not only gives the former confidence in the latter, but convinces him ultimately that there can be nothing in his own mind wholly alien to the mind of the analyst, or alien to those of the other patients from whom the analyst has learned. The analyst's understanding of " evil " is a tacit admission that he too has been " bad ". In effect, this means that the patient comes to realize that there is no intrinsic difference between himself and anybody else. Though emotional sympathy (counter-transference) may be held in the strictest check, this *understanding co-operation* is, to suitable patients, a most convincing proof of *love*, in the sense in which I use the word. It constitutes a rapport with the physician in which the patient can have the utmost confidence ; and under cover of this new-found confidence the true work of " reduction " may be commenced, namely *the reduction of grievances*. The patient then dares to face and admit his anti-social impulses, regressive and aggressive ; he voices his age-old challenge to the mother's love, and in so doing discovers that the social separation-anxiety to which it gave rise is in reality quite uncalled-for, since he was really loved and since his *protest* is kindly received. He sees then that his resentments, carefully hidden, do not in fact isolate him from the idealized parents and do not warrant his being

1**

"cast off". Then comes the deeper layer of grievances yet, where infantile anxiety has passed over into impulses of aggression, hatred and despair. These antagonisms, are, however, still nothing more than a protest against love-privation, but a reproach carried so far as itself to become guilty (in the primitive sense), and hence productive of anxiety.

The primal resentment against the parent, the ambivalent feeling, must at all costs be concealed, renounced and repressed. This has been accomplished long before the patient (usually) has come for treatment. Only when confidence in the physician-parent (positive transference) has grown to a high level can these unfilial rages be revealed to him or her (overcoming the resistance), since their mere expression in words seems to the child insulting and injurious to the highest degree, and therefore appears as a mere "tempting of providence" to inflict a crushing vengeance. (This protest-antagonism is of course the basis of "naughtiness" and what I call "protest" delinquency.) Little by little suspicion and anger (negative transference) is dispelled as the patient ventures to attack the physician-parent with sometimes wordless accusations of injustice and unkindness, and finds these *protests sympathetically understood, admitted and excused*. At last the patient is convinced that love is unconditional, and with the passing of anxiety, resentment is appeased. He has found security through the rapport with a physician who displays the ideal parental qualities, tolerance without moral weakness, equanimity without the indifference of self-isolation, firmness without punitiveness. The patient is now free to pursue his social development from the childish to the parental and, finally to the fellowship level, unfettered by the anxiety and resentment that had hitherto demanded the *securing of his title to the child rôle before venturing to surrender this in exchange for social adjustments that seem to the child more responsible and contingent,* more complex and " lonely "

This is my conception of the " modus operandi " of treatment by " overcoming hate with love " and by " the mastery of anxiety ". It seems to me more understandable if regarded as a " *social reconciliation at a primitive* level of development ", than if formulated in terms of the adjustment of conflict, etc. between abstract and hypothetical impulses and organizations, such as ego and super-ego, postulated within the patient's mind.

I do not of course consider this an adequate explanation of the process of recovery from infantile anxiety, or, what amounts to the same thing, of the process of unforced maturation. I am not concerned to offer my views of psychopathy and therapy here, but only to point out a systematic divergence between Freudian Theorizing and Freudian Practice. Freud the Theorist spends every effort in denying love—though theory should be free from strain and, still more, from mere negativism. Freud the Practitioner spends every moment in the " exhibition " of love—tempered certainly by anxious " withdrawals ", e.g. in the passive technique. What is the explanation of this divergence which leaves a theory isolated from, and even opposed to, its ostensible practice and empirical basis ?

It seems to me that Psycho-analytic Research affords a very simple answer. Patients are children; and if they are suffering they evoke our pity ; if they are frank and obedient they evoke our parental impulses. But the social environment, mankind, takes for us the place once occupied by our mother, and if we have been deprived of this place *by violence* this will engender a bitterness and repressed longing (for mother and tenderness) which will

make " the world " seem hateful to us and lead us
to deny the very existence of the objects of our
disappointed longings.   This pessimism, I maintain,
constitutes a taboo on tenderness and a *general*
inhibition upon feeling which varies with upbringing
between individuals and cultures.   It finds a
correspondingly varied expression in the cults and
customs of the different races and still more
conspicuously in the diverse ethical, philosophic and
religious conceptions of life and its purposes.   But it
finds expression even in science when this pretends
to offer us an ontology.   It is of course a legitimate
method to concentrate our study upon accessible
features of experience, as when Galileo concentrated
upon the " primary " qualities of matter, i.e. mass
and motion.   But such a pre-selection of fundamental aspects is extremely dangerous in the case of
psychology ; and I maintain that Freud, in leaving
love out of account, is but the counterpart of the
Christian Scientists who declare that evil (hate) is
a non-existent illusion of " mortal mind " which in
turn is held to be non-existent.   These not only
proclaim a future re-union with God but even *deny*
that *separation* has ever taken place or is at all
possible.   They regard themselves as emanations of
love, a sort of pseudopodia of the divine essence.
Like children *they deny creation—no changes are possible*
—and, significantly enough, they address the deity
as Father-God—Mother-God.*   This oedipus-free
regression naturally cures much anxiety by
reinstating primal infancy.   By contrast Freud is
the older, anxious, child who has suffered and
accepted *but not acquiesced* in severance from mother.
Hence his fear of death, antidoted by fantasies of
dissolution (Death Instinct=return to mother).
Hence his over-estimation of sex and sexual jealousy
and of the Oedipus Complex, which with him must

* See Chapter X.

explain all love and its conflicts. Hence his pessimism and pre-occupation with the problems of guilt and hate to the exclusion of positive factors in mind. Hence, also, his paranoid ideal of the father's rôle—almost an apotheosis—but laying emphasis upon rights, powers and privileges rather than upon parental tenderness. Hence lastly the metapsychology, the childish hymn of hate, when rage is not appeased by contact with patients and followers who accord to him paternal authority.

Note E.

The behaviourists achieve the unconscious double or ambivalent aim of return to the mother and revenge upon her more neatly than Freud's theory of Death-Aggression Instinct does. They too deny (the mother's) love and all feeling as distinct from knowledge. They deny also however (unconsciously) the existence of the (knowing) self. But if the self—as distinct from the objective world—has no existence then *it can never be " separated "*. Hence they achieve also the Christian Science ideal of unity with the universe and freedom from separation-anxiety.

CONCLUSIONS

THE justification (or otherwise) for inflicting such a tissue of hypotheses upon the public lies in the present need in psychology for new ideas which have been adequately tested in all the fields of the science of mind. It is not pretended that this testing has been done here ; this book offers merely a preliminary view, a " prospecting " exploration. Such results as emerge from these applications do, however, suggest that, if valid, the hypotheses here put forward will compel an extensive reorientation and supplementation of Psycho-analytic Theory. Their validity (or otherwise) can be judged on such grounds as these :

(1) By their capacity to furnish solutions to problems—biological, psychological, pathological and social—*which have hitherto defied analytic interpretation.*

(2) By their general applicability to all these kinds of psychological phenomena and *power to suggest further lines of study.*

(3) By their internal, logical, coherence, *provided this has arisen* (as I maintained in the Introduction) *from the convergence of independent lines of inductive research* and not as the result of an unconscious deductive process in my own mind.

It seems to me that on each of these three grounds the theories here propounded offer distinct advantages over Psycho-analysis and *that* without the over-elaboration of hypothesis and without the over-simplification (by selection) of fact which still characterizes the Psychology and Sociology of Freud.

To me the most striking results that emerge from this preliminary review are these :

(1) A greatly clarified view of the contrasts and similarities between human and animal mind and of the causes and mechanisms concerned in the production of our distinctive mind and culture.

(2) A new theory of the nature, origin and functions of " love " and " interest ", and an enlarged understanding of the jealousies and other conflicts that hinder individual development and mar social harmony.

(3) A new conception of the mind of the infant and of the factors and obstacles concerned in the initial *direction* of character-formation. We also have a suggestion *re* the mental differentiation of the sexes which may be worth pursuing.

(4) A positive conception of the social bond and of the process of socialization both in the child and in the race. The mechanism and functions of Repression appear also in a new light.

(5) A coherent interpretation of mental disease and of psychotherapy.

(6) A conception of the *function* of Religion as being a psycho-social therapy rather than as being a social disease.

(7) A Theory accounting for the inter-relationship of Culture and racial Character, and for the diversity of Peoples in these respects. This suggests also lines of research into such subjects as cultural antipathies and the degeneration of civilizations.

(8) A systematic explanation of the Freudian Failures and Successes.

Obviously the issues raised are numerous and of the very highest theoretical and practical importance, and this can be pleaded in further extenuation for the hasty, disjointed and often dogmatic and conjectural presentation of my interpretations of fact. The bulk of evidence and argument (particularly psychopathological) must be reserved for reasons of space and time. I therefore claim that these hypotheses are worth consideration on heuristic grounds, particularly as they are not in themselves complex or onerous. Indeed the principles upon which I base the whole theory might be stated very briefly and simply thus :

(1) That the mind of the infant is *adapted to its nurtured role* in life, and is not a bundle of instinct impulses like that of, e.g. the chick.

(2) That it must therefore be readapted during development to an independent, responsible, adult rôle, and that the surrender of the sheltered rôle entails emotional stresses.

(3) The initial (self-preservative) dependency upon others is never completely outgrown, but persists as a need for companionship, *apart from the organic satisfactions that may be derived therefrom* (i.e. persists in the form of " play " and " interest ").

(4) The renunciation or repression of the various wishes constituting infantile dependency can be effected *thoroughly* only by the loved object (mother) herself, and not by external interference.

(5) The mother's will and capacity to enforce the renunciation (" psychic weaning ") will vary directly, (*a*) with the quality of her own character and personality and (*b*) with her own domestic status and dignity in the child's eyes and inversely with (*c*) the importance of the *child* in her own emotional life relative to other attachments and interests (i.e. her dependency on the child).

Any social factors therefore which stunt the character-development of women, contract her interests or lower her prestige with her children will interfere with her function of promoting the maturation of her children and their independence of herself.

(6) Disturbances of this maternal function are the causes of " fixation ", " regressions ", " depressions ", jealousies and antagonisms which in turn are the root cause of mental illness.

(7) Psychotherapy is an attempt to " reduce these dislocations" of the love-life and to free interest for social purposes.

(8) Religions deal with these buried misconceptions of the parents' nature and relationship to the child. Their practices aim at the " institutional " expression (in ritual or other " innocuous " form) and control of the particular anti-social, anti-hygienic forces *which are most prevalent in the individual culture concerned.* " Matriarchal " and " Patriarchal " Cults, Cultures and Character vary fundamentally in the latter respect.

(9) Love should be regarded as something more than the sum of its expressions and the variety of its manifestations. Not indeed as an " essence " or " force ", but rather as an " x " analogous to the physical concept of " energy " or ether. This is a heuristically justifiable formula, particularly since love can *turn into* hatred, which is merely its negative or frustration aspect. From this it follows that " cure " of psycho-social ills (into which hate always enters) is theoretically easier than could be believed from the Freudian standpoint, which regards hate as proceeding from a " Primal, independent, instinct of destruction ", and hence as ineradicable.

It will then be seen that the primary assumptions I have put forward are not open to methodological objection. They are neither " ad hoc " nor transcendent, nor are they numerous and unrelated to each other, yet they afford us a considerable facility of interpretation over the whole field of behaviour. In fact it seems to me (in moments of enthusiasms) that they re-introduce common-sense into the science of psychology.

INDEX

This index is designed to facilitate reference to *topics* rather than *terms* ; consequently, in some cases, a term indexed may not actually be found on the page quoted.